THE PERFORMANCE OF LABOR-MANAGED FIRMS

Since 1970 the economics literature on the labor-managed firm has expanded greatly. Although it grew out of an initial interest in the Yugoslav system of workers' self-management, the literature is predominantly theoretical. Economists have tended to neglect the actual experience of labor-managed and cooperative firms throughout the world. This book is an attempt to remedy this defect by providing a blend of empirical evidence and economic modelling.

The major portion of the book is given over to a collection of studies of labor-managed, cooperative and participatory firms in eight countries. Each study is written by an author with considerable experience of the country under discussion. Taken together, the studies demonstrate the range of possible organizational forms which such enterprises may take. The empirical studies are supported by an introductory chapter in which the main themes of the economics literature are sketched and two chapters of a more normative character are written by Jaroslav Vanek and Branko Horvat.

This book is an important contribution to an expanding field of economic analysis. It presents in an accessible way evidence on an evaluation of the economic performance of participatory firms which will be useful not only to students of economics but also to students of sociology and industrial relations.

Frank Stephen, the editor, is a Senior Lecturer in Economics at the University of Strathclyde. He has visited Yugoslavia on a number of occasions to conduct research. He was a Visiting Fellow at the Program of Participation and Labor-Managed Systems at Cornell University, USA. He is a member of the International Association for the Economics of Self-Management. He has published articles in several major economics journals.

The Performance of
Labor-Managed Firms

Edited by

Frank H. Stephen

Senior Lecturer in Economics
University of Strathclyde, Glasgow

St. Martin's Press   New York

© Frank H. Stephen 1982

All rights reserved. For information, write:
. Martin's Press, Inc., 175 Fifth Avenue, New York, NY 10010
Printed in Hong Kong
First published in the United States of America in 1982

ISBN 0–312–60085–2

Library of Congress Cataloging in Publication Data

Main entry under title:

The Performance of labor-managed firms.

   Bibliography: p:
   Includes index.
   1. Works councils–Case studies. 2. Producer
cooperatives–Case studies. 3. Employees'
representation in management–Case studies.
I. Stephen, Frank H., 1946–   . II. Title:
Labor-managed firms.
HD5650.P422   1982   658.3'152   81–21216
ISBN 0–312–60085–2   AACR2

To Christine

Contents

Preface

This book has its origins in a symposium on labour-managed firms held at the University of Strathclyde, Glasgow, in June 1979. The eleven chapters of Parts II and III are based on papers which were prepared for that meeting (although, in the event, only ten could be presented). My reasons for organising the symposium were three-fold. Firstly, the economic literature on the labour-managed firm is heavily theoretical. Although some empirical work has been done, that has often been by non-economists. I hoped to bring together a number of theoreticians and experts on individual countries to try to relate theory and empirical evidence. Secondly, the theoretical literature has, until recently, been based largely on what I have called, in Chapter 1 of this book, the Ward–Vanek–Meade Model. This originated as a caricature of a labour-managed firm in a Socialist state (i.e. Yugoslavia) but increasingly was developed into *the* model of *the* labour-managed firm. It seemed to me that it did not represent the only type of labour-managed firm. I felt that it would be useful to bring together people with experience of different forms of organisation, which were basically co-operative in nature but different in structure and property rights, in order that each might become more aware (than was evident in the literature) of the diversity of such organisations. Thirdly, I hoped that a fairly informal working group might bring greater cross-fertilisation of ideas than is often possible in the almost adversarial, formal conference or the impersonal printed page. The reactions of the participants in the symposium suggest that some measure of success was achieved on all three fronts.

The apparent success of the symposium in the first two areas suggested the worth of publishing the papers as a collection. By presenting these with a theoretical introduction, I hope that this book will be a useful introduction to the economics of the labour-managed firm to a number of groups: specialists and students in fields other than economics who are interested in co-operatives;

students of economics looking for relief from the hegemony of the entrepreneurial firm; and economists who regard the labour-managed firm as a theoretical curiosity of little relevance outside Yugoslavia. I should also like to think that the intelligent layman interested in questions such as participation and social ownership might find this book interesting. Such a reader might, however, wish to confine himself to Parts II and III. In order to facilitate the use of this book by non-economists, when editing the symposium papers for publication, I have endeavoured to limit the technical nature of the presentation.

I am indebted to a number of people whose co-operation has made this book possible. The contributors themselves have been most helpful and understanding in allowing me to reorganise their presentation of material and trim their papers by an aggregate of about 30 per cent. I apologise to them in advance if this confuses readers as to the true meaning of any part of their contribution. Professor Andrew Bain made the symposium (and consequently this book) possible by a grant of funds from the Isadore and David Walton Benefaction to the Department of Economics at Strathclyde University. Without this it would not have been possible to bring together for three days participants from so many parts of the globe. Mrs. I. Leathard corrected the proofs and Donald Tait prepared the index.

Finally, but most sincerely, my wife Christine should be thanked for the help which she gave me in organising the symposium and for all she had to put up with during the editing of this book.

F. H. S.

Tillymet
August 1980

Notes on the Contributors

Eric Batstone graduated with First-Class Honours in Economics (and Sociology) from Cambridge University in 1966, and received his PhD in Sociology from the University of Wales in 1970. After holding various research posts at University College, Swansea, Sheffield University and the SSRC Industrial Relations Unit at the University of Warwick, he was appointed University Lecturer in Industrial Sociology, University of Oxford, and Fellow of Nuffield College. Dr Batstone's research has included shop steward organisation and strikes, industrial democracy in the British Post Office and a survey of the European experience of worker directors for the Bullock Committee on Industrial Democracy. Whilst on study leave in 1977/8 at the University of Paris, he studied plant industrial relations in engineering and producer co-operatives. He has jointly authored a number of books and contributed to others, is a member of the SSRC Working Party on the Political and Social Aspects of Accounting and is a member of the editorial board of *Economic and Industrial Democracy*.

Avner Ben-Ner was born in 1950 in Romania. In 1965 he emigrated to Israel, where he studied economics and philosophy at the Ben-Gurion University in Beer-Sheba and at the Hebrew University of Jerusalem. From 1977 until 1980 he undertook graduate studies at the State University of New York at Stony Brook, from which he received his PhD in Economics. He is currently a Research Associate at the Institution for Social and Policy Studies and Lecturer at the Department of Economics, Yale University. Dr Ben-Ner's research includes work on the economics of communalism and self-management and on economic and political cycles in Yugoslavia.

Katrina V. Berman holds a BA from Bennington College and MA and PhD degrees in Economics from Columbia and Washington State Universities respectively. She has carried out

Notes on the Contributors

economic research in the Antitrust Division of the US Department of Justice, the US Tariff Commission and other government agencies. Currently, she is Research Associate with the Center for Business Development and Research at the University of Idaho, having also taught at that university and at Washington State University. Dr Berman is a member of Hylarion Associates, a firm of consultants, and has acted as a consultant and expert witness in tax litigation for worker-owned plywood co-operatives. Her current research work includes an econometric study of comparative productivity of worker-owned and non-worker-owned plywood manufacturing plants as well as state and north-west regional water problems.

Juan Guillermo Espinosa is currently a Professor of the Inter-American Training Center of Economics and Statistics (CIENES), Santiago, Chile, and a Research Associate of the Program on Participation and Labor-managed Systems, Cornell University, USA. He qualified as a civil engineer from the University of Chile in 1965, and from 1966 to 1969 was Deputy Director of the National Industrial Development Agency in Chile. After completing his MA in Economics at Cornell in 1971, he took his PhD in Economics there in 1975. Dr Espinosa has held a number of advisory and consultancy positions with the United Nations, the World Bank and the Government of Peru. From 1975 to 1979 he was Senior Economist, Division of Development Programming of the Organization of American States. He has published a number of articles in academic journals and is joint author with Andrew Zimbalist of *Economic Democracy: Workers' Participation in Chilean Industry, 1970–1973*.

Saul Estrin holds a BA degree in Economics from the University of Cambridge, awarded in 1974, and he completed his DPhil thesis at the University of Sussex in 1979. Since 1977 he has been a Lecturer in Economics at the University of Southampton. His research work has concentrated on self-management and the Yugoslav economy but extends to an examination of planning in a market economy (France). Dr Estrin is a correspondent of the journal *Economic Analysis and Workers' Management* and from 1978 to 1980 was a member of the Council of the International Association for the Economics of Self-management. *Economica* and *Economic Analysis and*

Workers' Management have published papers by Dr Estrin.

Connell M. Fanning is a Statutory Lecturer in Economics of the National University of Ireland, at University College, Cork, where he has taught since 1978. He is a graduate of the National University of Ireland and was awarded his PhD in Economics from Cornell University in 1980. His areas of interest and publication are participatory firms and workers' co-operatives, and macroeconometric modelling. He is a correspondent of *Economic Analysis and Workers' Management*.

Branko Horvat is the Yugoslav economist whose work is probably best known to the western reader. After leaving school to join the Partizans to fight during Yugoslavia's National Liberation War he studied engineering, philosophy and economics at Zagreb University from 1946 to 1952. In addition to holding a doctorate from the University of Zagreb, Professor Horvat also holds a PhD of the University of Manchester. Post-doctoral studies took him to Harvard University and Massachussetts Institute of Technology. He was a member of Yugoslavia's Federal Planning Board (1958–63), the Federal Economic Council (1963–5) and numerous other government committees. In 1963 he founded the Institute for Economic Sciences in Belgrade and was its Director until 1970. He was founder, and remains editor, of *Economic Analysis and Workers' Management* and was the first President of the International Association for the Economics of Self-management. As well as serving on the editorial boards of a number of journals and being a visiting professor in universities throughout the world, Professor Horvat has published a large number of articles and books, the latest of which are *Self-governing Socialism* (joint editor), *The Yugoslav Economic System* and *Political Economy of Socialism*. He is currently Professor of Economics at the University of Zagreb and Research Fellow of the Institute of Economic Sciences, Belgrade.

Derek C. Jones is Chairman and Associate Professor, Department of Economics, Hamilton College, Clinton, New York. He obtained his BA degree from the University of Newcastle upon Tyne, UK, in 1968, an MSc from the London School of Economics in 1969, an MA from Cornell University in 1970 and his PhD also from Cornell, in 1974. He has taught at Hamilton College since 1972, was a visiting fellow in the SSRC

Industrial Relations Research Unit, University of Warwick, 1976–7, and was an Associate Fellow of the Program on Participation and Labor-Managed Systems at Cornell University in 1978. Dr Jones's research has focused on the experience of producers' co-operatives in Britain and the United States but has recently expanded to cover the wider European experience. He has published widely and his work has been translated into several languages. He has been a correspondent of *Economic Analysis and Workers' Management* since 1975.

Egon Neuberger is Professor of Economics at the State University of New York at Stony Brook. He has also taught at Amherst College, Michigan, and at the University of California at Los Angeles. Professor Neuberger has carried out research for the US State Department in Washington, at the US Embassy in Moscow and for the RAND Corporation in Santa Monica, California. He is a specialist in comparative economic systems and is the author of *Comparative Economic Systems: a Decision-making Approach.* Professor Neuberger has co-edited a number of books and written numerous articles on Yugoslavia, the Soviet Union, Hungary, the Yugoslav self-managed enterprise and the kibbutz, and theoretical and methodological issues in the study of economic systems.

Robert Oakeshott worked as a journalist, mainly for the *Financial Times*, after coming down from Oxford in 1958. From 1964 until 1970 he worked in Africa, first with the Government of Zambia and then in Botswana. In 1973 he was one of the founders of the building co-operative Sunderlandia in the north-east of England. He worked there full-time until 1966 and since 1978 has been the Director of Job Ownership Ltd, an organisation dedicated to facilitating the formation of co-operative enterprises. Apart from journalism, his publications include *The Bargainers* (joint author with George Cyviax) and more recently *The Case for Workers' Co-ops.*

Frank H. Stephen received his BA in Economics from the University of Strathclyde, Glasgow, in 1969. He worked for the Scottish Trades Union Congress, first as Research Officer and latterly as Head of its Economic Department until 1971, when he returned to the University of Strathclyde as a Lecturer in Economics. Since 1979 he has been a Senior Lecturer in the same department. In 1979 Dr Stephen completed his PhD on 'Investment in Labour-managed Firms'. He is currently a member of the Council of the International Association for the Economics of Self-management and has been a correspondent of *Economic Analysis and Workers' Management* since 1978. In 1980 he was appointed a member of the SSRC's Executive Panel on Work Organisation. Dr Stephen's research interests focus on the economics of the labour-managed firm but he has also published work in the field of regional economics.

Jan Svejnar holds degrees from the Universities of Geneva, Cornell and Princeton. He received his PhD in Economics from Princeton University in 1979. He is Assistant Professor of Economics and Industrial and Labor Relations at Cornell University and Deputy Director of the Program on Particip-ation and Labor-managed Systems. As well as labour relations and labour management, he has a research interest in the choice of technology.

Jaroslav Vanek has been a major contributor to the literature on the labour-managed firm. His book *The General Theory of Labor-managed Market Economies*, published in 1970, is a seminal contribution which has provided the basis on which the work of others has been built. He is Carl Marks Professor of International Studies and Director of the Program on Particip-ation and Labor-managed Systems at Cornell University, is a graduate of the Sorbonne and the University of Geneva and holds a PhD from MIT. After teaching at MIT and Harvard, he became a Professor of Economics at Cornell in 1966, and he has held visiting professorships at a number of European institutions. Professor Vanek has a considerable record of publication in international trade as well as in the labour-managed firm in the major economics journals. He is a correspondent of *Economic Analysis and Workers' Manage-ment* and is a member of the Council of the International Association for the Economics of Self-management.

Part I

Introduction

1 The Economic Theory of the Labour-managed Firm

Frank H. Stephen

This chapter sets the scene for the succeeding chapters by presenting a brief review of the theoretical literature on the economics of the labour-managed firm. It is hoped that this will provide an overview of how this field of scholarship has developed and the requisite theoretical framework for an understanding of the individual country studies.

After a somewhat slow start, the economics literature on the labour-managed firm (l.m.f) has expanded rapidly in the last twenty, and particularly the last ten, years. Because this is such a recent field of interest to economists, there are still many conceptual as well as analytical problems to be resolved. This is reflected in the fact that many of the papers being published currently deal with rather basic questions, e.g. what is the appropriate maximand in an economic model of an l.m.f.? Another distinctive feature of the economic literature on the l.m.f. is that it is largely theoretical. This is particularly true of the papers published in mainstream economic journals. Indeed, of the papers published following the First International Conference on the Economics of Workers' Self-management[1] in 1979, twenty-six are theoretical and thirteen empirical. This is probably a reflection of a general bias in economic research towards theory,[2] but it has had an important consequence for the economist's approach to the labour-managed firm: it has been treated as if there were only one such animal. An important purpose of this book is to demonstrate that there are a number of species within this genus which may behave in subtly different ways. Although there can be no purely *a priori* knowledge unconditioned by experience of the real world the dominant stream in the economic literature on the

3

l.m.f. is based on a purely theoretical notion of an l.m.f. which probably does not correspond exactly to any existing enterprise. It is the l.m.f. literature's analogue to the entrepreneurial firm of mainstream neoclassical economics. This model was first introduced by Benjamin Ward (1958), extensively examined and developed by Jaroslav Vanek (1970) and most succinctly reviewed by James Meade (1972). Given the seminal contributions of these authors, we shall refer to their model as the Ward–Vanek–Meade (W–V–M) Model.[3]

1 THE WARD–VANEK–MEADE MODEL

This model is developed from the following assumptions.

(i) The management of the firm is given over to the workers employed therein who are free to set output (X) and employment (L) at the level which they choose.

(ii) Non-labour inputs are hired at market-clearing prices. Initially, capital (K) is assumed to be the only non-labour input and it is hired at a rental r.

(iii) Decisions are assumed to be motivated by a desire to maximise net income (or dividend) per worker (π/L); workers are assumed to be homogeneous. To simplify analysis, it is further assumed that the output of the collective is sold at a parametric price (p).

(iv) There is no uncertainty.

This situation may be characterised[4] as follows: workers maximise:

$$\frac{\pi}{L} = \frac{pX - rK}{L} \tag{1}$$

subject to the production function:

$$X = f(K, L). \tag{2}$$

Maximisation of (1) requires that

$$\frac{\partial\left(\dfrac{\pi}{L}\right)}{\partial L} = \frac{pX_L}{L} - \frac{pX - rK}{L^2} = 0$$

i.e. $pX_L = \dfrac{pX - rK}{L} = \dfrac{\pi}{L}$ (3)

and $\dfrac{\partial\left(\dfrac{\pi}{L}\right)}{\partial K} = \dfrac{pX_K}{L} - \dfrac{r}{L} = 0$

i.e. $pX_K = r$ (4)

where X_L and X_K are the marginal products of labour and capital respectively.

Condition (4) simply says that capital should be employed up to the point where the value of its marginal product equals its price. This is the same as the long-run equilibrium condition for an entrepreneurial firm in conventional economic theory. However, condition (3) is rather different. It suggests that the membership of the collective should be expanded up to the point at which the value of its marginal product equals the dividend. This has important consequences for the way in which the W–V–M firm responds to changes in the price of its output or its capital, which can perhaps best be seen by referring to Figure 1.1. The curve ABC is the dividend curve showing how π/L varies as L (and consequently X in the short run) varies. EBF shows how the value

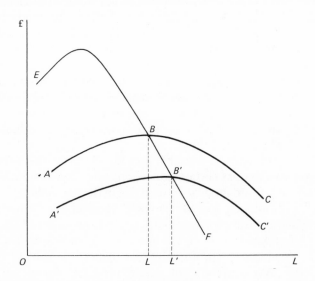

FIGURE 1.1

of marginal product of labour (pX_L) varies as L varies. The equilibrium labour force (that for which (3) holds) is given by the intersection of these two curves and is OL.

The equilibrium labour force for an entrepreneurial firm facing the same market conditions would be that where the value of the marginal product of labour equalled the competitively-determined wage rate.

The response of the W–V–M firm to changes in the rental of capital or the price of its output may be shown, approximately, by a shift in the divident curve ABC to, say, $A'B'C'$ in Figure 1.1. This change could be brought about by a fall in p or a rise in the price of K. The W–V–M firm would respond to such parametric changes by increasing the labour force to OL. Conversely, in response to a rise in price or a fall in the rental of capital the W–V–M firm would reduce the labour force. These responses to parametric changes are in the opposite direction to those usually associated with an entrepreneurial firm.

It should be noted that so far only the response of labour to a parametric change has been considered. Capital is held constant. This corresponds to the Marshallian notion of the short run.[5] As a consequence of this, it is suggested that the short-run response of a labour-managed firm to parametric price change is perverse. In the long run, capital will also adjust to the changed price and cost conditions. This long-run adjustment will be discussed further below.

The perverse short-run behaviour of the W–V–M firm is somewhat mitigated when there are multiple outputs and/or inputs. In the two output (X and Y) and single variable input (L) case, if the price of X increases relative to that of Y and production can be shifted easily in the short run, more of X may be produced. However, this would still be accompanied by a reduction in employment and total output.

When more than one variable input is used (say raw materials, M, as well as labour), certain conditions may lead to an increased demand for labour, in response to a rise in the price of the product. These conditions are that the marginal product of M does not fall rapidly as X is increased, and labour and the material input are highly complementary. If the price of X increases, the extra surplus generated by the difference between the cost of M and the price of X may overcome the desire to reduce the labour force.

However, as Meade (1972) points out, regardless of these more complicated cases, the output and employment of the l.m.f will be that which equates the value of the marginal product of labour to its average earnings: following on a price increase, one more worker will be taken on so long as he adds more to total revenue (net of additional costs of the other variable factor) than the existing dividend per head. Accompanying this new equilibrium situation there will be a higher dividend and a higher value of marginal product of labour. The essential point for the multi-product (as well as the single-product) W–V–M firm is that labour is taken on only when it increases the value of its marginal product: labour mobility will not therefore equalise the value of its marginal product between firms and industries in an economy (or sector) of labour-managed firms. In other words, in such an economy, wage differences are not competed away in the short run (see Chapter 2 below).

In the long run, both capital and labour are variable. It can be demonstrated that the W–V–M firm has a more limited set of equilibria on its production function than does its capitalist counterpart. In the case of the labour-managed firm, all income is distributed to the factors of production, i.e. the value of product is totally exhausted. Furthermore, in the long run all factors receive their marginal product. Traditional neoclassical theory has shown (e.g. Frisch, 1965) that these two conditions can be met, under the technology considered here, only at the 'technically optimal scale', as Frisch calls it, or the 'locus of maximum physical efficiency', as Vanek calls it. Along this locus, for a given set of factor input coefficients, the average product (of all factors) is at its maximum. It corresponds to the points for which the capitalist's long-run average cost curve is at its minimum, i.e. the locus of momentary constant returns to scale.

Figure 1.2 illustrates such a locus for two input factors, labour and capital. The curves I_1, I_2, I_3 and I_4 are representative isoquants. The technology being considered is one of increasing, followed by decreasing returns; thus there will exist a number of input combinations such as A, B, and C at which returns to scale are locally constant. There will be a locus of such points, such as EE, to the left of which returns to scale are increasing and to the right of which they are decreasing.

Along EE in Figure 1.2 Eulor's Theorem holds, i.e.

$$X = LX_L + KX_K. \tag{5}$$

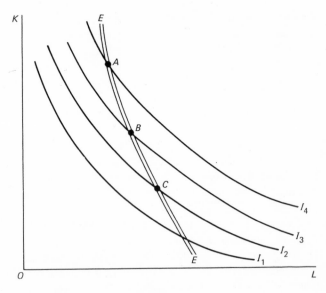

FIGURE 1.2

In the long run, with hired capital both labour and capital owners receive the value of their factor's marginal product, i.e.

$$X_k = \frac{r}{p},$$

$$X_L = \frac{\pi}{L}.$$

Substituting these in (5) yields

$$pX = \frac{\pi}{L} \cdot L + rK,$$

Therefore

$$\frac{\pi}{L} = \frac{pX - rK}{L}. \tag{6}$$

Along EE in Figure 1.2, equation (6) will be satisfied for different combinations of K and L and various values of r. Given a specific cost of capital, a collective seeking to maximise income per worker will select input combinations (K and L) for which equation (6) holds. Geometrically, this can be illustrated in Figure 1.3, which is

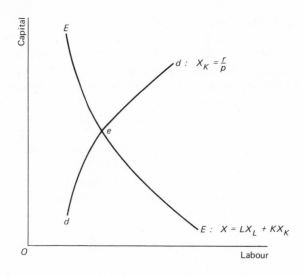

FIGURE 1.3

in the input plane. Along *EE*, as before, equation (5) holds. The locus *dd* shows those combinations of resources for which the marginal value product of capital (X_K) is equal to the market-clearing rate of interest (r). Clearly, the long-run equilibrium of the enterprise is given at *e*, the intersection of *EE* and *dd*. This equilibrium is unique once *r* is determined.

The point *e* would be the equilibrium for the zero-profit capitalist firm with the same production function, facing the same demand conditions and the same cost of capital. The labour-managed firm will never operate in the decreasing-returns region, except when it operates with an employment constraint. It is considerations such as this which lead Vanek to conclude that the problem of monopoly is likely to be less severe in a labour-managed economy than in a capitalist one. There is no financial incentive for the labour-managed firm to push its scale of operation beyond *EE* (by contrast with the case of the capitalist). On the other hand, this could lead to under-supply, in the absence of easy entry of new firms, and consequently to increased prices and welfare losses. The monopoly problem of a labour-managed economy is in achieving the number of firms necessary to meet demand, rather than restraining monopolisation by firms seeking to control output in order to maximise excess profit.

II OTHER MODELS OF THE L.M.F.

The W–V–M is the basic model of the l.m.f in the economics literature. However, its acceptance as a realistic predictor of how l.m.f.s would behave in the real world has been somewhat muted. Jaroslav Vanek, himself, clearly sees it as a prescriptive model showing the l.m.f. under ideal conditions. He has pointed out in a number of papers (Vanek, 1971a, 1971b) that, historically speaking, most producers' co-operatives have not hired capital at a market-clearing rental but have relied heavily on internally-generated funds. This has important consequences for resource allocation, as will be demonstrated below. A second factor is that producers' co-operatives frequently employ non-member labour (see, for example, Chapter 2, 3 and 4 below) which is excluded by assumption in the W–V–M model. Others have reacted, in particular, to the implications of the short-run perverse supply response by looking for forms of l.m.f which would not behave in this way or rejecting such behaviour as counter-intuitive and an indication that the maximand of the W–V–M model is too simplistic. A number of economic models of the l.m.f. reflecting these viewpoints will now be examined.

(a) THE INTERNALLY-FINANCED L.M.F

It has been argued, particularly by Vanek (1971a, 1971b), that labour-managed firms, or producers' co-operatives, in a capitalist environment are likely to rely heavily on internally-financed investment. Two reasons are usually given for this: firstly, the banking system is likely to be mistrustful of such an 'eccentric' form of organisation; and, secondly, that members of the co-operative are, themselves, likely to be reluctant, for idealogical reasons, to rely on established capitalist institutions. A reliance on internal financing of investment gives rise to two major problems. Firstly, there is a question of property rights: if members have no individual rights to income from the co-operative beyond their period of employment in it, and members cannot sell their membership rights to others,[6] the return from foregone individual earnings (i.e. collective savings) required by an economically-rational member of the co-operative will be greater than his simple rate of time preference. This arises because, where asset ownership is truly collective, the individual loses the principal of his investment. Thus, in evaluating prospective internally-financed investment, a member of the collective requires a premium above his simple rate of time preference to generate an acceptable return. The effect of this may be expressed in terms of the equilibrium condition for capital as

$$pX_K = R + D, \tag{7}$$

where R is the simple rate of time preference and D is the premium.[7] It is to be expected that R and r, the market rate of interest, are likely to be closely related. If so, (7) implies, on the assumption that the marginal product of capital diminishes, that the internally financed l.m.f. will employ, *ceteris paribus*, less capital than the externally-financed l.m.f. of the W–V–M model.

Secondly, Vanek argues that where all investment is internally-financed, the maximand of the l.m.f. is no longer (1) but

$$s = \frac{pX}{L} \tag{8}$$

since there are no current payments for the use of capital, i.e. r in (1) is zero.

Maximisation of (8) with respect to labour implies

$$\frac{dS}{dL} = \frac{pX_L}{L} - \frac{pX}{L^2} = 0,$$

therefore

$$X_L = \frac{X}{L}, \tag{9}$$

i.e. labour will be employed up to the point where its marginal product equals its average product. Average product is therefore maximised.

An important consequence of this is that equilibrium cannot be attained where there are constant returns to scale: (9) implies that

$$\frac{X_L \cdot L}{X} = 1. \tag{10}$$

The LHS of (10) is the output elasticity of labour (see Fergusson, 1969) which we denote by ε_L. Returns to scale may be represented in the two factor case by

$$\varepsilon = \varepsilon_L + \varepsilon_K$$

where ε is the function coefficient and ε_K is the output elasticity of capital. From (10), $\varepsilon_L = 1$ for the internally financed l.m.f., therefore

$$\varepsilon = 1 + \frac{X_X \cdot K}{X},$$

which implies that so long as X_K is positive, the equilibrium of the internally-financed l.m.f. occurs where there are increasing returns to scale.

If an internally-financed l.m.f. faces a technology which exhibits constant returns to scale, dividend maximisation implies that in the long run, the labour force (and thus the membership) will be run down. Vanek (1971b) describes such a firm as being subject to a number of forces which lead to its 'self extinction'.

(i) The *first self-extinction force* will arise because income per worker may be increased by reducing the labour force since there will be diminishing returns to labour. Even if there is no compulsory expulsion of members, this can occur via the non-replacement of members who leave or retire.

(ii) The *second self-extinction force* arises when via the reduction in the labour force in (i) the capital–labour ratio ceases to be optimal. Consequently, the size of the capital stock is reduced to re-establish the optimum ratio. However, when this ratio is attained, the first force is set off again. Thus, there is a repetitive cycle of forces (i) and (ii) which result in continued reductions of capital and labour until the collective is 'extinguished'.

(iii) The *'under-investment force'* arises because of the difference between conditions (4) and (7), which implies that the marginal value product of capital is always above the worker-manager's pure rate of time preference.

(iv) The *'never employ force'* arises since the adjustment from a suboptimal capital labour ratio is always achieved via increasing or decreasing capital or decreasing labour but never by increasing labour since that would reduce the size of the dividend.

When an internally-financed l.m.f. faces a technology exhibiting increasing followed by decreasing returns to scale, the dramatic nature of these forces is somewhat reduced. This is because in the increasing returns to scale zone, the benefits of reducing the size of the membership are counteracted by the loss of scale economies. Thus an equilibrium is attained at a positive labour force, capital stock and output. These, however, will be at socially inefficient levels. The change in technological assumption not only reduces the net effect of the four forces, but also a number of them are no longer universally present. When capital and labour are other than at their long-run equilibrium levels, adjustment may take place via increases (or decreases) in either (or both) of labour and capital. Thus, the 'first self-extinction' and the 'never employ' forces are no longer omnipresent. If an internally-financed l.m.f. is at a point such as Q_1 in Figure 1.4, it will move to its long-run equilibrium position a^* by increasing both capital and labour. The point a^* is at the intersection of the locus of points at which $X_L = X/L$, i.e. along which condition (9) holds and the locus along which $X_K = (R+D)/p$. This is in the increasing returns zone. The long-run equilibrium of the externally-financed (i.e. W–V–M) l.m.f. and the capitalist firm under perfect competition are at e, at which the locus of $X_K = r/p$ intersects with the locus EE along which constant returns to scale holds.[8]

Another defect in Vanek's four forces is that the circumstances

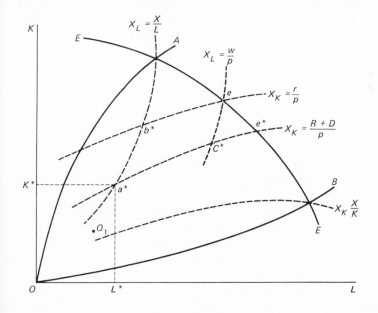

FIGURE 1.4

which allow the 'under-investment force' and 'second self-extinction force' to operate may be limited. These require that individual members have no claim on the assets of the collective but that the collective may consume its assets. The former is necessary for the 'under-investment force' to exist, whilst the latter is necessary for the 'second self-extinction force' to exist. For example, where individual titles to assets exist, as in a number of US co-operatives (see Chapters 3 and 4 below) and in the Mondragon system (see Chapter 6 below), there will be no under-investment force. On the other hand, where statute precludes even the collective consumption of assets, as in Yugoslavia (see Furubotn and Pejovich (1970), the second self-extinction force cannot be present. Thus Vanek's (1971b) self-extinction forces cannot operate in the way in which he describes them (even where there are constant returns to scale).

This is not the place to develop these points fully.[9] Suffice it to say that it can be shown that even under constant returns to scale, a Yuguslav self-managed firm will not 'self-extinguish'. Where the technology is of the increasing–decreasing returns to scale type, a wholly internally-financed l.m.f. of the Yugoslav type may even reach its long-run optimum along the locus EE at or to the right of e in Figure 1.4, whilst a co-operative where individual property rights exist will have its long-run equilibrium at b^* or even e^{10}.

Vanek's critique of internal financing points to a potential inefficiency that may arise from internal financing. The discussion in the preceding paragraphs, however, indicates that it cannot be applied in its totality to all producer co-operatives.

(b)   HIRING OF NON-MEMBER LABOUR

The economic consequences[11] of the hiring of non-members has only been tangentially discussed in the literature. Domar (1966), Pauly and Redisch (1973) and Carson (1977) have shown that a producers' co-operative which hires non-member labour reacts in the short run to parametric price changes in the same way as a capitalist enterprise. This may be illustrated using Figure 1.5 which shows the total revenue curve plotted against labour employed. The average revenue per worker for any value of L is the slope of the ray from the origin to the corresponding point on the total revenue curve. Thus, the value of L which maximises dividend per worker is that which maximises average product per

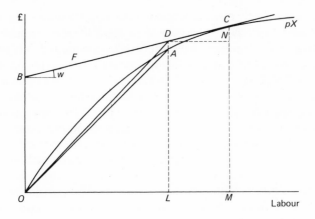

FIGURE 1.5

worker. Given the usual shape of the average product curve, this will occur at the origin, i.e. to use Vanek's phrase, the collective self-extinguishes itself.

Consider, now, an internally-financed l.m.f. with membership OL in Figure 1.5 which permits itself to hire labour. It would be willing to hire labour up to the point at which its marginal product equalled the competitive wage rate, w, which is shown in Figure 1.5 by the slope of BC. The optimum labour force for the collective is OM. With OL members (and LM non-member employees) the dividend per member is DL/OL or the slope of OD. It can be seen easily that it pays the remaining members to substitute hired labour for members where the latter leave the firm. Thus, the optimum number of employed members is zero. At this point a residual of OB is available for disbursement to the non-working members. Clearly the residual per non-working member is maximised when there is only one member.

McGregor (1977) has argued that the incentive to reduce membership is independent of the employment of non-members. Does this mean that Vanek's self-extinction forces apply equally to the cases of hiring and non-hiring as is implied by Derek Jones's analysis in Chapter 3 below? There is a subtle but important difference between these two cases. In the non-hiring case, the production unit disappears under CRS and operates where AP_L is maximised when there are increasing returns to scale. When labour is hired, the productive unit operates, in the short run at least, at the socially optimum output under CRS although it may cease to be truly labour-managed. Where individual members have a claim on the assets of the collective, as in many US plywood co-operatives (see Chapters 3 and 4 below), the social optimum output and K/L ratio will also obtain in the long run. A collective form of ownership will produce a lower K/L ratio than the optimum. Where there are increasing returns to scale, the long-run optimum combination of K and L will be the same for an internally-financed l.m.f. which hires labour as for an externally-financed l.m.f. or a capitalist firm, i.e. that given at e in Figure 1.4 where $X_K = r/p$ and $X_L = w/p$. The size of membership will, however, be reduced gradually. Where individual property rights are limited, as in French co-operatives,[12] the longrun equilibrium will be at C^* in Figure 1.4 where $X_K = R + D/p$ and $X_L = w/p$. In general, the hiring of labour takes the enterprise closer to the locus of constant returns to scale and maintains the productive unit in existence with an indeterminate but falling number of members. The firm does not 'self-extinguish' but the nature of its ownership changes. Thus there is an important qualitative difference between Vanek's analysis of internal finance and that when hiring takes place: the hiring of labour maintains output and employment close to the efficient combinations. When labour-hiring l.m.f.s 'disappear', it is only in the sense that a change in the form of ownership takes place, whilst in Vanek's analysis they somehow 'melt away'.

That the dynamics of the l.m.f. are altered when labour is hired may be seen by considering an externally-financed l.m.f. which hires members. Vanek, and by implication McGregor (1977) and Jones (Chapter 5 below), argue that it is the absence of a rental charge on capital which leads to the disappearance of co-operatives. McGregor emphasises this by stating that '(t)he incentive to reduce membership is independent of the employment of non-members'. He then argues that where a scarcity price is paid for capital there is no incentive to reduce membership because in the long-run equilibrium in this case (e.g. e in Figure 1.4) the dividend will equal the wage rate w: the income of members is unaffected whether or not the marginal worker is a member. However, this says nothing about how it is affected by the number of intra-marginal members. The size of membership is indeterminate: the desire to reduce membership (as opposed to the labour force) is not, as McGregor (1977) implies, neutralised by the capital rent. More significantly, however, if such an enterprise is not at the long-run equilibrium but at a point such as b^* to the left of e in Figure 1.4, it can expand along the locus $X_K = r/p$ to e by expanding membership *or* hiring labour. The existing members at b^* (or any point to the left of the locus $X_L = w/p$) will receive a higher dividend at each stage[13] of the movement from b^* to e if the move is made by hiring labour, since the value of marginal product of that labour is greater than the wage rate. In effect, when labour is hired the comparative static responses of the l.m.f. are exactly the same as those of an entrepreneurial firm. The only difference will be that in the case of collectively-owned assets it will use a less capital intensive input mix. In general, the choice of number of members becomes irrelevant to the input and output decisions, just as the number of shareholders is irrelevant to the corresponding decisions of the capitalist enterprise. The pattern of behaviour of a labour-hiring l.m.f. outlined here on the basis of deductive reasoning bears some similarity to the life cycle model of French producer co-operatives discussed in Chapter 5 below and which was derived from empirical observation.

(c) UNEQUAL SHARES

The hiring of non-members is one way in which the perverse short-run supply response of the W–V–M model may be removed. It does, however, result in a loss of internal democracy in the co-operative. A number of writers have examined models of the l.m.f. which modify the egalitarian membership rules of the W–V–M model. Meade (1972) refers to what we have called the W–V–M model as an 'egalitarian co-operative'. *Interalia*, he contrasts the behaviour of this model with what he calls an 'inegalitarian co-operative'. In the latter, the members have different shares in the surplus, and the rules of membership require that a joining (or leaving) member *and* the existing (or remaining) members must be agreeable to the change in membership.

The behaviour of the co-operative under these conditions may be demonstrated by some simple modifications to the maximand (equation (1) above) of the W–V–M model. Let the members now maximise

$$y = \frac{pX - rK - wL}{N} \tag{11}$$

where y is the dividend per share which each member receives in addition to the externally determined wage rate w per unit of labour supplied (it should be noted that y may be negative or positive). L is the number of labour units supplied (either man-days or man-hours); N is the total number of shares held by the members of the collective. This maximand is such that regardless of the number of shares owned by each member, maximisation of y maximises each member's income from the collective. The production function may now be written as

$$X = f(K, L, N). \tag{12}$$

Note that this implies that changing N with L constant affects X. In the W–V–M model, L and N are equal and $\pi/L = y + w$. However, in this model, L and N are not necessarily equal and the rate at which N changes relative to L is a policy variable for the collective. We may now examine the conditions under which (11) is maximised:

$$\frac{\partial y}{\partial N} = \frac{1}{N^2}\left[NpX_N - Nw\frac{\partial L}{\partial N} - (pX - rK - wL)\right] = 0$$

therefore

$$pX_N = \frac{w\partial L}{\partial N} + y \tag{13}$$

where $\partial L/\partial N$ is the partial derivative of the labour supply w.r.t. membership shares.

$$\frac{\partial y}{\partial K} = \frac{pX_K - r}{N} = 0$$

therefore

$$pX_K = r. \tag{14}$$

$$\frac{\partial y}{\partial L} = \frac{1}{N^2}\left[NpX_L - Nw - \frac{\partial N}{\partial L}(pX - rK - wL)\right] = 0$$

therefore

$$pX_L = w + \frac{\partial N}{\partial L} \cdot y \tag{15}$$

where $\partial N/\partial L$ is the partial derivative of the number shares w.r.t. the labour supply.

The partial derivatives in (13) and (15) are decision variables which in W–V–M model are equal to unity. In that model, therefore,

$$pX_N = w + y$$

and $pX_L = w + y,$

$$pX_L = pX_N.$$

Where hiring of non-members takes place, $\partial N/\partial L = 0$ and therefore (15) reduces to

$$pX_L = w.$$

The acceptance into membership of existing hired workers implies $\partial L/\partial N = 0$, reducing (13) to

$$pX_N = y,$$

i.e. that a hired worker's productivity must rise in order for it to be to the benefit of existing members to accept him into membership.

A simple rearrangement of (15) allows an examination of how shareholdings may be adjusted as the collective adjusts the labour force in the long run. From (15):

$$\frac{\partial N}{\partial L} = \frac{pX_L - w}{y} \tag{16}$$

Note that the jth member's income will be

$$w + n_j y$$

where n_j is the number of shares held by the jth member. The optimum values of N and L will obtain where (16) holds.

(1) If $w < pX_L$ and $y > 0$ then $\partial N/\partial L > 0$ and therefore the collective will benefit from expanding both the labour force and the number of shares which at the margin will be increased as indicated by (16). Expansion will take place so long as $pX_L > w$.

(2) Consider, now, situations in which from one or other party's view contraction is desirable.

   (i) If $w > w + n_j y > pX_L$, the jth member will wish to leave and the other members will be willing for him to leave since his current income $(w + n_j y)$ is greater than his marginal product's value. Rearranging the inequalities implies

$$0 > n_j y > pX_L - w$$

which implies $y < 0$ and $pX_L - w < 0$; therefore members will be released.

(ii) If, for all members,

$$w + n_j y > w > pX_L \tag{17}$$

the remaining members would benefit from someone leaving (since $w + n_j y > pX_L$) but no member would willingly leave (since $w + n_j y > w$). (17) implies

$$n_j y > 0 > pX_L - w,$$

$$\frac{pX_L - w}{y} < 0.$$

This implies from (16) that the number of shares in the surplus must move in the opposite direction to the labour supply; this seems paradoxical. What it really implies is that in order to persuade the jth member to leave, the remaining $j - 1$ members will transfer some of their share of the subsequent surplus to him. This could be effected by a lumpsum payment equal to the present value of annual sums of $n_j y - (px_L - w)$ (presumably financed against future earnings) or by allowing the departing member to retain a share in the surplus.[14]

(iii) Suppose, now, that for all existing members

$$w > pX_L > w + n_j y$$

$$\Rightarrow 0 > pX_L - w > n_j y. \tag{18}$$

In this case, an existing partner will wish to withdraw ($w > w + n_j y$) but the remaining partners will not allow him to ($pX_L > w + n_j y$), except on special terms. The special terms would be those necessary to make (16) hold. Given that $(pX_L - w)$ and $n_j y$ are negative, then $pX_L - w/y$ must be positive (assuming n_j to be positive). Also from (18),

$$\frac{pX_L - w}{y} > n_j.$$

From (16), the optimum requires

$$\frac{\partial N}{\partial L} = \frac{pX_L - w}{y} > n_j,$$

i.e. that the reduction in the total number of shares occasioned by the withdrawal of the jth (marginal) member must be greater than the shares which he holds. This may be looked upon simply, as in the previous case, as a requirement for compensation to be paid.[15] This time it flows from the departing member to the remaining members and will equal $(pX_L - w) - n_j y$.

Thus an inegalitarian co-operative avoids the perverse short-run supply response by always varying membership in the 'right' direction when $w \neq pX_L$. The efficient economic behaviour is, however, obtained at the loss of egalitarian income distribution within the collective. This compensation-based approach may be further adapted by considering a situation where membership of the collective is obtained via the purchase of a 'membership certificate' in a free market. A perfectly competitive market for such certificates has been shown by Sertel (1978) to produce, under certainty, comparative static responses to parametric prices and costs which are the same as those of the entrepreneurial firm. Mondragon (Chapter 6 below) and the US plywood co-operatives (Chapter 4 below) provide examples of such institutions in practice.

(d) THE UTILITY MAXIMISING CO-OPERATIVE

Some authors have responded to the W–V–M model's perverse short-run supply response by arguing that the maximand of that model is too simplistic. Generally, these alternative models set up the problem as one of utility maximisation. They differ in the factors which enter the maximand. Law (1977) and Estrin (1979c) include the number of members as well as the dividend, whilst Berman (1977) and Berman and Berman (1978) include, in addition, the number of hours worked by each member. Law (1977) and Estrin (1979c) use 'group' utility functions, whilst Berman (1977) and Berman and Berman (1978) use individual utility functions. Vanek (1970) argues that a group behavioural process is necessary to allow for variations in work effort. It can be shown,[16] however, that individual utility maximisation cannot yield a stable equilibrium. Stability can be attained only through some group decision process. Such a model in a simple form would be one in which the maximand is

$$U = U(y, N, H)$$

where $y = (pX - rK)/N, H$ is the number of hours worked by the total labour force, and the other variables are as defined earlier. The optimisation problem becomes

$$\text{Maximise} \quad V = U(y, N, H) - \lambda\left(y - \frac{pX - rK}{N}\right)$$

The optimising conditions yield

$$\lambda = -Uy, \tag{19}$$

$$-\frac{U_N}{U_y} = \frac{1}{N}\ [pX_N - y], \tag{20}$$

$$pX_K = r, \tag{21}$$

$$-\frac{U_H}{U_y} = \frac{pX_H}{N}. \tag{22}$$

Equation (22) expresses the short-run equilibrium condition: that the slope of the hours/income indifference curve is equal to the slope of the income per worker curve. So long as the substitution effect outweighs the income effect, an increase in p results in an increase in output. A point will, however, be reached where the supply of hours is reduced as income rises.

Equation (20) expresses the optimum condition for adjusting membership. This is assumed to take place over the longer run. If the collective exhibits no preference as to the size of membership, (20) is equivalent to the short-run condition of the W–V–M model, i.e.

$$pX_N = y$$

but in this case it does not represent a short-run condition.

This model, however, begs a number of questions. In particular: how is the group utility function to be determined? How are the H

hours distributed across members? The two are likely to be connected in that the 'shape' of the utility function most probably determines how the hours are distributed across members.

A similar problem arises in a more explicit form in Berman (1977) and Berman and Berman (1978), where the model is based on individual utility maximisation subject to a constraint that all workers adjust hours in the same proportion. In the simple two factor input case this yields the maximand

$$V_i = U_i(y_i, h_i, N) - \lambda \left(y_i - \frac{pX - rK}{n} \right)$$

where $X = X(H, K)$ and $H = Nh_i$, where h_i are the hours worked by the ith worker and the other variables are as defined earlier.

The first order conditions for maximisation yield

$$-\frac{U_H}{U_y} = pX_H \tag{23}$$

$$-\frac{U_N}{U_y} = \frac{pX_H h_i - y_i}{N} \tag{24}$$

$$pX_K = r \tag{25}$$

where X_H and X_K are the partial derivatives of output with respect to total hours and capital.

The first-order conditions (23)–(25) bear an obvious similarity to (20)–(22) except that the utility function now relates to individuals rather than the collective and that the relationship between h_i, N and H is specified. The latter accounts for the difference between (23) and (22). Berman and Berman (1978) argue that such a model describes a Pareto optimal situation in both the short and the long run; however, this is not a unique optimum since one will exist for each individual i. Berman (1977) argues that the proportionality of hours constraint is equivalent to an oligopoly collusion solution and thus produces stability. However, this is not the appropriate analogy. The situation analysed by Berman (1977) is as much a leadership model as a collusion model, since the proportionality rule is effectively the reaction function of the other members to a change in the ith individual's hours of work. The problem is that any member of the collective can choose to be leader with resulting instability. Berman's (1977) solution is unstable because it does not recognise that, given the nature of the labour-managed firm, the hours worked by *each* member must be subject to a collective decision and thus the appropriate utility function is that of the collective, not of an individual. Nevertheless, Berman (1977) and Berman and Berman (1978) do point to the importance of regarding hours worked rather than membership as the short-run variable in the development of a useful theory of the labour-managed firm (see Chapter 4 below).

III CONCLUSIONS

This chapter has set out the economic theory most relevant to the country studies which follow. It is by no means a full review of the literature, which would require more space than is appropriate to the current volume. It is hoped that it has been useful in summarising some of the main themes of the literature in a reasonably critical manner. Most of all it should indicate that it is possible to conceive of more than one form of l.m.f. and that, *a priori*, these may be expected to behave somewhat differently. The succeeding chapters of this book bear witness to this diversity.

The further development of the economic theory of the labour-managed firm may well focus on how the maximand is determined. Tyson (1979) has examined the l.m.f. using the tools of coalition theory and focusing on effort choice in a collective context. Ireland (1980) takes a different approach, based on individual utility maximisation which emphasises the utility (or disutility) to the worker of different forms of enterprise. Relatively little has been published in these areas thus far, but they are clearly of importance.

NOTES

1. These are published in *Economic Analysis and Workers' Management*, vol. XIII, 1979. This journal has become the first specialist journal in the field and is sponsored by the International Association for the Economics of Self-management.
2. It is interesting to note that although most western economists regard their subject as a positive science, the empirical testing and validity of economic hypotheses is accorded secondary importance in much of their work. A discussion of this subject is given in Katouzian (1980), Chapter 3. The

validity of the normative/positive distinction in economics is also discussed in Machlup (1969) and McLachlan and Swales (1978).

3. Ward's (1958) original exposition christened his subject 'the Illyrian Firm', a term which is still often used to denote what is referred to here as the W–V–M model. It is the present writer's view that the former title is best used to denote Ward's original simple model rather than the subsequently more fully-developed version.

4. It should be noted that in Ward (1958), workers receive a fixed wage and a dividend, i.e.

$$S = w + \frac{\pi^*}{L}$$

where $\dfrac{\pi^*}{L} = \dfrac{\pi}{L} - w,$

$$S = \frac{pX - rK}{L} - w + w$$
$$= \frac{pX - rK}{L}.$$

Thus the maximand is the same whether or not a fixed wage is paid.

5. Recently, however, this view has been challenged on the grounds that membership of an l.m.f. is not a short-run variable in the Marshallian sense. See Berman (1977) and Estrin (1980).

6. It should be noted that some organisations usually identified as labour-managed firms deviate from such arrangements, e.g. in US plywood co-operatives the right to membership may be transferred by sale (see Chapter 4 below); in Mondragon, members retain an interest in future profits in proportion to their foregone earnings (see Chapter 6 below).

7. For a more detailed discussion of this see Vanek (1971b), Furubotn (1971, 1976) and Pejovich (1969).

8. It should be noted that nothing in general can be said about long-run employment of labour and capital and output of the internally-financed l.m.f. compared with the W–V–M firm, as this will depend on the particular production function. The presumption in the literature would certainly seem to be that output and employment will be lower. (See, for example, Vanek, 1971b; Miovic, 1975; and Jones and Backus 1977.)

9. This may be obtained in Chapter 2 of Stephen (1979) where a distinction is made between 'constrained' and 'unconstrained' l.m.f.s and Vanek's (1971b) assumption of infinitely durable capital is relaxed.

10. The point e will be the long-run equilibrium if worker-members are concerned to maximise wealth rather than current income.

11. As opposed to the socio-political consequences.

12. In many French producer co-operatives, assets can be disposed of but the collective cannot consume residual assets when liquidated (see Chapter 5). This would suggest that in the internally-financed case a premium is required for investment to take place.

13. This assumes that the move from b^* to e is a gradual rather than discrete process.

14. The equivalence of the retention of some shares by the jth member and a sum of compensation can be fairly easily demonstrated.

Where $\partial N/\partial L < n_j$, the remaining members who hold, say, N' shares do not receive a dividend of π/N', where

$$\pi = pX^* - rK^* - wL^*,$$

where $*$ denotes the optimum values of the variables. Each share in the surplus is now $\pi/(N' + n'_j)$, where n'_j is the number of shares retained by the jth member after he leaves.

$$n'_j = n_j - \frac{\partial N}{\partial L},$$

$$y = \frac{\pi}{N' + n'_j},$$

therefore

$$\pi - N'y = n'_j y$$

i.e. the departing member received $\pi - N'y$.

$$n'_j y = n_j y - \frac{\partial N}{\partial L} y$$

For the number of shares to move its optimum

$$\frac{\partial N}{\partial L} = \frac{pX_L - w}{y},$$

therefore

$$n'_j y = n_j y - (pX_L - w);$$

since by assumption $(pX_L - w)$ is negative in this case, the jth worker is better off than if he had remained in the collective and received $n_j y$.

15. The analysis of Note 14 *supra* applies *mutis mutandis*.

16. See Stephen (1979, Chapter 1).

Part II

Country Studies

Introduction

Part I of this book has reviewed what might be described as the established economic theory of the labour-managed firm. There it is argued that the dominant theory of the literature, the Ward–Vanek–Meade model, has evolved largely through *a priori* theorising. An attempt is made in Chapter 1 to show that this model is based on a number of assumptions, both behavioural and institutional, which are not the only ones which might be admissible. The studies in Part II testify to the variety of institutional forms which labour-managed firms may take. A 'positive' economic theory of the labour-managed firm must surely reflect this diversity of experience.

The studies presented below do not provide complete coverage of countries where co-operative or labour-managed enterprises operate or have operated, e.g. Great Britain, Malta, Peru and the Scandinavian countries are omitted. Nor are all of the forms of enterprise examined usually covered by the term 'labour-managed' e.g. the West German Co-determined Firm and the Israeli Kibbutz. In the first case, a more limited coverage was necessitated by the logistics of organising a manageable symposium and set of essays. The inclusion of two rather different forms is justified on the grounds that they may be seen as bracketing the labour-managed or co-operative form along a continuum of degrees of participatory enterprise. Co-determination represents a, perhaps slight, modification of the capitalist form whilst the kibbutz involves, in theory at least, a more complete form of co-operation which extends beyond production into the area of consumption.

In Chapter 2, Saul Estrin, after providing a brief description of the organisation of enterprises in Yugoslavia and that country's economic-system, examines the question of income dispersion. He argues that the economic theory of the labour-managed firm predicts that after a change in input or output prices, dispersions in earned income between sectors will arise. These will not be competed away in the labour market and will remain until eliminated by changes in output prices brought about by the entry (or exit) of firms. This theory is then tested by examining inter-industry differentials for the period 1956–75 and intra-sector dispersions for the post 1965 period. This material is then combined to provide an overall picture. Estrin concludes that the data provide evidence that incomes had become endogenous to the firm and are consistent with the economic theory of the labour-managed firm.

Producers' co-operatives in the United States of America are discussed in Chapters 3 and 4. Derek Jones examines the performance of several groups of co-operatives whose members have been formed since the 1840s. These cover a number of industries and geographical locations. Jones examines the organisational similarities and differences of these groups. He then relates the performance of the co-operatives within these groups to the theories of Jaroslav Vanek and Paul Bernstein.

Katrina Berman focuses on a much narrower range of American experience in Chapter 4. There she uses her extensive experience of the plywood co-operatives of the north-western United States to examine those aspects of co-operative organisation which she sees as their strengths and weaknesses. After highlighting non-member employment, finance and share transfer as being problem areas and examining possible remedies, Dr Berman discusses the prospects for labour-managed firms in the United States.

More than six hundred producers' co-operatives belong to the French Société des Co-operatives Ouvrieres de Production. A sample of these are the basis for Eric Batstone's discussion of the French experience in Chapter 5. He argues that although the history and formal ideology of the French co-operative movement is based on the notion of a solidary collectivity of workers rather than a democracy of small capitalists, their constitutions generally place them somewhere between these extremes. Batstone then suggests a number of general hypotheses concerning co-operative performance which are tested by examining the performance of co-operatives relative to the industrial averages. The data, in general, confirm these hypotheses. In his concluding section, Batstone outlines a life-cycle hypothesis of co-operative behaviour.

Recently, much publicity has been accorded to the group of worker-owned enterprises centred on the Spanish Basque town of

Mondragon. The origins and performance of these enterprises is outlined in Chapter 6 by Robert Oakeshott. The evidence clearly points to these firms as having achieved economic success. Oakeshott argues that the Mondragon experience is of an attempt to achieve the necessary balance between 'genuine bottom-upwards control, and a genuinely efficient professional executive' as well as other divergent interests and values. He accepts that Mondragon has concentrated on achieving economic rather than social goals but rejects the view that the Mondragon experience is some kind of fraud and is clearly optimistic about the wider benefits of this type of organisation.[1]

In Ireland, co-operatives are widespread in agriculture but recently community co-operatives and industrial co-operatives have been established. In Chapter 7, Connell Fanning examines in detail the performance of three Irish industrial co-operatives as well as discussing other forms of co-operation. He concludes that two of the three co-operatives whose performance is analysed appear financially sound. The need for further research to widen knowledge on industrial co-operatives in Ireland is suggested.

Juan Espinosa draws on and extends his earlier work with Andrew Zimbalist to document the performance of and problems faced by co-operative enterprises in Chile. This chapter documents the changing economic and political environment of the last twenty years within which workers' participation was encouraged and then rejected. Espinosa documents the evolution of the System of Financing Self-Management and its role in supporting the co-operative sector. By 1979 this sector comprised 34 firms, each of which was relatively small in size. The author argues that the performance of these enterprises cannot be assessed in isolation from the general economic conditions prevailing in Chile.

The Israeli Kibbutz is the subject matter of Avner Ben-Ner and Egon Neuberger's study which comprises Chapter 9. The kibbutz is more than a form of enterprise, it is a comprehensive communal organisation. This chapter seeks to demonstrate that it is viable as such, traces its evolution and the factors which influenced this, and analyses the economic consequences of this form of organisation. Ben-Ner and Neuberger use a programming model to simulate the behaviour of an 'average' kibbutz in 1965. This model is then used as the basis for an economic interpretation of changes in the kibbutz movement.

Whilst the kibbutz is something more than a labour-managed firm, the West German co-determined enterprise is something less. Jan Svejnar describes the institutions of this system and examines its impact on wages and the share of power held by workers in the final chapter of this section. Previous work in this field has suffered from the difficulty of specifying a plausible objective function. Svejnar presents a relatively simple model of a utility maximising firm composed of workers and managers. This model is general in nature and may be applied to cases of different degrees of participation – from zero in the entrepreneurial firm to the fullest extent in a labour-managed firm.

It is thus a contribution to the literature on the labour-managed firm as well as to the understanding of co-determination. The empirical findings are that wages and worker power are not affected by minority co-determination but are affected by parity co-determination in the iron and steel industry but not in coal-mining.

In general, the studies in Part II testify to the diversity of form and performance of labour-managed or co-operative enterprises. They show that such firms can prosper but sometimes fail, and attempt to find explanations for such occurrences.

NOTE

1. A contrasting interpretation of the Mondragon experience is given in Eaton (1979).

2 Yugoslavia[1]
Saul Estrin

An important conclusion from the analysis of self-managed economies is that income dispersion between industries would significantly widen as a consequence of introducing such a system. This chapter examines whether the Yugoslav experience after the reforms of 1961 and 1965 (which permitted self-managed firms to operate in a market environment) conformed to these expectations. It will be shown that earnings' differences within and between sectors widened considerably after the Reforms, even when adjustments for skill are taken into account, and that the form of labour maket misallocation after 1965 conformed to that predicted in the literature (i.e. Ward, 1958; Vanek, 1970; Meade, 1972).

I BACKGROUND

The Yugoslav system of workers' self-management is probably the most extensive case of labour-managed firms to date. The system has gone through several phases in its development since the early 1950s and only at certain points in time has it corresponded to the model of labour-management discussed in the economic literature and outlined in Chapter 1 above. Stephen (1979) has argued that it is necessary to distinguish between the Yugoslav 'economic system' and the 'system of workers' self-management'. The former refers to the development of a broadly market-oriented resource allocation system whilst the latter is concerned with the internal organisation of the enterprise. The two aspects came together only to approximate the assumptions of the theoretical model in the period 1965 to 1972, though one should observe some of the problems discussed in this paper after 1957.

(a) INTERNAL ORGANISATION OF THE ENTERPRISE

Although workers' councils had existed in some factories in late 1949, their formal endorsement as part of the Yugoslav system came in a speech by Tito in mid-1950. In the early years their role was purely advisory, but gradually more and more power was accorded them. In part, this transition was effected by a new definition of property rights within the system. Workers were accorded a 'right of use'[2] which invested workers' councils with control over the way in which productive assets were used, as well as their sale or creation. However, workers were not allowed to increase current wages by liquidating assets, so individual assets had to be replaced, if sold, since they were social property rather than owned by the workers in the enterprise.

Formally, each enterprise was managed by its Workers' Council elected by and from the workers. That council appointed a Managing Board which met more frequently and was responsible for the more detailed specification of policies endorsed by the Council. The General Director (chief executive) of the enterprise was, in the early years of the system, appointed by the communal authority (i.e. from outside the enterprise) but gradually the Workers' Council was given an increasing and eventually determinant influence in his appointment. By the mid-1960s, the larger enterprises had reorganised along the lines introduced during the fifties, and were sub-divided into Working Units which had their own Workers' Councils as well as representatives on the enterprise Workers' Council. The organs of self-management throughout the period 1952–64 were subject to varying limitations on their powers. Space does not permit a detailed survey here. The interested reader is referred to Gorupic and Paj (1970) for a detailed Yugoslav account of the formal evolution of the system of workers' self-management within the enterprise.

Whilst this extensive system had provided the opportunity for an extremely large number of workers to participate in the 'management' of the enterprise, much evidence has been presented which suggests that policy making was dominated by a limited strata of workers within enterprises (see, for example, Gorupic and Paj, 1970; Adizes, 1971; Obradovic, 1973; Warner, 1975 and Stephen 1976). In particular, it was argued by Yugoslav policy makers that self-management was becoming increasingly bureaucratic. This eventually led to the new Constitution of 1974 and the Associated Labour Act of 1976 which formally abolished the enterprise to replace it with groupings of Basic Organisations of Associated Labour (BOAL). BOALs are based on groupings of workers with similar interests, who contribute to the production of a marketable output. Each BOAL is an economic entity in its own right, its primary economic relations being with the other BOALs with which it is associated through a 'self-management' agreement. The system is complex and in the early stages of development, and relates to a period beyond that of market self-management which is the focus of the empirical investigation reported in this chapter. For a more detailed discussion on this system the interested reader is referred to Sacks (1979a, 1979b), Dirlam (1979) and Stephen (1979).

(b) THE YUGOSLAV ECONOMIC SYSTEM

There was a decentralised planning system in Yugoslavia between 1953 and 1965, characterised by central control of investment, trade and most prices, though there were some markets for current commodities and nominal enterprise self-management. Over the period, firms were granted increasing autonomy over decisions, and the system was gradually decentralised until the major changes in 1965 abolished investment allocation and liberalised both internal and external markets. After that date, enterprises had both the resources and the power to make economic choices in their own self-interest. Thus, in the period between 1965 and 1972 the two components of the Yugoslav system – markets and self-management in the enterprise – became fully integrated.

The authorities maintained *laissez-faire* until 1972, when firms were persuaded to sign 'social contracts' so that their choices conformed more closely to the desired pattern of development. This innovation was concerned with growth and income inequality, and therefore entailed guidelines for the collectives' distribution of net revenue between income and investment. While nominally voluntary rather than imposed, they represented an effective reassertion of central direction over earnings (the three institutional systems are examined in more detail in Dirlam and Plummer (1973), Horvat (1971) and Neuberger (1970)).

Until 1958, incomes were determined centrally, though administered through the trade unions, but a new accounting system was introduced after that date in which enterprises could make collective decisions about the allocation of revenue, net of non-labour costs, between investment, wages and reserves. However, political control meant that these legal changes did not lead to immediate shifts of behaviour, and the proportion of net revenue involved remained small because of taxation to provide central investment funds. The amount available for internal distribution was increased in 1961, but almost immediately reduced again in 1962 because of the large wage increases that resulted. Even so, the pressures for enterprise autonomy were gaining momentum (see Milenkovitch, 1971; Rusinow, 1977) and culminated in the 1965 Reforms which increased both the resources at the disposal of the firms and their willingness to employ them. At the end of the period, the 1972 Reforms were pre-dated by moral suasion on enterprises to reduce income differentials, and entailed an incomes policy to provide norms for income distribution between skills and sectors.

Thus, one would predict a relatively narrow inter-industrial wage dispersion in 1958, because the authorities had the aim and power to ensure equality except for cases of political preference or labour scarcity. The gradual movement to self-managed auto-nomy would slowly widen the dispersion until 1965, with a discontinuity in 1961, after which it should rapidly widen until the late sixties or early seventies.

II THEORY

The economic theory of the labour-managed firm reviewed in Chapter 1 above, indicates that there will be a perverse supply response by an individual firm following from a parametric shift such as a change in product price, technical progress or change in capital rentals. In the long-run, a Pareto optimal allocation may be achieved by the movement of firms between sectors.

However, the resource misallocation in a self-managed economy after any parametric shift develops in the labour market and leads to a dispersion in earned income between sectors. The labour-managed firm chooses both employment and incomes, so each enterprise has only one demand point in wage-employment space which depends solely on the constraints in its optimisation problem. The equalisation of earnings cannot therefore rely on labour market forces, since potential recruits to high paying collectives cannot bid admission because existing members' incomes would be reduced by their employment (assuming they received an equal share of the surplus). Inter-sectoral income dispersion can therefore be eliminated only by shifts in the parameters exogenous to each firm (specifically, output price because of changes in firm numbers).

The income dispersion in a self-managed economy resulting from the absence of conventional labour market forces can be considered between and within sectors. During periods of resource misallocation, one should observe differences in earnings between industries, which derive from factors of relative demand, industrial concentration and technical advance. In the absence of any compensating changes in exogenous variables, these differentials can be maintained prior to enterprise mobility. Moreover, within each sector, differences in the efficiency of production which cause a dispersion in revenue per head at each level of labour input, despite a given price, must be translated into an earnings' distribution. The arguments are analogous to those employed to analyse profits' dispersion in capitalism, since average earnings represent profits plus the wage bill divided by the number of employees, so income distribution in a self-managed economy is skewed by the payment of the residual surplus (which may differ from that in capitalism because of the new maximand) to the employees in each particular firm.

These arguments suggest that the period 1965–72 in Yugoslavia should be characterised by a major increase in income differences within and between sectors, which would not be eradicated effectively by enterprise mobility over such a short time horizon. The remainder of this chapter examines how income dispersion changed between 1956 and 1975, and the differentials that developed during the period of market self-management.

Empirical work reveals that the Yugoslav market structure was severely imperfect in 1965 (Sacks (1973), Estrin (1978)), with significant differences in the efficiency of production between industries related to planners' preferences in the allocation of capital and import quotas. Once self-management was introduced, these should map into an inter-sectoral income dispersion (for evidence of these associations see Estrin (1979a)), which could be eliminated by enterprise mobility. While there is little evidence of new entry (Sacks (1973)), the data suggest considerable diversification by existing firms into new product markets (see Estrin (1978)) during the sixties, which should act to reduce income inequalities. Thus, though the period of market self-management was too short for the full eradication of income inequalities, one might predict some reduction towards the end of the period, before the state intervened with an effective incomes policy.

This represents the hypothesis about industrial earnings in Yugoslavia in 1956–75 given the institutional framework. Clearly, if Yugoslavia had remained effectively planned throughout the period, with differing degress of decentralisation, one would predict relatively constant and narrow dispersion measures. However, if the reforms had established a capitalist market system, the null is more complex since one would predict analogous income dispersion to the self-managed case if labour markets were not uniformly competitive. For example, if unions appropriated some fixed proportion of profits, the capitalist wage dispersion would differ from the self-managed one quantitatively, rather than qualitatively, and the two would be identical in a bilateral monopoly where unions appropriated all profit.

Therefore, although historical and institutional factors suggest that one can discount the possibility that capitalism was re-introduced in 1965, this work remains essentially empirical, and can establish consistency only with the predictions of self-management theory. It reveals that dispersion did increase after 1965, and details the scale and complexity of Yugoslav labour market misallocation after the Reforms, but cannot show causality between the two events.

III EVIDENCE

(a) THE DISTRIBUTION OF INCOME BETWEEN INDUSTRIES 1956–75

This section outlines the level and changes in income dispersion between sectors (approximately US two-digit industries) and industries (approximately US three-digit industries), as defined in the Yugoslav industrial classification. The material at the sectoral level is presented for unadjusted earnings per worker, skill types and job types, but the data on 75 industries are available only for unadjusted income dispersion measures. It should be noted that the film industry proved an outlier at both levels of aggregation, and has therefore been omitted from calculations unless otherwise mentioned.

(i) Dispersion at the sectoral level

Statisticki Godisnjak Jugoslavie provides material on the average level of gross monthly earnings per person employed by 22 industrial sectors for most years between 1956 and 1975. In 1956, the dispersion was narrow and skewed according to planners' preferences, as one would expect in a centrally-planned economy. The highest incomes were observed in heavy industry such as shipbuilding, ferrous and non-ferrous metals, and coal mining (around 115 per cent of the industrial average), and the lowest in the building, wood and tobacco trades (around 85 per cent of the mean).

Table 2.1 traces the movement in dispersion over the period, measured by the unweighted coefficient of variation (standard deviation over mean) and range from highest to lowest

TABLE 2.1   *Inter-sectoral dispersion of average incomes per head, 1956–75*

Year	Coefficient of variation (%)	Range (%)	Hourly earnings: coefficient of variation (%)
1956	12.1	146	12.0
1958	12.6	152	12.9
1961	18.3	191	
1962	16.0	179	
1963	17.0	171	14.8
1964	18.6	196	16.0
1965	18.0	203	19.0
1966	21.5	209	21.6
1967	26.5	234	
1968	24.2	226	22.0
1969	19.5	200	21.0
1970	19.3	203	
1971	20.0	215	
1972	17.0	173	
1973	16.4	182	
1974	17.1	186	
1975	18.5	202	

Source: Estrin (1981).

observation. There were data for only nineteen sectors in the two
years available prior to 1961, but the measurements can be
compared to those for hourly earnings by sectors from the same
source.

The pattern conforms closely to expectations, in that the
coefficient of variation gradually increased from a relatively low
level during the centrally-planned era to more than double the
previous value by 1967, after which it declined by one third to end
the period around fifty per cent above its initial value. The
measure increased in spurts in the years following Reforms (1961
and 1965), and declined considerably in 1972.

Moreover, the variability of the dispersion through time was
associated with changes in the sectoral rank order of incomes.
The gradual liberalisation shifted the pattern of inequality to
favour light rather than heavy industry, while the government
intervention in the early seventies to some extent reversed this
pattern. Thus, the rank order correlation coefficient for 1975 on
1956 was 0.759, but 1967 on 1956 was 0.563 and 1975 on 1967 was
0.654. The relative position of coal mining—a sector generally
favoured by planners—is a good illustration of this movement; it
declined from a rank of sixth in 1956 to fourteenth in 1969, after
which its position rose again to rank fourth in 1974.

The Yugoslav pattern of variability differs from the normal
pattern in other economies.[3] Coefficients of variation for western
capitalist economies have generally been stable over time and
lower than that of Yugoslavia during the period of market self-
management but higher than that during the planned period.
Comparisons with such economies might be unsuitable but when
the reference point is changed to eastern European and Mediter-
ranean countries, the conclusion remains unaltered. Moreover,
the coefficient of variation in other countries was generally below
that for Yugoslavia in the post-1961 period.

Therefore, there was a marked increase in Yugoslav inter-
sectoral earnings' dispersion after the 1961 and 1965 Reforms to a
relatively high level, with associated changes in rank order. These
represented abnormal phenomena by international standards.

(ii) The inter-sectoral dispersion for skill and job types

In the previous section, the sectoral income dispersion was
considered without adjustment for differences in the skill com-

position of the labour force. It is possible that the changes in unadjusted sectoral dispersion could be explained by shifts in either the proportion of the labour force in particular skill groups, or skill differentials. Therefore, the material below examines the sectoral dispersion for each skill group, and income differences according to labour type over the period.

Yugoslav sources categorise labour into eight groups: four white collar ones based on education from university to elementary level (ranked one to four), and four blue collar ones from highly skilled to unskilled workers (ranked five to eight). While they are not homogeneous labour types, it will be assumed that most members of each group could apply for posts in a similar classification and different sector, but would fail to obtain employment in a higher category and would not accept it in a lower one.

Table 2.2 shows the inter-sectoral coefficient of variation of gross average monthly earnings for each group, and the whole labour force.[4] The coefficient for each individual skill group followed the pattern observed for the whole labour force over time very closely, so correlation coefficients over the eight years between all groups and each particular one generally exceeded 0.9 for manual workers, and 0.7 for white collar ones.

The measure of dispersion between sectors in each skill group was always less than for the labour force as a whole, though they were generally high in comparison to the reported unadjusted

TABLE 2.2   *Inter-sectoral coefficient of variation of average incomes per head each skill group 1966–75*

Skill type		1966	1967	1968	1969	1970	1972	1973	1975
All groups		18.9	22.0	20.8	21.1	22.8	18.4	16.8	16.4
White collar	1	12.6	16.8	16.7	14.4	11.5	7.0	9.9	10.9
	2	11.4	15.0	15.9	12.1	13.1	10.5	12.5	10.9
	3	12.7	15.5	16.0	14.9	15.3	10.7	11.7	11.7
	4	12.7	15.6	15.6	13.8	18.0	16.8	13.5	9.9
Blue collar	5	16.0	19.1	16.5	17.7	18.3	13.6	12.3	13.4
	6	16.7	19.9	17.2	17.9	19.2	16.5	13.2	12.8
	7	13.6	17.2	18.9	13.7	17.7	13.8	15.2	12.2
	8	11.9	13.5	17.9	11.4	12.4	11.7	8.9	10.1

Source: Estrin (1981).

levels in other economies. The coefficient of variation was greater for blue collar than for white collar workers, and normally higher for highly skilled and skilled workers for whom the range, in 1967, reached over 200 per cent. This can probably be explained by labour scarcity factors, since competition for certain labour groups meant that lower paying sectors would have to widen their skill dispersion schedules to offer management and technicians an income that did not differ too markedly from the average.

Sociological studies (i.e.Gorupic and Paj (1970), Adizes (1971)) have suggested that skilled workers and the less qualified white collar ones represent the controlling group in Yugoslav co-operatives. If these acted as a majority coalition, effectively hiring the remaining labour types at a market wage, one would predict that the inter-sectoral income dispersion would be most marked for these groups. One can speculate that the effects of self-management on income dispersion could therefore be measured by the gap between the minimum and maximum coefficient of variation by skill type, which was around 6 per cent in the 1960s

Thus, the major changes in unadjusted inter-sectoral dispersion in Yugoslavia over the period could not have been caused by shifts in the sectoral composition of labour, since the distribution between sectors for each skill group closely followed that for the entire labour force, and the coefficient of variation was relatively large for certain labour types. An alternative explanation is that the reforms heralded changes in skill differentials,which altered the average earnings between sectors with different, though approximately constant, labour type proportions. Table 2.2 shows the industrial skill differentials, as a proportion of the incomes of the unskilled from 1956 to 1975.

At the start of the period, Yugoslav differentials from top to bottom were relatively narrow, but there was a major increase until 1961, which suggests that widening of inter-sectoral dispersion associated with the first liberalisation was partly caused by enterprises using their autonomy to broaden income differences between skill types. The previous differentials were restored by 1963, and dispersion by skill group did not increase at the time of the 1965 Reforms, though there was some drift at the end of the sixties. However, the reduction in inter-sectoral dispersion after 1972 must have been associated with the considerable narrowing in differentials at that time, which were reduced to a level below that achieved during the era of central planning.

TABLE 2.3   *Skill differentials 1956–75 (as a percentage of the unskilled)*

| | Skill type | | | | | | | |
| | White collar | | | | Blue collar | | | |
Year	1	2	3	4	5	6	7	8
1956	264							100
1959	316							100
1961	330							100
1963	261							100
1966	272	219	163	120	187	135	113	100
1967	262	217	160	121	188	133	110	100
1969	270	211	158	120	187	130	113	100
1970	299	225	170	122	199	135	115	100
1972	276	214	160	117	187	132	112	100
1973	246	198	154	122	177	132	107	100
1975	264	207	160	123	184	136	114	100

Source: Estrin (1981).

The table confirms the strong relative position of highly-skilled workers in Yugoslavia, who earned approximately double the income of the unskilled; more than most white collar workers; and around two-thirds of the incomes of the university-trained group. It should be noted that changes in the skill distribution generally affected these and the highest category of labour type, while the remainder faced stable relativities over time.

If one compares these findings with material derived from the UN: 'Incomes in Post-war Europe' and National Yearbooks, it appears that Yugoslav differentials were narrow by western standards, though rather wide compared with eastern Europe. However, insofar as data is available, it would appear that Yugoslav skilled workers were relatively better paid (as a proportion of the incomes of the unskilled) than anywhere except the United States. These results must be interpreted cautiously, because of probable differences in definition, but they suggest that neither the pattern of Yugoslav dispersion by sector over time, nor its level, were closely related to changes in either labour proportions or skill differentials.

Material on incomes by job type between sectors provides further information about labour market misallocation in Yugoslavia after 1965. Observed differences in income within relatively homogeneous categories must be explained by some constraint on labour mobility, such as suggested in the analysis of self managed firms, and could not be sustained in a competitive market economy. The dispersion was wide for most jobs, with a range between 165 per cent and 231 per cent in 1969, and 150 per cent and 253 per cent in 1973. The coefficient of variation was generally at a level comparable to that for unadjusted incomes by sector, varying in 1969 from 13.7 per cent for Technical Directors to 21.5 per cent for Administrative Staff.

The data confirm not only that there were large differences between the incomes paid for an identical job in different industrial sectors in Yugoslavia during the period of self management, but also that there was considerable variation in that income over time. There is less evidence of a decline in the dispersion after 1972 in this series, though this could be explained by the paucity of the data.

Finally, it should be noted that one can refute the argument that the inter-sectoral income dispersion was associated with differences in income by region. The inter-sectoral coefficients of variation of incomes in 21 sectors for each of the eight republics and autonomous provinces were generally greater than for Yugoslavia as a whole between 1962 and 1974 (except for Slovenia, where it was normally smaller). Moreover, the changes in the coefficient over time in each republic closely followed the national pattern, and the income rank orders were approximately the same in each republic in each year (the rank order correlation generally exceeded 0.9). There was no significant association between the level of regional development (measured by average income per head) and the sectoral dispersion, so one must reject on cross-section data, the argument that the observed distribution was associated with relative levels of development, rather than self-management.

(iii) Inter-industrial income dispersion

This sub-section uses the data from *Industrija Preduzeca* on gross average monthly earnings per worker by sector and industry to provide measures of income dispersion at the industrial level. It confirms previous findings, and shows that in Yugoslavia, as observed for other countries in the earlier sections, the income disparities become greater as the data become more disaggregated.

Table 2.4 shows the coefficient of variation and range of incomes by sector and industry between 1968 and 1974. The former series is included since the change in source means that, though consistent with the current material, they provide different measures to those in the previous tables.

TABLE 2.4 *Inter-industry coefficient of variation and range of average incomes (percentage)*

	1968	1969	1970	1971	1972	1974
Coefficient of variation						
21 Sectors	23.7	21.8	21.8	21.6	19.6	16.9
75 Industries	25.7	23.2	30.1	28.8	26.2	23.5
Range						
21 Sectors	225	209	205	205	195	189
75 Industries	335	332	367	277	236	217

Source: Estrin (1981).

The table shows that the coefficient of variation was always wider at the industrial than at the sectoral level, ranging between 23 per cent and 30 per cent over the period. These were very large by international standards, and the variability between years became more marked (with a change in the coefficient of 7 per cent between 1969 and 1970) and less cyclical. Thus, rather than declining from the midsixties peaks, the industrial dispersion was at a minimum in 1969 and peaked in 1970, while the effects of the 1972 Reforms were less marked than at the sectoral level.

The industrial dispersion was broadly based, with some 38 per cent of industries paying outside the range 80–120 per cent of the mean income in 1968, and only 28 per cent paying within the range 90–110 per cent of the mean. The decline in dispersion in 1969 and 1971 was caused by industries shifting from the 80–120 per cent to the 90–110 per cent range, while the extreme observations remained an approximately constant proportion over time. Thus, the industrial rank order correlation coefficient of 1974 on 1968 was relatively high (0.85), and the changes in the dispersion were caused by some narrowing of the differences between particular industries earning between 80 per cent and 90 per cent, or 110 per cent and 120 per cent of the industrial average.

One must assume there was a restructuring of employment from higher to lower paid industries in each sector to establish consistency in the pattern of dispersion over time at the sectoral and industrial level. Thus, while income differences between industries did not show a declining trend until 1972, the aggregation weights in each sector would have altered in favour of lower income groupings, so the sectoral dispersion appeared to have been narrowing after 1967. (This argument was loosely confirmed by examining the rate of growth of employment by industry 1968–72, which was negatively associated with earnings.) This relative shift of labour from high to low value marginal product uses is consistent with predictions from the theory of self-management.

(b) INTRA-SECTORAL INCOME DISPERSION

It was argued in Section II above that incomes in a self-managed economy may vary *between* industries according to differences in demand and industrial structure, and *within* sectors according to a dispersion in the efficiency of production. The focus now shifts to the latter dispersion in Yugoslavia after 1965, proxying inter-firm material by data on firm-size groups from *Industrija Preduzeca*. This provides information on incomes by sector in up to ten divisions according to firm size, categorised by net product, employment or capital. Because the categories span a very small range, and given the paucity of industrial enterprises (see Estrin, 1978), this adequately approximates the ideal classification, in that around 66 per cent of the categories contained fewer than five firms, and around 15 per cent only one producer.

The size groups are defined differently between years, so the series presented are not strictly comparable over time. In 1966, 1968 and 1972 the grouping was by net product, 1969 and 1971 by capital employed, and 1970 by employment.

If one considers industry as a whole, the annual industrial earnings per worker varied considerably according to the firm-size group of employment. The coefficient of variation between the nine or ten categories varied between 26.6 per cent in 1966 and 50.9 per cent in 1971, with the lowest range exceeding 300 per cent. Unlike western Europe (see EEC: 'Social Statistics; Labour Costs in Industry') incomes were not positively monotonically associated with the scale of production, but high earnings were received in both the largest and smallest companies.

The most important feature of the all-industry data by firm size was the variability of incomes over time in a given size group category. There was stability in the middle categories, but the relative position in those with very large or small firms was constantly changing. For example, in small firms, average earnings changed from 10 per cent of the industrial average in 1966 to 293 per cent in 1972, while in the medium-sized ones they only varied between 95 per cent in 1969 and 100 per cent in 1970.

Turning to the intra-sectoral income dispersion, the data may be analysed to show the proportion of sectors with particular intra-sectoral income ranges between 1966 and 1972, as a per-centage of all sectors. In 1966 only 4 per cent of sectors displayed a range of less than 150 per cent, while 64 per cent contained an income range by firm-size groups in excess of 200 per cent. Similarly, in 1969 the intra-sectoral range was below 150 per cent in 35 per cent of sectors, but in excess of 200 per cent in 40 per cent of them.

The data show that the majority of sectors, in most years, had an internal income range between 150 and 300 per cent, with a sizeable minority (reaching 40 per cent in 1968) displaying one in excess of 300 per cent. Generally, the extreme observations used in calculating the range occurred in categories with only one, or very few, firms so these figures adequately proxy an inter-enterprise dispersion. The sectors with lower income ranges normally contained more producers in each size class, so the averaging probably disguised further dispersion.

The changes in the definition of categories make inter-temporal comparison difficult, but if one considers 1966, 1968 and 1972, with net product size-groups, one can discern the familiar pattern of increasing then declining dispersion within sectors. Even so, after the 1972 Reforms, 14 per cent of sectors showed an intra-sectoral range in excess of 300 per cent, while only 18 per cent had ranges below 150 per cent.

There was no significant association between either the level, or rank order, of earnings by sector and the intra-sectoral range. The correlation coefficient ranged between -0.217 (1968, rank order) and 0.232 (1971, level) with no consistent pattern. Thus one can refute the hypothesis that dispersion in a sector was related to the average income in that industry, relative to the mean.

There is little international evidence on wage dispersion within sectors, but some material is available for the UK mechanical engineering industry (derived from the Economic Development

Committee for Mechanical Engineering: 'Company Financial Results 1967–1972'). The coefficient of variation between 33 firms was 1.5 per cent with the range between incomes approximately 130 per cent.

Therefore, the data, which proxies for inter-firm evidence within sectors, reveals considerable income dispersion in every year, with major changes in the location, though not level, of income differences. The earnings' range in a sector exceeded 10:1 per cent in several instances, and was at least 2:1 per cent in a majority of sectors in most years. It is interesting to note that incomes were not monotonically associated with the scale of production, so self-management favoured some small as well as large firms. There was little evidence of similar income dispersion levels within industries in other market economies, and these findings are entirely consistent with the arguments concerning earnings in a self-managed economy.

(c) RESOURCE MISALLOCATION IN YUGOSLAV LABOUR MARKETS UNDER SELF-MANAGEMENT

The material on income dispersion between sectors and within them according to skill and firm-size groups are now combined to provide an overall picture of the specific income inequalities which developed after the introduction of self-management.

Commencing with the income dispersion between firms and firm-size groups in different sectors, Table 2.5 summarises the matrix by showing the proportion of firm-size groups in particular earnings ranges (as a percentage of the average industrial

TABLE 2.5   *Intra-sectoral disperson: the proportion of sectors in different firm-size group income ranges*

Income range in sector (%)	Proportion of sectors (%)					
	1966	1968	1969	1970	1971	1972
<150	4	5	35	18	23	18
151–200	32	35	25	32	18	41
201–300	46	20	20	27	27	27
>300	18	40	20	23	32	14

Source: Estrin (1981).

income) for the years of constant definition – 1966, 1968 and 1972.

In any year, the imposition of a non-systematic variation by size category upon the familiar inter-sectoral pattern meant that the bulk of groups were paying within a relatively narrow income range. More than 40 per cent of the categories paid between 80 and 120 per cent of the industrial average because, in practice, there was little difference between the minimum incomes in high paying sectors, medium incomes in middle income sectors, and maximum ones in the worst paying industries.

However, the overall income range proved to be very large, exceeding 1000 per cent in every year and reaching a peak of 7160 per cent in 1966. When the most extreme observations are excluded, the maximum range lay between 650 and 750 per cent, and these were generally between categories containing one firm.

An example of this process is a comparison of the oil and textiles industries (the highest and lowest paid sectors) in 1966: the highest earning group in textiles earned around the average for oil, and the worst paid group in oil around the average for textiles, but the overall range between the two sectors increased to around 500 per cent.

Combining the relatively large sectoral and intra-sectoral income dispersion shows that many firm-size groups actually paid within a relatively narrow range, but the gap between the rewards for the small number of successful and unsuccessful co-operatives (10 per cent of the categories paid outside the range 51–200 per cent of the industrial average in 1966 and 1972, 14 per cent in 1968) was very wide – generally in excess of 1000 per cent. These findings are consistent with the arguments in Section II, that, while one might not expect the profits or losses accruing to labour in the majority of cases to prove large, they would considerably widen the overall range in a small proportion of firms. The introduction of self-management would therefore flatten out and increase the span of the income distribution between firms.

Finally, one can combine the income dispersions by sector and skill groups to investigate whether the monopoly power of co-operatives in the labour market proved comparably important to differences in skills in determining earnings in post-reform Yugoslavia.

At the peak of the dispersion in 1967, the inter-sectoral range was around 200 per cent, and the skill one around 290 per cent, so the overall range from electrical managers to unskilled metal workers was around 5:1. Since this was similar to that observed between skills elsewhere, this and the findings of Table 2.5 help to explain why the overall Yugoslav income distribution, measured by the Gini coefficient, has been shown to be relatively egalitarian (see Chenery *et al.*, 1974, Table 1). However, this paper has concentrated on the peculiar character, rather than absolute level, of inequality, and there were serious anomalies because the sector in which the individual worked was of comparable importance to the skill level in determining incomes.

For example, highly-skilled workers in electricity supply or oil earned more, on average, than the highest paid groups in two-thirds of Yugoslav industry. They also received higher incomes than the second white collar group (technicians) in all sectors but their own, while the least-skilled groups in these aggregated industries earned above the average income, and more than skilled labour in one third of Yugoslav industry.

Conversely, management in the metal industry on average earned less than skilled workers in around one-third of Yugoslav sectors, and more than 33 per cent less than highly-skilled blue collar labour in the two best paid sectors. Management in the tobacco industry earned 50 per cent less than highly-skilled labour in electricity supply and only 50 per cent more than unskilled workers in that industry.

The range between sectors, and especially skill types, narrowed significantly in the early seventies, but because the former movement exceeded the latter, the anomalies generally remained. For example, in 1973, highly-skilled oil or electricity supply workers still earned at least as much as the best educated group in around 75 per cent of the sectors, while the former group earned less in tobacco than highly skilled workers in around 20 per cent of Yugoslav industry.

Therefore, at the peak of the post-reform income dispersion, the most highly educated labour type in the bulk of Yugoslav industry could have increased their incomes, on average, by resigning to undertake skilled manual labour. More generally, the incentive system was inadequately directed towards the acquisition of personal skills since individuals could raise their earnings more by shifting employment between sectors and firms than by investing in human capital.

The fact that these large sectoral differentials emerged, yet did not adequately generate labour mobility to equalise incomes, is consistent with the previous discussion about the behaviour of self-managed firms in terms of collective monopoly power in the labour market.

IV DISCUSSION

This paper has examined evidence on the proposition that the Yugoslav income dispersion would assume unusual characteristics after the introduction of self-management, because wages would become firm-or industry-specific and competitive labour market forces would prove inadequate to eliminate the resulting differentials. Therefore, both the changes in income dispersion by sector over the period 1956–75, and the particular inequalities which developed between 1965 and 1972 have been investigated, and compared with international experience.

It has been shown that there were considerable increases in inter-sectoral income differences after 1965, which cannot be accounted for by changing skill proportions, differentials, or job location by region. The Reforms heralded changes in the sectoral income rank order, and the resulting dispersion proved wide by international standards, even when skill types, job types and regions were taken into account.

The material on dispersion within sectors, and the overall measures, provide the strongest evidence that incomes had become endogenous to the firm, rather than a market-determined parameter, after 1965. While one observed a maximum range for a given job type between sectors of 2.5:1, the range within sectors generally exceeded 2:1, and reached 10:1 in some years. Thus, the overall dispersion of unadjusted average incomes between firm size groups once exceeded 70:1, with some 10 per cent of categories outside the range of 4:1. Moreover, the sectoral dispersion proved to be of comparable importance to the skill dispersion in determining incomes, which led to major anomalies between labour types by industry.

Therefore, there is considerable evidence for the suggested widening of income dispersion, and weakness of conventional labour market forces in Yugoslavia after the introduction of self-management in 1965. While some of these findings are consistent with the introduction of any market system in a planned economy, the scale and nature of the differentials which emerged point to the particular resource misallocation which arises in self-managed economies because labour incomes are an enterprise choice variable.

NOTES

1. This chapter is an edited version of the paper 'Income dispersion in a self-managed economy' presented at the Walton Symposium, June, 1979. The full paper included a lengthier discussion of international comparisons and is available as Estrin (1979b), and a revised version will appear in *Economica* (1981). The permission of the editors of *Economica* to reproduce Tables 2.1 to 2.5 of this chapter is gratefully acknowledged.
2. For a more thorough discussion of property-rights in the Yugoslav system see Milenkovitch (1971, pp. 94–9) and Wiles (1977, pp. 41–5).
3. For more detailed comparisons see Estrin (1979b).
4. The measures for the whole labour force in Table 2.2 differ from those of Table 2.1 because of a change in source. Table 2.2 is, however, internally consistent.

3 The United States of America: a Survey of Producer Co-operative Performance[1]

Derek C. Jones

Although the 1970s have witnessed widespread interest in workers' participation in management, little attention has been paid, thus far, to the American experience with a form of participation which involves a radical shift in organisational ownership and control: the producer co-operative (for exceptions see Shirom, 1972 and Jones, 1977). This chapter demonstrates that there have been a surprising number of co-operatives (PCs) throughout North American history. Contrary to common belief, many survived for more than 20 years. This chapter proceeds by first describing the nature of a number of these co-operatives. In the second part, two models of co-operative performance are presented and these are evaluated against the evidence of North American co-operative performance. The evidence shows that for long periods of time, PCs have grown, been profitable and provided considerable job security for members. On the other hand, mature PCs have a tendency to under-invest and this factor may have contributed to the eventual demise of even the seemingly most successful.

I BACKGROUND

In this chapter, a Producer Cooperative is defined as an autonomous enterprise in which (a) many workers (or members) own

53

stock, (b) ownership is widely distributed, (c) worker-members participate in the enterprise's management and control, and (d) they share in the distribution of surplus (profits).

Hundreds of PCs were formed in the US during the nineteenth and twentieth centuries. Not all are examined here.[2] Those selected may be divided into seven clusters (see Table 3.1.). Four of these clusters – Foundry, Cooperage, Shingle and Plywood[3] – are distinguished by the nature of their final product. A fifth (KOL) consists of PCs that were initially financed, at least in part, by local assemblies of the Knights of Labor. The remaining two clusters – Early General and Late General – include otherwise unclassifiable PCs founded between 1860 and 1889 and between 1896 and 1937, respectively.

Table 3.1 provides estimates of the number of PCs in each cluster by decade of formation. (Note especially the high activity during the 1880s.) Most early PCs were in the east. Foundry PCs, for example, were concentrated in Illinois, Massachusetts, New York, Ohio and Pennsylvania. For later groups we see a drift to the west. This is apparent even with Cooperage PCs, but is particu-

TABLE 3.1   *PCs by cluster and decade of formation*

Decade formed	F[a]	C	EG	KOL	LG[c]	S	P	Total
1840s	4							4
1850s	0							0
1860s	(15)[b]	1	12					(28)
1870s	(10)	3	38					(51)
1880s	(11)	9	55	200				(275)
1890s	(7)	2			1			(10)
1900s		1			1			2
1910s					7	20		27
1920s					11		1	12
1930s					18		1	19
1940s							3	3
1950s							27	27
Total	47	16	105	200	38	20	32	458

Notes

[a] Column abbreviations are as follows: F = Foundry; C = Cooperage; EG = Early General; KOL = Knights of Labor; S = Shingle; LG = Late General; P = Plywood.
[b] Figures in parentheses are less reliable than other entries.
[c] Entries for the Late General group refer only to respondents to BLS surveys.

larly evident in the Shingle and Plywood clusters, both of which were predominantly located in the Pacific coast states. Overall, the geographical scope of American PCs has tended to be wide.

The industrial distribution of PCs has also been diverse. The KOL cluster encompassed more than 30 distinct activities, including coal mining, plumbing, and banking. In general, the trades involved have tended to be of a craft nature and have been characterised by a high skill content.

There are inter- and intra-cluster differences in the PCs' formal organisational rules and regulations. Discernible uniformities appear to be the result of some clusters having used a single, earlier, co-operative as a model, e.g. the Co-operative Barrel Company served as a prototype for Cooperage PCs, and Olympia Veneer fulfilled a similar function for the Plywood cluster. Additionally, in certain clusters, like Plywood and Shingle, the firms were members of a federation. Most Shingle PCs for example, belonged to the Mutual Lumber Mills, which acted primarily as a central marketing agency. On the other hand, KOL PCs, among others, neither used a prototype nor developed a general association.

More specific organisational similarities and differences among the clusters are discussed below.

(i) MEMBERSHIP

PC membership, in most instances, was determined by whether one supplied capital rather than whether one worked in the organisation in question. Many workers were excluded from membership (e.g. unskilled workers in the Foundry and Cooperage PCs and managers in some Plywood PCs). The Cooperage, Shingle, and Plywood PCs confined membership to current workers. Other PCs, however, made stock available to some organisations and individuals outside the workforce. This was the case with Foundry PCs, which often sold stock to individuals in the local community, while KOL PCs usually allowed trade unions to own stock. In all cases, except perhaps the Foundry PCs, admission of new members required approval either by the board or at a general meeting. Finally, though many groups of PCs, particularly earlier clusters, were closely connected with trade unions, in only KOL PCs was union status a normal condition of membership.[4]

(ii) VOTING PROCEDURES

The by-laws of most Cooperage, Shingle, Plywood and Late General PCs[5] provided for a system of one member, one vote, irrespective of stock ownership. An additional requirement for most Shingle PCs was that worker-members owned equal amounts of stock; normally no shareholder may hold more than 5 per cent of the total stock in a Plywood PC. In the remaining three clusters, ultimate control of the firm (by voting at annual meetings) usually was based on a system of plural voting, where voting rights reflected differential stock ownership. However, except for Foundry PCs, the dominant practice was for by-laws to impose restrictions on maximum shareholdings by an individual.

These differences concerning voting rights and practices are further reflected in elections to the board of directors. In all cases, shareholders elected the board at the annual meeting. Sometimes, as with the Early General cluster, the general manager and all principal officers of the society were then appointed by the board. In other cases (e.g. Shingle and Cooperage), such positions were ordinarily filled directly by the membership. With Plywood PCs, it was the board who appointed the general manager, other key officers being directly elected by members.[6]

(iii) FINANCE

As indicated in (i) above, initial capital in most cases was supplied as equity by members who worked within the firm. In certain cases (e.g. Foundry, KOL and Late General PCs), some foundation finance was provided by trade unions and/or outside individuals. Sometimes (especially in Plywood PCs) the initial capital stake required of a member was in excess of $1000. Often, founder members were unable to fully pay up all the stock to which they had subscribed. In the case of Cooperage PCs, frequently only 15 per cent of the initial capital stock was fully paid; the balance, including interest, was paid off by weekly assessments.

(iv) DISTRIBUTION OF NET INCOME

Plywood PCs stand almost alone among PC clusters in distributing profits to members on the basis of their functional role as workers. The Cooperage PCs distinguished between profits resulting from 'ordinary' gains, such as sales of barrels, and 'extraordinary' gains, such as those resulting from an increase in the value of the firm's land. Ordinary profits were distributed on the basis of number of hours worked, while extraordinary profits were distributed equally to members as capital suppliers. No profits were distributed to hired labour. In some other clusters (e.g. the Early General PCs), a profit-sharing scheme existed whereby part of the profits were distributed to labour. In all of these cases the basic determinant of claims on profits was capital ownership.

These organisational differences among American PCs may be summarised as follows: on average, the Plywood, Cooperage and Shingle clusters were the most co-operative in terms of initial organisation. Membership in most of these PCs was confined to workers; control was based on the principle of one member, one vote; and profits were distributed on the basis of work role. The Foundry and KOL PCs were in general the least co-operative. Here membership often included non-workers, power tended to be unequally distributed, and profits were shared on the basis of ownership of capital. No strong patterns are visible among the remaining two clusters.

I THEORY

Much of the theoretical literature in economics dealing with PCs focuses on the Yugoslav experience and is not directly applicable to that of the United States (see Steinherr, 1978, for a literature review). Other research (e.g. Berman, 1967; Bellas, 1972) treats only a single group of co-operatives. There are, however, two influential discussions of relevance to American PCs: those of Bernstein (1976) and Vanek (1975). The differences in the two models essentially reflect intellectual preferences derived from each author's discipline. So far as approach is concerned, Bernstein's is primarily inductive and focuses on isolating factors necessary for sustained workplace democratisation. Vanek's perspective is deductive and concerned with the determination of necessary conditions for sustained economic viability.

Bernstein examines a variety of cases of workplace democratisation, including American Plywood PCs and PCs elsewhere. He then presents a model comprising six factors, o: 'key components', which he argues are necessary for the mainten ance of democratisation. The basic requirements are: (i) particip ation by workers in decision making; (ii) frequent feedback o economic results to all workers (in the form of money, not jus information; (iii) full sharing with workers of management-leve information; (iv) guaranteed individual rights; (v) an independen appeals system; and (vi) a particular set of attitudes and value: (participatory consciousness). These were determined by examin ing how well various cases of workplace democratisation satisfie three criteria – economic viability, democracy, and adherence t a humanistic standard.

In explaining variation in success among and between PCs an the comparative performance of PCs and capitalist firms, Vanel (1975, pp. 34–5) enumerates a list of fundamental rules fo efficient labour-managed firms. By implication, PCs which com closest to satisfying these conditions will be most efficient, in bot economic as well as social terms. The most important of thes rules for American PCs are the first, third and seventh, whicl provide that: (i) 'All control, management and incom . . . should remain in the hands of those who work in a give enterprise . . . ; the underlying operational principle being fully democratic rule on the basis of equality of vote'; (iii ' . . . capital . . . is entitled to adequate remuneration at rat reflecting the relative scarcity of that factor in the economy'; (vii 'It is imperative to establish a shelter organization . . . whos express function would be to fund and promote the self-manage sector . . .'.

The absence of scarcity rents for the use of capital (Vanek': third condition) is deemed to be of fundamental importance i explaining the tendency of PCs to self-destruct. Vanek (1971b compares the long run equilibria for a PC firm which does pa owners of capital a scarcity reflecting remuneration (called labour-managed firm by Vanek) and a PC which pays no capita rents (which he calls a worker-managed firm). Whereas labour managed firms are assumed to maximise average net (afte capital – as well as material – costs) income, worker-manage firms maximise average income, because no charge is made for th use of capital. The model predicts that the firm which does no extract capital rents will: (i) under-invest; (ii) produce at a smal scale of output; and (iii) with a 'U' shaped technology, produce i

he inefficient zone of the production function, i.e. the zone of
ncreasing returns to scale. In examining the disequilibrium
ehaviour of the worker-managed firm, four self-extinction
orces are identified. These tendencies are: (i) to reduce the
umber of members; (ii) to dis-invest and consume capital; (iii) to
nder-invest; and (iv) never to admit new members.[7]

In the next section, after examining the performance of PCs in
he United States in general terms, the models of Bernstein and
Vanek will be used to explain it*.

II PERFORMANCE

n this section, five indicators are used to assess the PCs'
ocioeconomic performance. For the sake of discussion, we have
sed the same indicators for PCs and capitalist firms, despite the
act that they have different goals.

i) ECONOMIC VIABILITY

A powerful and persistent belief about American PCs is their
lleged inability to survive (Millis and Montgomery, 1945). As
he data in Table 3.2 demonstrate, however, that belief has little
asis in fact. The evidence shows that in each cluster, except KOL,
t least three PCs survived for more than 20 years.[8] On the other
and, many PCs have quickly succumbed, so that in only two
ases (Plywood and Late General) has the median lifespan
xceeded 10 years. Indeed, Plywood is the most stable cluster by
ar. Of 32 PCs formed since 1921, 17 still existed in 1978. And, if
he three PCs that sold out to capitalist corporations are
xcluded, the survival rate becomes 17/29. Though we do not
ave access to comparable information on capitalist firms, this
eems to suggest a 'low' mortality rate.[9] The least resilient cluster
s KOL, where all measures of PC lifespans are under 10 years.

ii) GROWTH AND SIZE

t is often argued that PCs are smaller, and if they grow at all, they
vill do so more slowly than capitalist firms (Atkinson (1973)).

Editor's note: The relevance of Vanek's formal model and its four forces to the US
xperience is also discussed in Chapter 1.

TABLE 3.2 *PC Lifespans by cluster*

	Foundry	Cooperage	Early General	Knights of Labour	Shingle	Late General[c]	Plywood[d]
Range (years)	1–>24	1–53	1–>38	(1–<10)	1–>27	13–37	1–>35
Average (years)	(<10)[a]	12	–[b]	<5	<10	19	21
Median (years)	(<5)	4	–[b]	<5	<10	18	25
Number PCs with known lifespan:							
10 years	1	2	2	0	0	4	8
20 years	4	0	4	0	4	2	18
30 years	0	0	0	0	0	1	3
40 years	0	2	0	0	0	0	0
50 years	0	1	0	0	0	0	0

Notes

[a] Figures in parentheses are less reliable than non-parenthesised entries.
[b] No data available.
[c] Entries refer only to respondents to 1933 BLS surveys.
[d] Many Plywood PCs are still extant; hence these estimates will likely change.

he experiences of Foundry, Cooperage and Plywood PCs
present only partial support for this contention. On the basis of
heer numbers, Foundry PCs never grew to be a significant factor
n the overall industry. Census of manufacture data for 1850–
900 show that only once did PCs account for more than 1 per
ent of all establishments in the industry.[10] The Foundry industry
'Cs were also smaller than the 'average of all firms'.[11] This is
particularly true when capital stock is used to indicate size. Also,
'oundry PCs tended to have lower capital-output ratios than
heir capitalist counterparts. Yet, although not all PCs in this
luster experienced growth, some increased quite rapidly. The
Kingston foundry in Plymouth County, Massachusetts, the
Equitable Foundry Company, Rochester, NY, and the Molders
Co-operative, Cincinnati, more than doubled their capital in less
han a decade.

Cooperage PCs, according to census data, often accounted for
nore than half of the local Minneapolis/Hennepin County
barrel-making firms. Furthermore, between 1880 and 1910 they
accounted for 10–15 per cent of the Minnesota cooperage
ndustry. As with the Foundry cluster, certain economic indi-
ators were calculated for Cooperage PCs (specifically, for Co-
operative Barrel, Hennepin, and North Star) and compared with
imilar 'all-firm average' statistics computed at the state and local
ounty/town level. In two cases (Hennepin and North Star), the
beginning capital was less than the state and county/town
averages for existing firms. In all three cases, the starting labour
orce apparently was larger than the 'all-firms' counterpart. All
hree firms displayed a tremendous capacity for sustained
growth.[12]

Plywood PCs have constituted a significant part of the plywood
ndustry for many years. Unfortunately, available data are not
ufficiently detailed to allow valid comparisons of indicators of
growth and size between these PCs and an 'all-firms average' for
he industry. Certain estimates do exist, however (Berman, 1967;
Bellas, 1972). The total market share of Plywood PCs since 1940 is
believed to be in excess of 10 per cent, and, for some years, more
han 20 per cent. In terms of the proportion of mills, the same
stimate (10–20 per cent) holds. However, no new PCs have been
ormed since the fifties, while the number of conventional
plywood firms has continued to grow.

(iii) EFFICIENCY

PCs are sometimes assumed to be more efficient, particularly with respect to the use of labour, than other organisations. Advocate predict improved productivity as a result of establishing a clos link between worker participation in control and managemen and worker participation in the determination of the distributio of profits (Jones, 1977). Most orthodox economic opinion i America, however, regards PCs as inherently inefficient, par ticularly because of the co-operatives' alleged failure to ap preciate the separate and distinctive contribution of the en trepreneur (Jones, 1977).

The efficiency of PCs is evaluated here in terms of labou productivity (Q/L) and profitability.[13] For the three Foundr PCs for which Q/L could be calculated (Equitable, 187C Leonard, 1880; and Somerset, 1880), productivity per worker i PCs was always greater than that in the comparable capitalist al firms county average for foundries – by 42, 5 and 21 per cen respectively. Moreover, these levels of Q/L are all greater than th national averages for 1870 and 1880; indeed, they even exceed th national average for 1900. On the other hand, the Q/L for the tw barrel-making PCs for which we have observations (North Star 1877; Hennepin, 1888) was probably well below both the loca town/county and state averages for barrel makers. However, i both of these cases, the PC data are not for the same year as th town/state averages – a significant consideration given the pro duct market volatility. Furthermore, productivity per worker i the Hennepin co-operative in 1888, though less than that of th state average in 1880, was greater than the national average fo 1880. Existing research on Plywood PCs indicates that, wit respect to labour productivity, these PCs out-perform thei capitalist counterparts (Berman, 1967; Dahl, 1956). Howevei differences in productivity may be dropping (Bellas, 1972; but se also Bernstein, 1977).

(iv) PROFITS

Data on Foundry PCs reported in Table 3.3 show that selecte firms could make profits, and did so for periods as long as te years. For the period 1875–84, the Somerset (Mass.) foundry, fo instance, recorded an average annual rate of return on total asset

TABLE 3.3 *Foundry PCs profitability*

Firm/group		Period	Rate of return on total asset (%)	Rate of return on investor equity (%)
NY	Equitable	1870	36.0	(>36.0)
Mass	Somerset	1875–84	9.9	22.7
	Kingston	1878–84	1.2	2.0
	Leonard	1873–74	4.7	8.8
Arithmetic average for foundries		1870–84	7.1	13.5

Note.

Profit rates are calculated from data reported in Massachusetts Labour Inspectors, *Seventeenth Annual Report* (1887), except for Equitable Foundry Company, for which calculations are derived from US Bureau of the Census, *Decennial census for 1870*.

of 9.9 per cent. For the same period, the average annual rate of return on investor equity was 22.7 per cent. Similar estimates of profitability exist for certain Early General cluster firms in Massachusetts during 1875–84 and are presented in Table 3.4. For three industries (footwear, cigar making and furniture manufacture), the average profit rate, either on total assets or on investor equity, was positive, though there are several instances of firms making no profits, and one example of losses. Taken as a whole, though, the available evidence indicates that these PCs can be profitable.[14] Of 15 PCs sampled in 1963, Berman (1967) reports that 13 recorded positive profits, with rates of return on capital as high as 50 per cent. (In that study, no comparisons were made with the profitability of capitalist firms.) Dahl's (1956) finding that, for the period 1952–6, less than half of the Plywood PCs investigated (all in Washington) registered any profits, is most likely a statistical illusion following from the tendency of PCs to pay out labour incomes at rates considerably in excess of capitalist averages.

(v)   GOVERNANCE AND DECISION MAKING

Although PCs frequently are expected to degenerate into non-co-operative institutions, little is known about their informal governance (but see Greenberg, 1978; Perry, 1978). As indicated above, however, there are certain minimum formal requirements

TABLE 3.4   *Massachusetts PCs' profitability*

Industry	Period	Average annual rate of return on total assets (%)	Average annual rate of return on investor's equity (%)
(a) *Footwear*			
Stoneham	1875–84	6.9	16.7
Middlesex	1876–84	3.6	11.5
Essex	1875–6	0	0
Marlborough	1877–8	21.0	21.0
American	1883–4	1.3	2.6
Franklin	1884	0	0
Wakefield	1884	0	0
Orient	1877	0	0
N. Adams	1875	0	0
Arithmetic Average	1875–84	5.0	10.9
(b) *Cigar making*			
Phoenix	1876–82	4.7	10.8
Mass.	1875–8	2.5	20.2
E. Co-op. Assoc.	1875–7	1.3	0.5
Nat. Cigar	1876–7	2.8	6.8
Westfield Cigar	1875–6	0	0
Springfield	1875	5.1	17.6
Arithmetic Average	1875–82	3.1	13.8
(c) *Furniture*			
E. Templeton	1875–84	0.3	0.6
Athol	1880–4	−6.0	−5.0
Co-op. Furniture	1880–2	15.6	65.5
Arithmetic Average	1875–84	1.7	9.9

Note

For sources, see Table 3.3.

that may be advanced as basic to the democratic organisation of co-operatives: (i) a majority of the members are workers; (ii) a majority of the work force are members; (iii) voting on the basis of one member, one vote, or, in those cases where plural voting based on stock ownership prevails, an absence of concentration of stock ownership in the hands of a few; and (iv) at least some of the profits are distributed to worker-members in their capacity as workers. The data needed to evaluate the various PCs on these criteria are incomplete. For those clusters where information is most plentiful, the record is mixed.

Some data exist for eight Foundry PCs. In five, the co-operative structure degenerated – i.e. was transformed, according to our measures, into something other than a co-operative structure. For example, though a majority of the workers in the N. Dighton foundry were members in 1886, by 1909 this was no longer true. The Equitable Foundry Company began by distributing much of the profits to labour, but within 15 years all profits went to capital-suppliers. The co-operative Stove Works at Troy, which began with all members having one vote, quickly degenerated into plural voting based on capital holdings. Moreover, from the start, many Foundry PCs did not satisfy all four formal requirements. Despite the pattern of rapid degeneration in this cluster, two firms (the Somerset and Leonard foundries) decayed only slightly (between 1877 and 1883), and this was caused chiefly by increased concentration of stock holdings.

Evidence for the Cooperage cluster is limited, but it indicates that the first, third and fourth conditions of democratic governance were maintained over time; on the other hand, the proportion of the work force who were not members tended to increase. At the North Star Barrel Company, after 11 years of operation, 36/90 were non-members. At the Hennepin Co-operative, after eight years, 43 per cent of the workers were non-members, and after 25 years the figure had increased to 48 per cent. At the North West Barrel Company, within five years between one-quarter and one-third of the labour force were non-members. However, this apparently frequent and rapid erosion of one aspect of co-operative organisation does not seem to have seriously compromised the formally co-operative nature of Cooperage PCs.

For many Early General PCs in Massachusetts, the tendency for the co-operative structure to degenerate was especially pronounced and rapid – usually occurring in a decade or less. In only three out of nine cases did workers constitute a majority of the membership, and in only five of nine cases were most workers members of the firm.[15] Moreover, in five cases there was a tendency towards concentration of stock ownership during the late eighteen seventies and early eighties. Many Late General PCs also seem to be characterised by a disintegrating co-operative structure. Thus, in two cigar factories, though most workers were members, most stock-holders were not current workers. The available data for the Shingle cluster suggest that these PCs tended to lose their co-operative features through slow erosion. Janes (1924) reports that there were no PCs in which all workers were shareholders, but he also notes that three firms came very close to this standard. In the Olympia Mill, the proportion of the work force that was non-member grew from zero to about two-fifths between 1915 and 1922. At the Mutual Mills, Marysville, only 78 per cent of the work force were members by 1922. But it is not until some years later (as the BLS survey data for 1929, 1932 and 1936 indicate) that we find situations where, on average, most workers in Shingle PCs were not members.

For Plywood PCs, Berman (1967) reports Dahl's estimate that, on average, 13 per cent of the work force were not members, and Bernstein (1976) finds that usually 85–90 per cent of workers were members. Also, there are documented accounts of individual instances in which Plywood PCs were transformed into institutions with other than formal co-operative structures, notably Olympia Veneer and Mutual Plywood. It is clear then, that the Plywood cluster has not suffered rapid degeneration, though some gradual transformations have taken place.

(vi)   JOB CREATION

At least initially, PCs have been successful in creating and maintaining jobs. Besides the positions created by the formation of wholly new co-operative enterprises, there are many instances of workers preserving jobs by buying plants that were threatened with closure. This was the origin of the Acme and National Barrel companies.

Examination of individual firm labour force profiles over time reveals that the capacity for job preservation often was not sustained, particularly for many non-member workers. Most American PCs seem to go through a life cycle with three distinct phases, though of varying length, depending on the particular PC. During the typical first phase, both the size of the total labour force and the number of worker-members increase. In the second phase, the proportion of workers who are members decreases. During the last phase, both groups decline in numbers, and the proportion of workers who are members may increase or decrease. Hence, the absolute performance of mature PCs has been less impressive, though it is not necessarily inferior to that of ageing capitalist firms.

Labour force profiles for American PCs are not sufficiently detailed for any confident inferences to be made about stability and regularity of employment. However, the available evidence suggests that these firms performed well on both counts. Slumps in product demand would first be met by general belt-tightening and lowering labour incomes; only if these measures proved insufficient would workers (usually non-member workers) be let go and then, so far as possible, by voluntary attrition.

We now turn to a discussion of North American experience in the light of the models of Bernstein and Vanek outlined in Section II. Although Bernstein fails to define many of his key terms precisely (e.g. what constitutes 'meaningful participation' in decision making?), it is still possible to test the PCs' experiences against his model (see Table 3.5). For each cluster we checked for the presence of the key components at the time a PC commenced business and again after some (where possible, ten or more) years of operation. Incomplete PC data compound the problems posed by Bernstein's imprecise definitions; for any category of PC we seldom have data relating to more than two of the three criteria and five of the six key components. However, as the table demonstrates, the available evidence does support Bernstein's model. For Cooperage, Shingle and Plywood clusters – all PCs where Bernstein's criteria for work-place democracy are generally met – the data also indicate the presence of the key components. In the remaining cases – Foundry, the two General categories, and KOL – Bernstein's criteria do not seem to be satisfied, nor are his key components continually present.

Earlier we provided evidence on the tendencies for the number of worker-members and the proportion of the labour force that are workers to decrease in PCs over time. Indeed, except in the cases of Cooperage, Plywood and perhaps Shingle PCs, usually the reduction in the number of worker-members quickly proceeded to the point at which control of the PC lay outside the domain of worker-members. These phenomena are consistent with Vanek's first and fourth self-extinction forces. Not much available data bear on the predictions of dis-investment and under-investment. However, the fact that long-lasting Cooperage PCs were reducing their output between 1900 and 1910 (and presumably reducing their capital stock by not replacing worn out capital), while the average cooperage firm in Minnesota increased its capacity, suggests some support for these predictions. Note also the fact

TABLE 3.5 *Bernstein's model and the experiences of American PCs*

Criteria	Foundry		Cooperage		Early General		Knights of Labor		Late General		Shingle		Plywood	
Economic viability[4]	−		++		−		−		−		++		++	
Industrial democracy[5]	−		++		−		−		−		+		++	
Humanistic values[6]													(+)	
Components	A	B	A	B	A	B	A	B	A	B	A	B	A	B
Participation in decision making[5]	−	−	++	++	−	−−	−		++	(+)	++	++	++	++
Feedback of economic results[7]	−	−	++	++	++	−	−		−				++	++
Sharing information[7]	−		++	++	++				++	++	++	++	++	++
Guaranteed rights[7]	−		++	++					++	++	++	++	++	++
Appeals system[7]	−		++	++	++				++			+	++	++
Attitudes[6]							+							++

Notes

1. ++ is used to indicate complete fulfilment of a criterion and −− to indicate complete non-fulfilment. Other designations show degrees of partial fulfilment.
2. A blank element means data are not available; parenthesised entries are less reliable than others.
3. Entries in column A are assessments made initially or soon after the PC (or groups of PCs) was formed; entries in column B are determined after a long interval, usually more than 10 years.
4. Average PC earns a surplus for ≥5 years; if data on surplus are not available, median lifespan ≥5 years.
5. Average PC satisfies three conditions for democratic governance and decision making (as defined in the text) for a period of ≥5 years.
6. A statement exists in the literature to this effect.
7. Sources indicate that institutional provision for this feature does (does not) exist.

that unlike capitalist firms, no Plywood PCs have invested recently in new mills.

The tendency toward dis-investment, where members experience an increasing desire to extract their equity, also receives some confirmation in the available data. Three Plywood PCs were sold to capitalist concerns within 30 years of their commencing operations, for sums that realised worker-members substantial capital gains. Similarly, when the North Star Barrel Company was sold by aged worker-members, large capital gains were recorded.

The experiences of the three long-lasting Cooperage PCs (discussed earlier) tend to support Vanek's prediction that payment of scarcity rents for the use of capital is needed for efficient PCs, each firm showed a tremendous capacity for growth during its first 20–30 years such that, in 1900, for the two cases for which we have information, the average output of each firm exceeded the state average by more than 150 per cent. But within 20 years, one of the two surviving firms was producing at an output level half that of the state average, and the other firm's output was even smaller. In general, PCs which came closest to satisfying the fundamental rules for efficient labour-managed firms have performed best. Particularly noteworthy is the positive relationship between degree of participation and economic performance.

Finally, since no group of American PCs has operated under the protection of what Vanek designates as a shelter organisation, it is problematic whether or not the need for such an institution can be tested well using North American evidence. Tentative support for the proposition may be drawn from the fact that Plywood PCs, which have been served by an institution that has undertaken some of the functions envisaged of a shelter organisation, performed better than any other cluster. Also, one of the clusters that performed next best–Shingle PCs – was served for a time by a federation. Moreover, it could be argued that the existence of a shelter organisation would have prevented successful Plywood and Cooperage PCs from allowing members to recoup their accumulated equity by selling to outside interests.

IV CONCLUSION

In general, and by various measures of socioeconomic performance, it is PCs in the most co-operative grouping – Plywood, Shingle and Cooperage clusters – that performed best. Moreover, the available evidence on socioeconomic performance is broadly consistent with key features and predictions of Bernstein's and Vanek's models. However, we are not persuaded by the American experience that either of these models constitutes a necessary and sufficient set of conditions either for the maintenance of workplace democratisation or for efficient labour-managed firms. For example, the Minneapolis cooperages, which Bernstein's model would likely adjudge as a successful instance of sustained work-place democratisation, are now defunct. Since available data indicate that all key components continued to be present in these PCs until their demise, the model appears incomplete.

Alternatively, it could be that the criteria used for making the model operational are not precise. For example, is five years really a sufficiently long period to appropriately assess an organisation's economic viability? Is this assessment done properly by looking at the ability of the firm to generate a surplus during this period? Perhaps a longer time period is needed and one that employs diverse measures of economic performance, rather than relying solely on profitability. It may also be that the evaluation of work-place democracy should include more than an examination of the opportunities available to members. The proportion of the work force that assume membership status must also be considered. Furthermore, perhaps it should be explicitly stated that the opportunities available to members be on an equal basis. It is likely that other conditions of formal organisation and structure (such as the requirement that scarcity rents be paid for the use of capital which is not collectively owned) need to be incorporated in Bernstein's model. Analogously, to the extent that the key components of Bernstein's theory are not clearly spelled out in Vanek's model, it too needs to be augmented.

The experiences of American PCs suggest that in seeking optimal forms, theorists begin by integrating the findings of Vanek and Bernstein. The new model could then be expanded to include factors necessary for the subsequent maintenance of work-place democratisation or efficiency in labour-managed irms, such as smallness, institutional assistance, and leadership. Some contextual/environmental factors might also be included. In his regard the American experience, wherein even the seemingly most successful PCs have eventually succumbed, suggests that institutional assistance and support from an agency or (an) individual(s) outside the immediate PC may be of prime importance in sustaining work-place democratisation. The development of a satisfactory model in the future clearly requires additional research on past and present PCs within and without the United States.

NOTES

1. This chapter is based on a paper entitled 'Producer cooperatives in the US: an examination and analysis of socio-economic performance' presented at the Walton Symposium, Glasgow, June 1979, which in a revised form has appeared as 'US producer cooperatives: the record to date', *Industrial Relations*, vol. 18, no. 3, Fall 1979. Details of the numerous sources used in compiling Tables 3.1, 3.2 and 3.5 are given in this paper. Permission of the Regents of the University of California to use material from the latter is gratefully acknowledged.
2. Omitted PCs include the self-help co-operatives of the nineteen-thirties and refuse collection firms in the San Francisco area. Also excluded are those PCs which resulted from owner-initiated conversions of viable capitalist firms, such as the Columbia Conserve Company.
3. A more detailed discussion of the Plywood PCs is presented in the next chapter.
4. Even for KOL PCs there were exceptions, as with the Detroit Shoemakers. In the Early and Late General clusters, the incidence of unionism varied greatly.
5. Most PCs register under company rather than co-operative laws; co-operative features are introduced typically via by-laws.
6. Little systematic information is available on board size. Boards of Early General PCs were typically 10 strong, but a glass manufacturing co-operative at Baltimore had a board of 23 members. Similarly, not much is known about directors' remuneration. Whereas directors of KOL PCs generally received no payment for their services, directors of Early General PCs were usually rewarded.
7. Vanek's (1971b) analysis is discussed more fully in Chapter 1. McGregor (1977) identifies five forces, three of which overlap with Vanek's model. The others are: (i) an increasing desire on the part of members to extract their equity; (ii) a tendency to abandon co-operative ideals and hire wage-earning employees. Both forces are implicit in Vanek's model.
8. The varying reliability and availability of data is reflected in the arrangement of the table. While we know that some Minneapolis cooperages

survived for one year and that the PC with the longest lifespan survived 54
years, with Shingle PCs we know only that the oldest survived for more than
27 years. With KOL PCs, it appears unlikely that any survived for more
than 10 years.

9. Data on mortality rates both for PCs and other more conventional
   organisations are meagre. For most groups of PCs the available data do not
   show conclusively whether the mortality rate for PCs, compared to
   conventional organisations, is better or worse.
10. However, over time, the number of PCs was declining, while the number of
    conventional firms increased dramatically. The data are as in Table 3.6.

TABLE 3.6

Year	Number of establishments (all firms)	Number of PCs	Number of PCs as per cent of total
1850	1391	1	0.07
1860	1412	15	1.06
1870	2654	13	0.49
1880	4984	14	0.28
1890	6500	11	0.17
1900	9325	2	0.02

11. Data for the 'all-firms' groups were derived from censuses of manufacture
    for 1870 and comparisons were made by county. Usually, observations for
    six PCs were available; in only one case, the Equitable Foundry Company,
    were we able to compare data for 1870 itself. In other cases, comparisons
    were made for years as close as possible to 1870, usually later.
12. In 1865, both the labour force and the capital stock of the Co-operative
    Barrel Company were two to three times the town average and seven to eight
    times the state average; in 1900, its output was about two and one-half times
    the town average. In 1888, sales of the North Star Barrel Company were
    substantially below the town average (**$48 000: $75 584**); but by 1900 the
    town average had been eclipsed (**$265 200; $93 903**).
13. To use Q/L alone as a valid indicator of comparative performance requires
    that equal amounts of other inputs, particularly capital, are used in
    production. Unfortunately, there is no way of determining if this is the case,
    though, as noted earlier, there is some reason to believe that PCs
    (particularly mature PCs) tend to have lower capital–labour ratios than do
    capitalist firms. Likewise, the usefulness of profitability as an index of
    performance is problematic. If, as one would expect, 'pure' PCs attempt to
    reward workers with incomes greater than the wages employees would
    receive in comparable capitalist firms, then true 'profits' are understated.
    (Of course, during slumps in demand, the reverse may be true.) Even in
    'impure' PCs, where return on capital may be an important concern of
    members as capital suppliers, to the extent that members as workers receive
    incomes greater than the wages they would receive as employees in

comparable capitalist firms, a similar problem prevails. To employ profitability as a useful index of PC performance requires that profitability be calculated using capitalist-equivalent wages, rather than actual earnings received. In practice, this is difficult with many American PCs, mainly because of incomplete data. The computations cited used unadjusted profitability data.

4. There is less evidence available on profitability for the other clusters. The BLS surveys report several Shingle PCs registering positive profits in 1925 and 1929. Those same surveys also indicate that in 1925–36 many PCs in other industries also experienced positive profits. However, as with the data for Shingle mills, it is difficult to estimate rates of return on capital because often profit and capital data do not exist for the same firms. A notable exception, however, is a footwear PC which reported a return on investor equity of 46.6 per cent for 1929.

5. The nine firms are: E. Templeton, Athol, Stoneham, Middlesex, American, Franklin, Wakefield, Brockton and N. Dighton. All but the first two, which were manufacturers of furniture, were boot and shoe concerns. Data on membership and stock ownership are in Massachusetts Department of Labour and Industry (1887, pp. 194–229) and Berman (1967, pp. 13–15).

4 The United States of America: a Co-operative Model for Worker Management[1]

Katrina V. Berman

This chapter examines in detail the experience of US plywoo manufacturing co-operatives who form one of the groups identi fied by Derek Jones in the previous chapter. This group is worth of special consideration since its history is the best documented o all groups of US co-operatives and the institutional arrangement (e.g. transferable share ownership, and non-member employ ment) differ significantly from cases examined elsewhere in thi book. After an examination of the institutional arrangements an the size and nature of this group of firms, and a discussion of th relevant theoretical model, this chapter focuses on three problem encountered by these producer co-operatives, non-membe employment, capital shortage, and share transfer problems, an suggests some relevant policy implications.

Since the descriptive story of the worker-owned plywood co operatives is dealt with extensively by Berman (1967, 1975) an Bellas (1972), only brief details will be reviewed here, befor shifting the focus to performance strengths and weaknesses an the implications of these for policies to promote effective an economically viable labour management in a private enterpris economy. The chapter concludes with an assessment of th prospects for labour management in the United States.

I BACKGROUND

At least 27 enterprises wholly owned and managed by thei workers have manufactured and sold softwood plywood in th

acific north-western United States for periods of 8 to 37 years, in
ompetition with conventionally-managed enterprises. Probably
5 such co-operative enterprises are in operation at present.
Vorker co-operatives have played an important role in produc-
on and technological development of the softwood plywood
idustry since its beginning.[2]

The pioneer co-operative was organised in 1921, in the
idustry's infancy, by 125 workers who each contributed $1000
nd built their own plant. Although immediately successful, this
xample was not followed until just before the Second World
Var, when three more co-operatives were organised by workers
/ho built their own plants and developed highly successful
ompanies (one of which is still operating as a co-operative).
1ost of the co-operatives were organised in the early 1950s, none
nce 1957. Co-operatives accounted for 20 to 25 per cent of
idustry production during the 1950s and 1960s, but since the
iid-1960s (when 24 were operating), and especially in the last few
ears, their number has decreased. The surviving co-operatives
)day account for less than 10 per cent of industry output, but still
ave the major share of the market for finished 'sanded' plywood.
. few of the lost co-operatives sold out at a profit, but most have
uccumbed to financial difficulties. Their problems have stemmed
irgely from stringent raw material shortage for companies
'ithout timber-lands, which has seen them seeking sources in
.laska and the Philippines. Sharply higher equipment require-
ients and costs have also contributed toward eliminating the
ibour-cost margin on which co-operatives depend.

The co-operatives were organised on the initiative of groups of
'orkers, sometimes with community assistance; individual pro-
ioters hoping for stock sales commissions, profits, or manage-
ient or product-sales contracts; or corporations wishing to sell a
lant found inadequately profitable (usually because of
bsolescence, or depletion of timber supplies). Although some
apital was available in a few instances from loans, community
ssistance, or credit from selling corporations, almost all the
apital has been supplied by the workers themselves through
oregone earnings supplementing some initial investment. Most of
ie companies were originally organised as ordinary
orporations, with co-operative features spelled out in by-laws,
ut have shifted to more specific co-operative organisation
ecause of tax considerations.

Perhaps half of the co-operative organisations took over previously operating plywood plant. In some of thes conversions, the co-operative was helped by financial assistanc or sales contracts from former owners, but at least as many take overs burdened the workers with inflated plant prices or un satisfactory sales agreements. Some worker organisations wer also victimised by promoters, and one speculative promotio resulted in convictions for fraud.

The plywood co-operatives have been diverse in many impor ant respects, such as size (60 to 300 members or 500 total worker with the average size close to the average industry plant size employment of non-members (zero or close to it to over 50 pe cent), and member activism versus managerial dominance However, they have shared common organisational feature mainly following precedents set by the pioneer company. A member of the plywood enterprises is a person who has bought c contracted to buy a share of stock (or specified equal block c shares) *and* is working in the plant. Such members and only suc members, vote to elect the board of directors (which appoints th general manager) and to decide major matters which are reserve according to the by-laws for decision by membership meeting Each member has an equal vote. There is constant commun cation between rank-and-file members and directors, who wor side by side on the same machines.

No dividends, or at most minimal amounts, are paid on share so a share's value derives from the right to employment an earnings, and there are few non-working shareholders. Member shares are transferable, and are bought and sold in individua transactions. However, the selling member must first offer th shares to the company, and if the company does not buy it mu approve the purchaser, usually requiring a probationary perio of work in the plant.

The proceeds of the enterprise above costs paid out to othe (which include any costs of outside capital or non-membe workers) are allocated to members according to hours worke during the period. (This is the 'business done' by each with the cc operative organisation.) Almost universally, distribution pe hour has been equal, regardless of job performed by th individual member, from 'off-bearer' to head lathe operator c sales manager. Some of the amounts allocated to members ar paid out during the year as 'hourly advances'. Of the remainde

ome is paid out at end of the fiscal year, and some may (by
iember vote) be retained by the company for investment or
:serves, although allocated to individuals (to be reported by
iem as income) for tax purposes.

Members' principal jobs are assigned according to a bid
ystem. Members bid for vacant jobs, and get them according to
me elapsed since the individual's last successful bid, except that
ome key jobs are awarded by the board of directors.

The worker-managed plywood enterprises conform to the
rinciples of co-operative organisation: subordination of capital
i control of the company and limited return to capital; one man,
ie vote, basis for management authority; and distribution of
roceeds of the enterprise according to the contribution of each
iember in business done with the organisation. Except for this
eneral adherence to the co-operative model, organisational
:atures and operating methods of the plywood co-operatives
ave developed without benefit of preconceived ideology, theory,
r model, and without assistance or influence from government
r any organised group. Although affected by characteristics of
he industry, and to a lesser extent by legal, especially tax,
onsiderations, operating methods of the plywood co-operatives
ave evolved through the 59-year practice of self-management.
his gives the practices a legitimacy entitling them to special
onsideration from persons interested in self-management.

I THEORY

he plywood co-operatives conform in important respects to the
iodel of the labour-managed firm developed by Berman and
ierman (1978). This model, outlined in more detail in Chapter 1
bove, predicts Pareto-optimal adjustment to changes in para-
ietric costs and prices, under the assumptions of perfect
ompetition under either private enterprise or socialism. What
ias been called, in Chapter 1, the Ward–Vanek–Meade model,
vhich occupies a central position in the literature, is inap-
•ropriate to an examination of the plywood co-operatives,
•rimarily because of its assumptions that short-run adjustments
o market and cost conditions are made through membership
hange and that such adjustments are not made by variation in
vorking hours.

In the plywood co-operatives, hours of work are variable by enterprise decision and are changed for short-run adjustment to market and cost conditions, primarily by varying amounts of overtime. Adjustment of membership is not a short-run option for the co-operative, since a membership share carries the right to employment for the member in the plant (if it is operating). Although a member may elect to work elsewhere and sometimes does when the co-operative's member return is below outside employment alternatives, he must be readmitted to work at the plant on equal terms at his option. Even if a member is discharged from plant employment for cause according to established procedures, the member retains and will sell his share, and no decrease in the number of members results. However, membership can be adjusted in the long run. Companies can buy and retire shares when members wish to sell, and have used this method to decrease membership slightly to accommodate labour saving technological advances. Membership increase is also possible in the long run, through issuing previously authorised or newly authorised shares of stock to worker purchasers. In practice, however, institutional difficulties and the availability of the non-member employee option have limited plywood co-operatives' expansion through the addition of members.

Some correspondence with the Berman and Berman model is also found in respect to capital input. Incentive to invest in the enterprise is provided for members by the individually-owned transferable shares giving individual members opportunity for full realisation of the future income generated by the investment. Members have power to borrow, as well as to liquidate unprofitable investment, although institutional imperfections in capital markets have impaired the availability of loans in practice.

Departures from the theoretical assumptions of perfect competition in raw material markets as well as in capital markets have caused serious problems for plywood co-operatives. The co-operatives buy logs where available, but usually bid on standing timber and contract out the logging. Private timber ownership is highly concentrated in large timber companies; the co-operatives are largely dependent on timber sales from government-owned lands. Even with respect to government timber, small companies and independent companies without timber lands suffer competitive handicaps in procurement.[3] The product market for plywood is reasonably competitive, despite the presence of some

arge firms. Strong distribution organisation has eased marketing
problems for the co-operatives.

II PERFORMANCE AND PROBLEMS

a) MANAGEMENT PARTICIPATION

Labour management is practised to the fullest extent by the
members of the plywood co-operatives. Members have decision
authority, without external restriction, for the entire range of
management decisions. Indications are that most individuals
participate actively in decision making, and not merely through
the election of directors.

b) FINANCIAL RESULTS

Although financial performance has varied among the different
co-operatives, it has been good for the co-operative group as a
whole, with some being extremely successful. Average hourly
return has been above union average pay for plywood workers
most of the time in most of the co-operatives and 50 per cent or
more above union averages consistently in some plants, although
others have managed to exceed union pay only at times.
Continuous operation and employment have been a feature of the
co-operatives in an industry plagued with seasonal and cyclical
unemployment. For this reason, plus substantial overtime
operation, annual incomes of members have been higher even in
the low-rate plants than incomes of plywood workers generally.
In successful companies, incomes have reached the $25 000 to
$40 000 range. Continued operation, with satisfactory incomes to
workers, of plants that would otherwise have closed is another
credit to the co-operatives. Many of the low-rate co-operative
plants were those scheduled to be closed before co-operative take-
over; some of these plants have now closed, but they operated
successfully for 15–25 years. Most of the co-operatives remaining
at present (including some co-operative take-overs) that have
survived recent difficulties (primarily scarcity and escalating cost
of raw material) are strong enterprises, with per capita income for
members substantially above plywood workers' average pay.

On the negative side, only about half of the plywood plants tha have operated on a worker-owned and worker-managed basis are operating as co-operatives today. Financial difficulties have resulted in the closing down of most of the co-operatives that have disappeared, and have also been responsible for several decision: to sell out to non-co-operative interests. Furthermore, some co operatives have yielded low incomes for the members, par ticularly in terms of hourly pay rates.[4] However, a majority of the co-operatives that have disappeared for financial reasons have done so in the last five or six years, after well over twenty years o co-operative operation.[5] To a large extent, the companies have succumbed to unusual and recently accelerating pressures in the western plywood industry: environmental demands requiring large capital expenditures; locally depleted timber supplies; and raw material prices increasing 400 per cent over a seven-year period and as much as 90 per cent in a single year. Escalating raw material and equipment costs have drastically reduced the labour-cost share where superior labour productivity can be effective. These difficulties proved too much for companies without adequate capital and reserves.

(c) PRODUCTIVITY

The major basis for co-operative success, and for survival of capitalistically unprofitable plants, has been superior labour productivity in the co-operative plants. Studies comparing square-foot output have repeatedly shown higher physica volume of output per hour, and others, made for tax purposes, of value productivity show higher quality (value) of product and also economy of material use.[6] Recent tax settlements have conceded to co-operatives value productivity 30–50 per cent above that ir non-co-operative plants, with evidence in some cases supporting far higher productivity premiums. Members of co-operatives not only work harder and more carefully, but perform supervisory executive, maintenance and plant improvement functions, as wel as becoming able and being willing to do a variety of production jobs as needed. Continuous high-level operation also lowers unit costs. Co-operative production concentrates on the produc items requiring relatively more labour ('sanded' rather than 'unsanded' plywood) to gain most advantage from superior labour productivity which can offset cost disadvantages in other directions (such as obsolete plant or distance from markets or raw material sources).

Co-operative survival has also been aided by a lower disutility of labour under co-operative conditions. In financial exigency, members have been willing to work for lower hourly return than plywood workers elsewhere, sometimes for lengthy periods. Thus low labour costs offset high costs elsewhere or sharply reduced prices. Co-operative members have also chosen regular work-weeks longer than those of workers in non-co-operative plants.

The superior productivity of plants operating on the co-operative model has provided members with secure and continuous employment and income, and some with high incomes. It also offers higher output for society from given resources of capital and labour. Co-operatives operate at a lower capital/labour ratio with more output from given plant. This economy of capital use may be particularly important for capital-scarce underdeveloped societies.

(d) NON-MEMBER EMPLOYMENT

Self-management is not complete for the work force in the plywood co-operatives because non-member workers are employed who do not have the responsibilities and rights (or assume the risks) of members. They have no rights to participation in management or permanent employment, and contribute no capital. These workers are paid at or slightly above union wage rates, which have sometimes been more than members receive. Where non-member employment is substantial, employees are covered by union contract. Probably all of the plywood co-operatives have some non-member employment. It varies from less than 10 per cent to more than 50 per cent of all workers.[7]

There are several reasons (with differing policy implications) for non-member employment.

(i) The companies have almost universally employed non-member general managers, and a company with a member manager will employ a non-member plant superintendent. This is partly because managers, with the alternative of non-co-operative employment, can command a higher salary than the remuneration to co-operative members.[8] The principal reason for non-member managers and superintendents, however, appears to be preference for an outsider to give orders to members, rather than one of themselves. Although the manager is of course subordinate to the elected member board of directors, and in some companies managers have had short tenure, the illusion, however transparent, of outside authority may be the plywood co-operatives' way of overcoming the difficulty with producer co-operation considered insuperable by early twentieth century writers on co-operation and socialism: maintaining necessary discipline when a manager is subject to the direction of those he must direct.[9]

(ii) In addition to managers, non-members with other particular skills, training, or certification are often employed. Skills such as those of electrician and millwright are essential to the plant's operation. These transferable skills also frequently command a higher pay rate than the co-operative member rate. Although some plants have members with these skills, others do not and must hire and pay the going rate. An alternative would be to pay for a member's training in the needed skill (and subsidising such training could be a function of an agency promoting co-operatives), but with more remunerative outside employment available there is no assurance that the trained worker would remain in the co-operative.[10]

Presumably this problem could be eased by abandoning the hourly pay equality among members, common in the plywood co-operatives, so that persons whose skills command a higher pay rate in outside employment could get a larger share of co-operative proceeds.[11] There is, however, in the plywood co-operatives, a strong sentiment against unequal shares. Equal pay status is considered essential for co-operative solidarity, to avoid dissension. Plywood co-operatives take pains to promote equality in all respects. Members not only receive equal pay rates, have equal votes and own equal amounts of stock, but also attempt to equalise annual incomes by offering overtime work to members with fewest work hours credited.

Argument over justified pay differentials could be time-consuming and divisive.[12] (This problem would be even worse where there was no 'outside' employment to suggest pay standards.) Elitism of higher-paid members, and reaction against it by others, could create antagonistic factions. A worker co-operative is highly vulnerable to damage from factionalism, as members are more closely and continuously interdependent than in almost any other joint activity. There is evidence supporting the plywood co-operatives' view of the importance of equality, as dissension and divisiveness from unequal status appear to be important reasons for failure of Vermont Asbestos Group and difficulties in other non-co-operative worker-ownership efforts.

Different income shares for different jobs would also jeopardise the productivity that is the basis of co-operative survival and success. Much of the productivity stems from flexibility of job assignment. Most plywood co-operative members learn to do most jobs in the plant and can be shifted as needed. Frequently an individual member will regularly perform jobs in different pay classifications, such as maintenance on the production machine he operates, or plant clean-up when his production work is slack. Members also shift principal assignments around, bidding for vacant jobs. These measures (similar to those recommended by management experts for combatting job 'alienation') eliminate idle time and need for some positions, as well as improving job satisfaction and performance by relieving the boredom of mono-tonous work. They are not readily reconcilable with different pay classifications.

(iii) Some non-member employment is temporary, to fill in for members on vacation or to supplement member labour for seasonal peaks. With primary product use in construction and raw material dependent on logging, plywood is a highly seasonal industry. Berman and Berman (1978) argue that vari-ation of member work-hours will adjust plant output to market-condition fluctuations. Although work-hours of plywood co-operative members vary positively with product price (for example) as that theory suggests, with seasonal demand member-hour variation may not be sufficient. If membership were large enough for member-labour to meet all peak demands, work-hours per member at slack times of year would be too low to provide adequate income. Income could be averaged over the year, but this alternative (or maintaining added storage to even out production fluctuations) would decrease member annual incomes and put co-operatives at a competitive disadvantage.

(iv) A similar problem of cyclical variation in demand and production leads to non-member employment to meet cyclical peak demand. An important reason for membership in a worker co-operative is assurance of continuous employment, over busi-ness cycle variations as well as over the year. Co-operatives therefore wish to limit membership to the number that can reasonably be assured of remunerative employment in low demand periods.[13] High demand is then met by hiring additional workers. Members afraid of unemployment in the cyclical plywood industry may tend to estimate too conservatively the basic labour need determining membership. A margin of non-member workers may then be maintained as a cushion against unemployment on a fairly permanent basis, when upward membership adjustment would be the theoretically appropriate response. (Membership expansion also presents institutional difficulties; see (vi) below.)

(v) Many plywood co-operatives with a large percentage of non-member employees are companies that took over a failing conventionally-organised plant. The number of co-operative share buyers in such take-over cases may not be adequate to staff the plant, so non-member hired workers fill the gap. There may also be unwillingness to deprive of their jobs existing workers who do not feel they can subscribe to shares. Similarly, when a plant is organised *de novo*, the number of share-buying workers may be inadequate to staff the plant. In these ways, a plant from its initial organisation may be adjusted to operate with a large percentage, even a majority, of non-member workers. While employees could be given the chance to buy shares gradually by deductions from pay, initial establishment of the co-operative requires substantial contributions of capital, probably necessitating some pressure or incentive for substantial down-payment such as the member/non-member distinction provides.

(vi) Similar considerations apply in cases of major expansion. Theory postulates long-run adjustment by membership change. In practice, slight membership change downward has occurred to accommodate technological displacement, but expansion has taken place by increase in hired labour, although not on the scale that destroyed the co-operative character of the initial plywood co-operative and earlier co-operatives in other industries.[14] In cases of major expansion also, companies are likely to need major infusions of capital in order to finance the new equipment. Expansion by increase in membership would then require substantial down-payment contributions by the share buyers. There is no market mechanism for selling co-operative shares (resales are handled on an individual basis), and in the absence of such organisation as was provided by the initial organising group, promoter, or failing-plant work force, co-operatives may be legitimately dubious of their ability to raise sufficient capital by selling new shares. A new share issue would also incur the expense and delay of security registration procedures. Furthermore, member admission procedures which require individual evaluation and probationary periods for prospective new partners would be severely taxed. For these reasons, co-operatives have tended to finance plant and equipment expansion by internal funds or loans where available, and man the expanded facilities with additional non-member labour where necessary.

Employment of non-member labour in the plywood co-operatives should not be dismissed as evidence of corruption. These problems of necessary skills for which the outside world competes, of seasonal and cyclical fluctuations greater than member-hours variations can accommodate, of needs for capital to buy or build, are problems of real-world implementation of worker management that must be faced by worker-managed enterprises, certainly by those operating in a non-labour-managed society and probably by those in such a society as well. Also real are problems of acceptance of authority and legitimacy of status differentials, of maintaining cohesiveness and flexibity, that complicate responses to the more strictly economic difficulties. Member income equality, found vital by the plywood co-operatives throughout their history, should not be dismissed as unimportant, or foreclosed as a viable option by implementation methods. Complications arising from limitations of capital sources and methods may be more easily approached.

(e) CAPITAL SHORTAGE

Evidence suggests that a major cause of difference between successful and unsuccessful co-operatives is capital investment.

Worker-owned companies have tended to be starved for capital. In general they have been dependent on capital contributed by members; initial down-payments on shares; and withheld earnings. Although short-term credit appears to have been available, markets for long-term capital have not adequately served the co-operatives' needs. Outside equity capital is nearly impossible to obtain for a worker co-operative (although some companies have sold non-voting stock in their communities) because of the divorce of outside investment from any management control. Loans have been infrequent, and are not usually

available when most needed. Real financial problems are aggravated by the conventional lender's distrust of worker
management. However, loan capital is now available for companies with records of success. Capital shortage was most acute at
the companies' start-up, but has continued to impair their ability
to modernise obsolete plant and adapt to a fast-changing
technology, to invest in timber, and to maintain adequate reserves
to cushion market down-turns.

Although capital markets have proved inadequate for the
needs of worker co-operatives (probably due to discrimination),
members' willingness to invest is also a factor. With retained
earnings almost the only source of capital, willingness to invest
becomes a crucial factor. Investment lag and low income tend to
be mutually reinforcing, since reinvestment of members' earnings
is difficult when earnings are near subsistence level, which itself is
often the result of prior under-investment. Some of the co-
operatives, however, have overcome the handicaps of low
income, lack of timber, and obsolete plant (including plants
closed under capital management) to obtain modern plants and
high income. Conversely, high member income has not always
guaranteed adequate investment. Workers who become co-
operative members tend naturally to think like workers rather
than owners, concentrating on take-home pay. Even when they
have learned to think of the welfare of the enterprise as a whole,
many have failed to appreciate the importance of investment to
the company's success. This may be the crucial difference between
successful and unsuccessful co-operation. The inherent conflict
between immediate and long-run income maximisation is the
exception to the efficiency tendency of worker-managed
operation.[15]

(f) SHARE TRANSFER PROBLEMS

The member's individually-owned share of stock, freely
transferable, carries a right to participate fully in future earnings
of the enterprise. It thus provides the maximum incentive to invest
in the co-operative, since by selling his share when he retires or
leaves the company, the member can receive the full value of the
future earnings stream as estimated independently by market
forces. In view of the importance of re-investment, and worker-
managers' difficulty in perceiving it, maximum incentive is

obviously desirable. There is no inherent incompatibility between labour management and private individual equity ownership by members (i.e. the worker owns his own tools) as long as management rights are equal.

Other methods of handling members' capital contribution and re-investment have adverse consequences for investment, company solvency, and labour-management solidarity. If there are alternative investment opportunities, investment in the co-operative will be deterred if a member, on retiring or leaving the co-operative, must forfeit his capital contribution or retained re-investment earnings.[16] The same is true if he receives only the value put in. Addition of interest payments on his invested amounts will not eliminate the disincentive, as interest will be less than the expected return from the investment or other equity-type investment. The degree of disincentive here will depend on the interest rate, which has no objective basis for determination. Accrual of interest in internal individual accounts leads to differences in objectives between longer-term members and others, with respect to interest rates and other matters. Long-term members with large accrued accounts could exercise undue influence by threatening to pull out.[17] (Non-cash settlements of accrued accounts to minimise this problem would further dampen investment incentives.) The same divisive conflicts would threaten if existing members sold shares to the company for resale instead of directly to individuals, even if arbitration or independent appraisal for the share's price could be agreed on. With company obligation to buy shares, although retirements could perhaps be predicted and covered by reserves or insurance, exit of members for other reasons (probably when the company was already financially hard-pressed) could seriously strain the enterprise's solvency.

Individually transferable shares carry problems for labour-managed operation, however. Individual share ownership, with either private or company-brokered share transfers, provides a way to co-operative extinction through the company buying up and retiring individual shares, until the longest-lived few remain as owners of a company relying on hired labour. The pioneer worker-owned plywood company (as well as early worker co-operatives in other industries) lost co-operative character in this way. Later plywood co-operatives, however, have not followed this route. (Limits on non-member employment would prevent this result, as would other easily-implemented restrictions.)

Difficulties with share transfers and inadequacies of capital markets can lead to sell-out of co-operatives to non-co-operative interests. Market mechanisms are lacking for bringing together potential buyers and potential sellers of co-operative shares, for financing transfers, and for evaluating shares. Inadequacies cause particular difficulty when substantial numbers of shares must be sold at one time: at the time a co-operative is organised to buy or build a plant; when major expansion is projected; or when a substantial number of shareholders approach retirement age simultaneously. The first two situations lead to non-member employment, as noted above. The last has been a factor in the sell-out of co-operative plants to non-co-operative interests (as well as, perhaps, some plant closings, as a one-generation lifetime would seem to suggest).

With the capital value of a successful company's share higher than a worker can manage out of savings, a privately-financed transfer requires the seller to accept a long-term contract for payment from the buyer's future earnings. If a majority of owners is approaching retirement, sale of the entire company to an outside interest may obtain immediate payment in full in cash or a more negotiable investment instrument. A higher price for the individual share may also be realisable. In recent plywood co-operative sell-outs, especially those not under economic duress, speculative considerations based on timber holdings and other special circumstances resulted in buying offers above the share prices based on production profitability otherwise realisable.

Lack of co-operative access to loan capital is a factor in the high price of co-operative shares. With some of the asset value offset by debt requiring servicing, share values would be more within reach of worker purchasers because of smaller workers' equity and lower expected future worker-owner income. (Plywood co-operative members believe, however, that a substantial down-payment is desirable as an indication of commitment to the company's future.) It might also be noted that co-operatives can avoid the mass retirement problem by making sure, as some now do, that members are of different ages.

Individual share transfers also suffer from lack of a market for evaluation of shares. Co-operative members have not always obtained a fair return for deferred earnings.[18]

(g) MANAGEMENT PROBLEMS

Financial failure and difficulties have resulted in many co-operatives from management problems, of which investment decisions are one aspect. Worker-owners tend to think as workers, not owners, and do not have the background and tools needed for making business decisions. Neither owners nor hired managers have a clear understanding of their relative roles and functions in decision making. Excessive manager turnover is one indication of this confusion. For these reasons, the co-operatives have probably made more than their share of bad decisions, on investment and other matters. The recent adverse changes in the plywood industry have put additional stress on management difficulties.

IV CONCLUSIONS

(a) POLICY IMPLICATIONS

The major problems of the plywood co-operatives discussed above stem from inherent difficulties and dilemmas of worker-managed operation in a real world lacking the perfect competition conditions postulated by theory. Thus they suggest policy implications for labour management generally.

i) Financing

The need for a source of capital to supplement private capital markets is a clear policy implication for implementation of labour management. Capital shortage problems of the co-operative model, and problems deriving from capital requirements, could be met by a financing agency, public or private, without sacrificing the characteristics of individual ownership and equal direct decision authority that make the model appropriate and attractive to workers in a private enterprise economy.

For initial financing of a co-operative to buy or build a plant and equipment and commence operations, a Bank for Worker Co-operatives could lend the necessary amount in a lump sum to the company, perhaps with a lien on the tangible assets as security. The company would issue shares of stock on an equal basis to each worker in the company who agreed to deduction from his 'pay' of regular amounts up to a cumulative total equalling the assigned value of the shares. A worker could also buy the share outright, or pay out of withheld earnings at a faster rate; perhaps incentives to faster purchase should be built in, to build up the company's equity capital more quickly. The company would repay the loan to the Bank on a regular schedule, or with a faster repayment rate option, as money from individual share-purchase deductions accumulated. If part of the Bank's loan was treated as an ordinary loan, so that, for example, only half was converted into equity capital, share value for initial purchasers could be kept lower. The company would be free to obtain loans from other sources as well. Perhaps a guarantee from the Bank would be sufficient to make capital available from private sources, or the Bank could be used as a lender of last resort.

A worker who had agreed to the capital contribution deductions from his gross remuneration would be a member (perhaps after a probationary period) with full voting rights and right to employment. Members collectively would have full and exclusive decision authority.

The member would be free to sell his membership share, subject to the purchaser taking over the pay-deduction agreement, and perhaps to approval of the buyer by the company. Re-investment in the company through retained earnings decided on by the membership would be reflected in appreciation of share value and realised by a member selling his share on leaving the company.

Major expansion requiring new capital could be handled in the same way.

As an exception to the members' decision autonomy, it would be appropriate for the loan agreement to prohibit sale of the company to non-co-operative interests, but liquidation would be permitted. Provisions could be written into the loan agreement limiting earnings pay-out and requiring accumulation of reserves for equipment replacement. However, restrictions on members' decision authority impairs self-management.

(ii) Non-member workers

With use of the financing method suggested above, there would be no reason for a non-member work force to arise in the initial

rganisation or major expansion of a co-operative, since the
orkers needed for plant operation would not need to contribute
apital or be persuaded to buy a share outright but merely to
gree to deduction from earnings as a contribution to capital.

The first four reasons for employing non-members discussed
arlier, however, suggest the advisability of allowing a worker co-
perative a certain percentage of workers with a different status
1an that of members, not subject to equal-treatment limitations
r advantages. With remuneration less dependent on company
erformance and no permanent right to employment, these
orkers would have less entitlement to equal voice in long-run
ecisions. Participation in short-run decisions would be ap-
ropriate and could be required, although a distinction would be
ard to draw. The percentage of such special workers might vary
ccording to the needs and seasonal or cyclical nature of the
1dustry. It would seem appropriate, however, to limit the
ermitted number of workers without full participation rights, if
ny special capital or other assistance was provided. Dangers of
xploitation', either in economic terms or in terms of manage-
1ent participation commensurate with their economic role, are
ot significant for skilled overhead workers or temporary or
easonal workers. To prevent cyclical-peak workers from becom-
1g a permanent second-class group, companies might be re-
uired after a certain period of employment to either offer the
orker membership (perhaps with credit toward share cost for his
ears of employment) or eliminate the position. The initial
umber of shares authorised could include a margin for future
1ember additions.

iii) Share transfer

n agency concerned with financing worker co-operatives could
lso ease problems of share transfer. A Worker Co-operative
ank could provide an organised meeting point for would-be
ellers and buyers of co-operative shares. It could also act as
1iddle man in financing the transfer, paying full value of seller's
quity immediately to sellers, with the buyer's purchase agree-
1ent then being with the agency. Full disclosure could be
2quired to aid accurate valuation by the private parties, or the
ank could provide appraisal. If considered desirable, the agency
ould subsidise transfer to lower the purchase price to the buyer.

(iv) Education and information

Providing information and education for worker co-operativ
members on economic essentials (particularly the need for re
investment) and basic management tools, skills and methods is
vital function that could be performed by a labour-managemen
promotional agency. Organising help, an experience clearin
house, and information on democratic decision-making method
are other possibilities. Expert management consultation o
individual enterprise problems would be a significant further ste

(b) PROSPECTS FOR US LABOUR MANAGEMENT

Plywood co-operatives have shown that the co-operative mod
based on private individual ownership works for achievin
labour-management for members, and for survivin
economically, without subsidy or external assistance, in a priva
enterprise economy in competition with conventionally-orga
nised capital-managed enterprises. Particularly significant
survival as co-operatives of plants found inadequately profitab
under capital management.[19] The adherence of the plywoo
companies to private ownership with individually transferab
shares demonstrates the appeal of individual ownership t
workers in a private enterprise economy. Although individu
shareholding has worked as a method of finance, sources c
capital additional to those provided by conventional capit
markets could ease many of the difficulties experienced by work
co-operatives. This and other measures could solve problems c
the co-operative model without need for structural departu
from the model.

Other US enterprises involving several hundred workers that a
organised on the co-operative model, are the northern Californi
refuse collectors and Oregon reforestation contractors.[20]

In recent years, unemployment insurance, welfare, and great
worker protection through unions have lessened the urgency c
economic motives for self-employment in industry, and th
willingness to sacrifice (as previous co-operative founders did) t
achieve it. The drive for self-employment has been most strong
manifested by individuals with little experience in industri
employment, with the result being proliferation of small cc
operatives in non-industrial fields. Recent actual and threatene

lant closures, however, have once again called workers' atten-
on to self-employment possibilities for industry.

Unfortunately, the instances of worker ownership that have
esulted have not been modelled on co-operative principles of
worker equality in decision making, and beneficial results for
dvancement of labour management are dubious. Management
uthority in these recent take-overs is based on share ownership,
nd share ownership by workers is unequal and weighted toward
igher-paid employees. Some management structures are de-
berately biased to minimise 'blue-collar' influence. Perhaps most
mportant, most 'worker ownership' take-overs of failing plants
ave involved indirect ownership with little or no management
articipation, through Employee Stock Ownership Plans
ESOP).

The idea of worker ownership appeals to legislators as well as
o workers. A number of laws to encourage worker ownership in
ndustry through 'employee stock ownership plans' have been
assed.[21] Government loans have helped Employee Stock Owner-
hip Trusts take over closing plants, and other worker-owned
ompanies have also used ESOPs as their worker-ownership
tructure. More laws to provide government assistance are being
onsidered.[22]

The legislative endorsement of worker ownership has not so far
ncluded worker management; ESOPs are designed to filter any
management participation by workers through the ESO trust and
rustees. (Only workers believe that workers can manage indus-
rial plants, as they show by attempting it when they get the
pportunity. Acceptance by workers of ESOPs for 'worker
wnership' may show recent diminution of that faith, or merely
onfusion.) ESOPs are designed and regulated as pension plans.
lthough some improvement over the usual ESOP structure is
ossible, it remains doubtful that viable or effective labour
management on a basis of equality of participation can be
stablished through ESOPs. In directness and complexity also
iminish the quality of the participatory experience and the
conomic incentive effects of participation, particularly in early
ears.[23]

Some of the proposals for government assistance endorse
mployee-community control'. This is an ambiguous concept, as
s 'community control' itself. Unanalysed questions abound: how
he 'community' can be defined; who are its legitimate

representatives; what the community's objectives are; wha happens if community and workers' objectives conflict, as i likely.[24] 'Community' participation in control (with more than minority interest) conflicts with the efficiency tendency of worke management and so with potential for survival and success, a well as with workers' self-management. Much of the impetus fo 'community' participation in control stems from distrust c worker management. If promotion of worker management is th goal, 'community' participation should be limited to minorit representation at most, so that workers have clear decision making control.

While preoccupation with ESOPs has diverted worker-owner ship development away from worker management, worke management without worker ownership is being approache through conventional industry's experiments with worke participation, job enrichment, job redesign, and similar efforts t combat worker alienation. If this interest in worker participatio and appreciation of its human and economic benefits could b integrated with the 'worker ownership' movement, labour man agement based on worker ownership could take a great lea forward in the United States. The co-operative model of th plywood and other worker co-operative enterprises provides proven and socially acceptable structure for implementation Measures such as those suggested in this chapter would solve th problems that have been shown in the plywood experienc making the co-operative model even more effective for labou management.

NOTES

1. This chapter is a revised version of 'Worker management in US plywoo manufacturing co-operatives: a co-operative‧ model for labou management' presented at the Walton Symposium, Glasgow, June, 197!
2. The softwood plywood industry – distinct from hardwood plywood developed in the Pacific north-west because of the properties and ad vantages of coast-type Douglas fir in construction, although other wood from other areas are now used. Softwood plywood manufacture in th north-west 'Douglas fir region' uses heavy machinery and in part a high speed production line, and had investment in plant and equipment (boo value) of $14 000 per worker in 1971 (less in earlier years). The manufactur ing process comprises log procurement (usually by bidding on standin timber and contracting out the logging), 'peeling' the log into venee clipping the veneer for size and defects and drying it, gluing and pressing th veneer together into panels, and trimming, patching and finishing. With th

north-west region historically dependent on the lumber and fishing industries, 'rugged individualism', and self-help, independent enterprise, and radical unionism are all part of its tradition. Unions have had no part in the co-operatives' development.

3. See Mead (1966).

4. In earlier years, one co-operative plant operated for only a year; one burned after several years and was not rebuilt; two closed after 13 and 17 years of operation; one sold out. An additional plant closed after 10 years because of dereliction by its exclusive sales agent (and former owner) which resulted, too late, in a $1.5 million damages judgement. Other co-operatives – some that survived and some that did not – were hampered by deliberate efforts to take advantage of workers' inexperience, in terms of unjustified plant selling prices, sales agency and management contracts, and promoters' fees.

5. Bellas (1972), for example, found that members' hourly remuneration in the 'low performance' half of his reporting sample averaged below the industry average wage for 3 years of his 4-year period, although hourly income in the 'high performance' half averaged considerably above it. See also Berman (1967).

6. A study currently under way (in early stages) by the author will compare productivity of co-operative and non-co-operative plywood plants in terms of value added by manufacture on a more comprehensive and statistically sophisticated basis.

7. Employment of some non-members is paralleled in other types of co-operatives which sell to non-members or sell produce of non-members, with non-members in such cases paying or receiving market prices without member patronage dividends.

8. Co-operative members have managerial capability; several managers, in both co-operative and non-co-operative firms, are former co-operative members of other firms.

9. On why producer co-operation is 'impossible' for this reason, see S. and B. Webb (1930) and E. Bernstein (1909) as quoted in Berman (1967, p. 2).

10. The necessity for highly remunerated professionals and specialists is a common problem in many types of co-operative organisations. Contracting for the needed service is a possible solution and could also be used for temporary workers, but is essentially a subterfuge.

11. Equal sharing is not required by co-operative principles; other types of co-operatives divide proceeds according to value as well as quantity of business done with the organisation.

12. Settling questions of pay differentials could be an important function of a labour union under worker management (see Berman, 1978), but changing the arena would not eliminate the damaging effects of dispute.

13. Some adjustment of member labour does take place in response to cyclical fluctuation, by members who leave the plant for outside employment when outside pay is higher than the co-operative return (usually being replaced by hired labour), returning to demand their guaranteed employment when conditions improve for the co-operative plant. This has happened only in the least prosperous co-operatives, and co-operative members try to avoid a situation where this response is appropriate.

14. The original worker-owned plywood company bought two other mills

which were staffed almost entirely by non-members. This contributed to the decline in the percentage of working owners, which cost the company its co-operative character by the time it sold out (after progressively retiring shares) with only 4 or 5 working owners remaining. Cf. Berman (1967 Chapters 2 and 6). Bellas (1972) considers this to be the normal pattern for successful co-operatives, holding that worker co-operation is 'basically unstable' because a successful co-operative will expand by acquiring other production units and increasing use of non-member workers, until owners are a small minority, perhaps not working in the plant, and participatory character is gone. This equating of success with inevitable massive expansion, and more particularly with acquisition of other mills, finds no support in the record of subsequent plywood co-operatives, which have shown no disposition towards multi-unit operation (except for setting up some small veneer plants near timber supplies). Absence of the empire-building drive is another social and economic advantage of worker co-operatives.

15. Pareto-optimal efficiency in resource use is demonstrated for the model of labour management outlined by Berman and Berman (1978).

16. Cf. Furubotn (1976).

17. Such problems are anticipated in Mondragon (see Chapter 6).

18. Although share prices for successful plywood co-operatives presently operating have probably stabilised, past prices of plywood co-operative shares do not appear to have borne a consistent relationship to earnings prospects, sometimes varying with speculative considerations and temporary industry circumstances.

19. An interesting question is why the viability of producer co-operation has been thus demonstrated in the United States, when development of other forms of co-operation is less extensive than in many other countries. Reasons may be suggested by two aspects of US working life: the North American tradition of individual proprietorship that has found widespread outlet in gasoline and other independent servicing and retail proprietorships as well as farms; and the relative lack of class consciousness of North American labour. A worker co-operative with ownership and management prerogatives for individual workers is a group expression of the individual proprietorship and upward mobility ideas. The idea of equality in co-operative group activity is well embedded in North American society in the myriad of voluntary associations, despite the lack of Rochdale structures.

20. Members of Sunset Scavenger Company and the other refuse co-operatives are workers owning individually transferable shares of stock, who have equal vote and receive their return in equal payments per hour worked. A worker becomes a member of Hoedads or other tree-planting co-operatives by joining a crew and agreeing to a deduction for capital reserves of a percentage (up to a certain total) from his share of contract proceeds, distributed in proportion to trees planted by each individual. Crew representatives chosen by equal vote from the central contracting organisation which maintains performance bonding reserves; some operating equipment is owned by crews, and some members individually. Hoedads has made loans from capital reserves to other co-operative organisations.

21. Principally Pension Reform Act 1974, also Tax Reduction Act 1975, Trade Act 1974, Regional Rail Reorganisation Act 1973.

22. Cf. *Self-management*, vol. vi, no. 3, Spring 1979, pp. 35–6.
23. ESOPs are primarily used by conventional corporations to augment their capital at government expense, but have also been used in the South Bend Lathe case and others for government financing to keep a plant open under nominal worker ownership. Worker-owned and partially worker-owned companies without government financing have also used ESOPs.

In an ESOP, the loan (government or private) is made to an employee stock ownership trust (ESOT) which uses it to buy stock from the company, whereby the company obtains new capital. The trust pays off the loan with scheduled payments made to it by the company, which also guarantees the loan. Payments, repayments of principal as well as interest, are deductible expenses (within limits) for corporate income tax purposes. This advantage means that, if the company is profitable, the new capital is contributed by the government through its reduced tax take.

Company shares owned by the trust are allocated to accounts of individual workers usually in proportion to pay rates (equal allocation is usually legally possible, and would happen if pay rates were equal) but only in proportion as the loan is paid off. The worker gets ownership to the allocated shares according to another 'vesting' schedule based on his years with the company. The worker is actually issued his shares only when he retires, or if he leaves the company after his shares are 'vested'. Voting rights of stock held by the ESO trust are exercised by the ESO trustees, usually appointed by company management.

An ESOP could probably be constructed to effectuate worker management as well as indirect worker ownership with specific provisions to make participation more direct than in the usual structure: requiring stock in the trust to be voting stock, with majority control, and voting rights to be passed through to the worker-beneficiary, on unallocated as well as allocated stock. For one man, one vote, stock would need to be allocated equally, or vote made independent of stock. Management control, but less direct, could be achieved by worker election (by equal vote) of the ESOP trustees who would vote the stock, or vote the unallocated stock which would remain even with immediate vesting of allocated stock.

An ESOP is a complex and roundabout method of establishing a worker-owned enterprise and providing it with capital. It does not open a new source of capital if government is the source of funding, although it offers a possibility of supplementing private lending with government funds through reduced corporate tax payments. The tax benefit, however, is helpful only if and when the company is profitable, substantial only with sufficient corporate income to incur the full corporation tax rate, and unnecessary if a worker-managed enterprise is organised as a co-operative since a co-operatives do not pay corporate income tax on profits derived from members' work. An ESOP offers workers the apparent advantage of gaining stock ownership without specific deduction from 'pay' for capital contribution; in a wholly worker-owned company under an ESOP, however, the same effect of lower individual take-home pay would result from reduction of distributable company income by the amount of payments to the ESO trust to retire the loan.

Under an ESOP, problems would arise of redemption of shares of workers retiring or leaving the company. If dividends and voting rights were absent or limited to preserve worker management, the company would be the only market for the stock issued to a worker on retirement, or on leaving the company earlier, and the company would have an obligation to buy at a price compensating for increased capital value built by unrealised reinvested earnings, both for equity reasons and to preserve an incentive for investment. While retirements could perhaps be handled by insurance or reserves, workers leaving for other reasons would be unpredictable, and could put serious strains on company solvency.

Equity problems, both on leaving and in participation during tenure, are posed among workers with different lengths of employment, who would get equal value per share though contributing unequal amounts to that value, and who would have unequal voting power while in the plant because of unequal number of years of share allocation, even if allocations were equal in each year. Organisational structure at end of the loan period poses further potentially serious problems of equity and participation.

The indirectness of worker ownership, with the company owned by the trust rather than the workers, appeals to some advocates of labour management who are ideologically opposed to individual ownership with transferable shares. However, the filtering of ownership and participation through the trust necessarily diminishes the equality of the participatory experience and the incentive effects leading to the greater productivity basic to worker-management survival and success. For several crucial early years of a worker plant take-over through an ESOP, for example, worker participation would be almost non-existent. The complexity of the structure and its many involved problems further alienate the worker from the enterprise.

ESOP laws and regulations are designed to provide a semblance of worker ownership without worker intrusion on management. Even ESOPs set up for worker-ownership control through a government loan embody this negative attitude toward worker management. ESOP provisions are part of pension law, and trustees' obligations to protect workers' pension rights do not harmonise with worker management. The differing objectives and orientation make it unclear whether ESOPs, to establish genuine worker management, would receive the required governmental approval or survive governmental supervision. With all the drawbacks, uncertainties and complexities of the ESOP method, it seems clearly inferior to the direct co-operative model of worker management as amended in this chapter.

24. The 'community' is hard to define on any but a geographic basis. Legitimate representatives of the geographic community are the elected local government officials (cf. Dewan and Frieden, 1978). These persons have no expertise or interest in industrial management, and might use their authority in the enterprise to foster unrelated and possibly antithetical personal objectives. Community objectives have never been defined and are quite likely to conflict with workers' goals, beyond the apparent initial concensus on the general objective of keeping open or starting a plant. Likely community objectives such as maximum employment or local purchasing could destroy the survival chances of the enterprise.

5 France[1]

Eric Batstone

The aim of this chapter – by a non-economist – is to look at certain aspects of the economic performance of French co-operatives and seek to assess the utility of formal economic models of self-management in understanding these data. The first section briefly outlines aspects of the history and constitution of French co-operatives and seeks to draw from this a number of general elements of 'motivation'. Subsequent sections look at the scale and usage of funds; the nature of production and organisation; rewards to labour; and more dynamic aspects of performance, making comparisons with French industry generally and between co-operatives.

The data presented here derive from a study of co-operatives belonging to the Société des Co-operatives Ouvrières de Production (SCOP). The latter comprises over six hundred co-operatives which employ, in total, about thirty thousand people, mainly in construction and printing. The study concentrated upon a sample of sixty co-opertives located in the Paris region. These constitute about a third of the co-operatives in the area and about ten per cent of all SCOP affiliates. In addition, further data derive from SCOP documents and publications, and case studies of five co-operatives.

I BACKGROUND

With some oversimplification, two contrasting notions of the producer co-operative can be identified in the general literature. The first of these promotes the concept basically in terms of what can best be described as a democracy of small capitalists, seeing the merging of the roles of capital and labour as a means of fostering a more co-operative, 'responsible' and energy-releasing approach on the part of workers (e.g. Jay, 1976; Oakeshott, 1978). In brief, while recognising notions of self-fulfilment through co-operative production, a central theme is that it makes unnecessary the conflict orientation associated with trade unions.

At the other extreme, co-operatives have been seen as a step towards socialism; protagonists of this kind therefore conceive of the co-operative much more as a solidary collectivity of workers (e.g. see Coates, 1976). Co-operative production assumes significance as a stimulus and example, involving the reduction, if not the eradication, of the role of the conventional capitalist or shareholder. Within both these broader perspectives there are those who are pessimistic about the real validity of the co-operative and its ability to survive without changing its nature and failing to meet its dreams (see Jones, 1976; Mandel, 1975).

These differing perspectives, if nothing else, suggest that the orientations of co-operatives – and, therefore, the assumptions required of any economic model – are likely to vary considerably. Indeed, even a brief and superficial perusal of, for example, the British experience of (degrees of) worker management shows this clearly. In this section, therefore, the history and constitution of French co-operatives is considered in an attempt to identify where they lie between the extremes of 'a democracy of capitalists' and 'a solidary collectivity of workers'. For example, if the movement were primarily concerned with the former, it would clearly be absurd to consider the extent to which it has been able to pursue priorities other than those of capital. Co-operatives will vary in their commitment to more radical goals, but nevertheless it is meaningful and useful to consider two aspects of the co-operative movement as a whole – its history and constitutional requirements – to develop some idea of the broad orientation of French co-operatives.

(a) HISTORY AND IDEOLOGY

For the present purpose, it is sufficient to demonstrate that the movement has its roots in socialist ideology.[2] In the first half of the nineteenth century, the need to transform workers into co-owners was argued by Fourier and supported by Leroux, Buchez and Coûsidérant. Louis Blanc put forward most clearly the ideals of producer co-operatives (still supported by SCOP today): 'what the proletariat lacks for self-emancipation are the instruments of work'. Carbon developed the idea of the Labour Association, which he described as the industrial parallel of political revolution: 'it is the substitution in the heart of the workshop of a democratic for a despotic situation'.

The real growth of co-operatives in France dates from 1848 and received support from the first International and from writers such as Prudhon. The early experience of co-operatives was delicate: at times they were suppressed by the state, while at other times they received its support as a means of integrating craft workers into society. Nevertheless, as their origins really lie in the 1848 revolution, so they also received strong support in such periods as those of the Paris Commune. Then in 1876 the first workers' congress in Paris encouraged the formation of co-operatives which were seen as complementary to trade unionism.

Despite this origin within the socialist tradition, many French socialists and trade unionists are opposed to the establishment of co-operatives. Nevertheless, it seems that most co-operatives have been established by active trade unionists, particularly in periods of social upheaval, and often as a consequence of lock-outs or redundancy. There have also been a number of co-operatives established largely on ideological grounds, particularly by professional workers since 1968. The diversity of reasons for setting up co-operatives has been noted by Vienney on the basis of a study of the period 1884 – 1950. He notes the following characteristics of periods in which there has been a high co-operative birth rate:

> these periods . . . correspond: on the one hand to periods of post-war reconstruction, marked by a strong rebirth of the spirit of 'social experimentation'; on the other hand by periods of economic crisis. The observation therefore strongly confirms the two fundamental elements of the experience of worker co-operatives . . . the communal exercise of the craft (safeguarding jobs in a period of unemployment) and surpassing the status of wage labour (experience of self-management). (Vienney, 1966, p. 153)

Given that co-operatives are often formed as a consequence of plant closure, it would seem that, if only indirectly, workers are seeking to reject the priority of profit. Moreover, SCOP still maintains its socialist orientation which may be expected to influence individual co-operatives.

The present manifesto of SCOP stresses its base in 'the real French socialist traditions' and that its aim is to reverse the order of priorities in industry; for in a co-operative, 'capital does not use men but men use capital'. As a consequence, the financial surplus 'is not the profit of the capitalist' and its division between various uses ceases 'to be a choice of a class nature'. Consequently, the nature of a co-operative is such that

> the work of the co-operators is not simply a marketable commodity but a personal contribution to the pursuit of common objectives . . . For producers who are firmly masters of their own destiny, work ceases to be an intolerable subjection. It is no longer a necessary evil . . . If the worker is no longer resigned executor of a task the aims and means of which are foreign to him, work becomes an active manifestation of association with a voluntary community. It is therefore the condition and the means of the blossoming of the humanity and craft of he who devotes himself to it.

The history and formal ideology of the French co-operative movement, therefore, indicate its formal commitment to the idea of a solidary collectivity of workers rather than a democracy of small capitalists.

(b) THE CONSTITUTION OF A SCOP CO-OPERATIVE

The actual constitution of a co-operative may be expected to reflect its priorities (Tivey, 1978). Certainly, if we look at worker-managed firms generally, a wide diversity of constitutional arrangements can be found. Moreover, a relationship between these arrangements and the informing ideology can be suggested. For example, if the aim is to establish a democracy of small capitalists then individual shareholdings might appear the best structure. On the other hand, if the aim is a solidary collectivity of workers, then a more desirable structure might be one of collective rather than individual ownership. Similarly, if emphasis s placed upon democracy among workers, then one might expect a restriction upon non-working shareholders and also a requirement that all workers be full members – in terms of holding shares either individually or as part of the collectivity – rather than there being anyone who occupies solely the role of employee. It is clear that other considerations will impinge upon the exact constitution of a co-operative: a shortage of funds may lead to the existence of non-working shareholders. At a minimum, however, the constitution may facilitate or obstruct the movement of a co-operative in a particular direction.

In terms of the two main features mentioned in the preceding paragraph – the nature of shareholdings and the distribution of membership – the French co-operatives have an 'intermediate' status. While shares are held individually, the constitution also requires the development of collective funds. In addition, any capitalist orientation is further limited by, first, a restriction upon the sale of shares which can be sold only at their nominal value, and, second, the requirement that, in the event of closure, the assets should be donated to another co-operative or similar body. On the second point, outsiders may own shares but they may be bought out at the wish of working members and their right to representation on the board of directors, even if they were to own a majority of the shares, is limited to a third. On the other hand, while workers may demand, after a certain period of employment in a co-operative, that their application for membership be considered, there is no rule requiring that all workers should be members (i.e. own shares). Moreover, workers who are not members cannot be discriminated against in terms of jobs or conditions and they are assured a share of the financial surplus.

Furthermore, two constraints upon the role of capital are worthy of note. First, voting occurs on the basis of 'one man, one vote' among members, no matter what the size of their shareholdings. Second,[3] the constitution requires that the return on capital be limited to six per cent and that the proportion paid to 'labour' should exceed that paid to 'capital'.

We turn now to how exactly democracy is conceived within the constitution of a SCOP co-operative. In general terms, subject to the points made in the preceding paragraphs, the internal organisation of a co-operative is comparable with that of any *société anonyme*. The direction of the company is the responsibility of a board of directors, elected by the shareholders, and this, in turn, elects a managing director. As a consequence it is possible that the internal structure of a co-operative is little different to a conventional company. This may, in part, reflect a perceived need for specialist skills and patterns of authority. But it is also, perhaps, a logical derivative of the concept of the conventional shareholder as a 'mandator' (Abrahamsson, 1977). For if the capitalist shareholder is identified as a major problem in the conventional enterprise, then his substitution by worker-owners can be seen as the most efficacious means of redirecting the enterprise to more valued ends. In any event, the constitution – although this is to be distinguished from practice – provides for the exercise of democratic rights solely through the mandator role associated with the ownership of shares.

In addition, co-operatives are subject to laws concerning industrial relations which provide further potential means for worker influence (if only of a limited kind). If there are more than eleven workers, enterprises are legally required to recognise *dèlègués du personnel* elected by the work force; if there are over fifty workers, a works council must exist, nominated (where relevant, and in the first instance) by the unions and elected by the work force. Similarly, the unions can have a section in a co-operative. Clearly the role which these institutions play can vary significantly. In all, just over sixty per cent of the sample of sixty co-operatives had some form of collective representation – union section, *dèlègués* and/or *comité d'enterprise*.

The structure of the French co-operative recognises the importance of individual shareholdings whilst imposing a number of significant constraints upon the powers associated with capital ownership. Nevertheless, an important distinction exists between employee and member: while the former has certain rights and is guaranteed a share of the financial surplus, constitutionally only the shareholder has democratic rights. In terms of internal organisation, the law provides for the conventional roles of a board of directors and a managing director. The law also provides rights to conventional forms of worker representation. In brief, the French co-operative constitutionally occupies a place mid-way between the solidary collectivity of workers and the democracy of small capitalists. However, within this constitutional framework, actual patterns of organisation may vary considerably.

I THEORY

Vanek (1975) has pointed to the variety of objectives put forward in economic models of co-operatives. The preceding discussion – stressing the socialist orientation and the frequent origin of co-operatives in fights against unemployment – suggests that the individualistic notion of maximisation of income per worker is not apposite. There is a considerable – although incomplete – emphasis upon the collectivity. However, given the way in which membership tends to tie the worker to the enterprise, there is a tendency for the interests of the collectivity to be identified with the co-operative.

A number of general hypotheses may be derived from the history and ideology of the French co-operative movement. These are first outlined in general terms and then specific behavioural hypotheses are detailed and examined against the evidence. The nature of the French co-operative movement suggests there is a condsiderable emphasis upon factors other than simple monetary income. In addition, the very establishment of the co-operative frequently appears to contradict market forces: the fact that workers seek to protect their jobs suggests that their actions within the co-operative will tend to focus, above all, upon continued job preservation or security. This suggests the adoption of a long-term perspective and the desire to protect the enterprise from adverse risk: hence, one might expect a limited resort to external financing (particularly other than through shareholdings) and high levels of liquidity. Consequently it might be expected that individual co-operatives will seek to dampen market forces. Thus it is to be expected that their employment will expand less rapidly than those of capitalists under favourable conditions and be maintained when other firms are declaring workers redundant.

It is being suggested, therefore, that, to a degree, co-operatives will seek to reverse the conventional priorities as between capital and labour. Relatedly, this suggests not only that wages and other forms of financial reward may be higher, but also that the experience of work will differ as compared with the capitalist enterprise. (Certainly 'the practice of the craft' is an important element in the history of French co-operatives.) Furthermore, skill levels will tend to be higher in co-operatives (this further acting as a counterbalance to the lower level of capital which may

result from the bias against external financing) and at the same
time the notion of 'community' and associated 'responsibility'
suggest that levels of supervision will be lower. In brief, at least
relative to the capitalist enterprise, the co-operative will be
concerned with a collective notion of the interests of labour
involving, as a primary condition, a partial insulation from the
vagaries of the market. Given this, workers will find higher
instrumental and effective rewards while the 'high-trust' (Fox
1974) fosters superior levels of performance. A further set of
implications follow: that co-operatives will have a higher level of
survival than conventional enterprises; and that the co-operative
sector as a whole will tend to grow rapidly, particularly in periods
of recession as new co-operatives are formed.

Although in practice the goals of co-operatives may be
expected to vary considerably, those which demonstrate a more
democratic structure (in terms of levels of membership and
possibly, collective representation) may be expected to fit more
closely these general hypotheses.

The more specific hypotheses are examined using data derived
from a sample of sixty co-operatives in the Paris area. About half
of these are engaged in construction, and a further seventeen per
cent in printing. The remainder range from professional activities
to engineering to baking. Levels of membership – i.e. the proportion of workers who are shareholders in the co-operatives – varies
considerably: five per cent of the cases have one hundred per cent
membership; a further forty-two per cent have between ninety-
nine and fifty per cent membership while at the other extreme
twenty-seven per cent have less than a quarter of their work force
in membership.

III EVIDENCE

The general hypotheses discussed above may be conveniently
grouped under three headings:
 (i) Scale and Usage of Funds;
 (ii) Nature of Production and Organisation;
(iii) Rewards to Labour.

Detailed hypotheses are now specified under each heading and
the evidence from the sample considered.

i) SCALE AND USAGE OF FUNDS

We first consider the performance of co-operatives *vis-à-vis* capitalist counterparts. Four hypotheses suggest themselves:

(a) that co-operatives have a lower level of funds;
(b) that their funds are of a more long-term nature, and internal financing is more important;
(c) that co-operatives will have a lower level of capital intensity;
(d) that co-operatives will have higher levels of liquidity.

General comparisons across industry are not particularly useful here. Thus, the performance of co-operatives in the Printing and Construction industries (the two largest groups in the sample) is compared with general data for each industry (INSEE). Table 5.1 presents the performance of the co-operative sector in each of the two industries relative to the industry as a whole. For indicators appropriate to hypotheses (a)–(d), the data broadly confirm the hypotheses.

The nature of French co-operatives is such that it would be wrong to expect more democratic co-operatives to conform more closely or strongly to the above hypotheses than their less democratic counterparts. Where membership is higher, it is likely that funds will be higher and, automatically, funds per worker are higher. Accordingly, they will be able to maintain a higher level of both liquidity and of capital intensity.

TABLE 5.1 *Performance of co-operatives relative to industry (co-operative performance as percentage of industry)*

Hypothesis	Measure	Printing (%)	Construction (%)
a)	Total funds per worker	56	67
b)	(i) Percentage of funds of a long-term nature	152	163
	(ii) Share of external sources	76	84
	(iii) Level of internal funds	79	> 110
c)	Capital equipment per worker	68	79
d)	Average level of liquidity	168	172
h)	Proportion of skilled to total manual workers	129	100
i)	Proportion of supervisory personnel	50	100
m)	Labour cost per worker	104	108

Three hypotheses on inter-co-operative performance ar
suggested:
  (e) the more democratic will have higher levels of funds pe
      worker (but not necessarily per member);
  (f) they will have higher levels of liquidity;
  (g) they will have higher levels of capital intensity.

The sample reveals that there is virtually no variation in the leve
of funds per *member* by level of membership of the existence o
collective representation. However, high membership co-operat
ives (more than half the work force in membership) have a highe
level of funds per *worker* – nearly twice as many have fund
totalling more than 25 000f than do their low membershi
counterparts. No variation exists in terms of the existence o
collective representation. High membership co-operatives als‹
tend to have less resort to external sources of funds, although thi
variation is not very strong.

Given higher funds per worker in high membership co
operatives, it is not surprising that they have a higher net (an‹
gross) value of capital equipment per worker, both generally an‹
within specific industries. For example, in construction twice a
many high as low membership co-operatives have equipmen
valued at over 20 000f per worker. At the same time, on average
liquidity tends to be twice as high in high membership as in lo\
membership co-operatives. There are similar, though weake›
relationships with the existence of collective representation. Th
hypotheses therefore receive support from the data.

(ii) NATURE OF PRODUCTION AND ORGANISATION

In this category two major hypotheses on the performance of cc
operatives *vis-à-vis* capitalists are examined:
  (h) skill levels will tend to be higher;
  (i) the level of supervision and professional management wi
      tend to be lower.

Caution has to be exercised here over the reliability of comparat
ive data on occupational breakdowns across industries.

The evidence on hypotheses (h) and (i) is shown in Table 5.\
Some support is shown in the case of the printing industry bt
none in construction.

The comparable hypotheses for inter-co-operative compa›

sons are, again, somewhat more complex. First, it seems reasonable to suggest that more skilled workers than unskilled will be prepared to become co-operative members so that the direction of causality of any relationship between levels of skill and membership is complex. But, in any event, it seems reasonable to suggest:

(j) high membership co-operatives will tend to have fewer unskilled workers;

(k) more democratic co-operatives will have lower levels of professional management and supervision.

Hypothesis (k) does not extend to directors. Given the way in which directors are selected, a proportionately higher number would indicate a greater degree of democracy. Accordingly:

(l) high membership co-operatives will tend to have proportionately more directors, fewer of whom will be non-members (i.e. the level of 'professional' management will be lower).

Table 5.2 presents evidence from the sample of co-operatives on hypotheses (j)–(l). The data are consistent with these hypotheses.

TABLE 5.2 *Comparative performance of high and low membership co-operatives (percentage of co-operative in each group)*

Hypothesis	Measure (%)	Membership	
		High (%)	Low (%)
j)	Unskilled workers >10 of work force	< 45	63
k)	Supervisory personal >5 of work force	43	69
l)	(i) Number of directors >10 of work force	70	40
	(ii) Some directors or managers are not members	8	50
r)	Reduced labour force in last 3 years	34	46
t)	(i) Payments to capital ÷ payments to labour >0.5	33	57
	(ii) Specific 'bonus' paid to management	30	55

(iii) REWARDS TO LABOUR

Following from the earlier discussion, four hypotheses on the rewards to labour in co-operative relative to industry as a whole are examined:

(m) wages will tend to be higher;

(n) differentials will tend to be lower;

(o) job security will be higher;
(p) the nature of the work experience will be superior in co-operatives in terms of lower levels of, and different kinds of, supervision, and a greater sense of commitment.

Data on wages in the co-operatives are not available and thus labour costs per worker (including social security payments etc.) is used. The test of hypothesis (m) is shown in Table 5.1. These figures do not, of course, take account of the occupational structures of enterprises. The higher proportion of skilled workers in some co-operatives is counterbalanced by the lower proportion of supervisors. Moreover, the case studies undertaken along with data obtained from SCOP officials suggests that the differentials in co-operatives between the highest and lowest paid are much smaller than in industry generally (hypothesis (n)). For example, the lowest range in the five co-operatives studied was 1.8:1 between the highest and lowest wage, and the highest found (in a co-operative employing several hundred people) was only 5:1 – much lower than in France generally (Cf. Silvestre, 1974)

In the area of job security, difficulties are again confronted since the data available on industry refers to a changing population of firms whilst that on co-operatives refers to a constant population. Nevertheless, these data suggest that between 1970 and 1975, construction co-operatives actually increased employment by five per cent while in the industry employment fell by over twelve per cent. While some co operatives have disappeared in this period, it is also the case that many new ones have been established. At a minimum, the available data does not contradict hypothesis(o).

While, as has been shown, levels of supervision appear to be lower in co-operatives, it cannot be said that they have engaged in many radical changes in the typical pattern of work organisation However, French companies have been, traditionally, highly hierarchical and centralised. As the managing-director of one co operative explained, 'We've achieved quite a success by getting the idea of delegation to other directors, let alone anything else' Management tend to develop proposals, and members, beyond being able to vote out directors, tend to have a formal say only on the most crucial issues. This is, however, a considerable improvement upon the rest of French industry. Similarly, the institutions of collective representation seem to operate in a much more meaningful manner in the co-operatives than in the rest of industry, where they tend simply to match the minimal requirements of the letter of the law (see e.g. Batstone, 1978). Further, as is clear from much of the remainder of this paper, 'social' considerations appear to play a significant role in the policy formulation of co-operatives.

In terms of day-to-day work, the co-operatives appear to be distinctive in a number of respects. There is a greater emphasis upon the self-discipline of workers and such disciplinary action as occurs tends not to be of a punitive kind but rather a case of 'discussing the communal nature of the enterprise'. Managers are aware of disciplinary problems but they tend to be of a peculiar kind – namely, how do you tell a worker (shareholder) not to take ten minutes off when he has already exceeded the planned work rate? Indeed, a study of a sample of time sheets in an engineering co-operative indicates that over half the jobs were completed in about half the estimated time. This is part of a 'high-trust' syndrome in which workers will often advise on job costings, etc.

Unfortunately, we do not have data of a systematic nature on the conventional indicators of morale such as turnover, absenteeism, etc. But in all the interviews conducted it was claimed that these tended to be lower in co-operatives than in industry generally. Moreover, a survey (Chevalier, 1974) of co-operative workers found that while about 40 per cent joined co-operatives by chance and nearly a quarter joined because of the levels of wages, about 40 per cent also stressed the attractions of working in a co-operative or 'a good atmosphere'. Similarly, the major reasons put forward for staying in co-operatives were: interesting work; 'a good atmosphere'; good management–worker relations; and good team spirit. These somewhat qualitative and patchy comments appear to give support to the superior nature of co-operative work experience (hypothesis (p)). Other hypotheses could also be developed but, unfortunately, the data available permit no kind of testing. However, some of these issues are capable of investigation with the available data as far as inter-co-operative comparisons are concerned. Hence:

(q) labour costs per worker will tend to be higher in high membership co-operatives;

(r) job security will tend to be higher in high membership co-operatives;

(s) consistent with the commitment to self-fulfilment, the more

democratic co-operatives will spend more on general
training and on training in the principles of co-operative
production;

(t) in high membership co-operatives, proportionately more
of the financial surplus will be paid to labour than to
capital, and less will be paid specifically to management.
However, through the use of participation agreements
whereby workers receive a 'bonus' which is then held and
used by the co-operative for a number of years, the higher
proportions of the surplus paid to labour does not detract
from the funds available to the more democratic co-
operative.

Hypothesis (q) receives some support since labour costs in high
membership co-operatives are about 12 per cent higher than in
low membership co-operatives. Table 5.2 includes data which are
consistent with hypotheses (r) and (t). Where collective representation exists, nearly twice as many co-operatives spend at least the
legal training levy on internal training than where it does not
exist; a similar, although less strong, relationship is also found
with level of membership (hypothesis (s)). While only one in
twenty of co-operatives who have no collective representation
have any form of training in principles of co-operative
production, almost half of those with such representation do. A
similar, but weaker, relationship exists with the level of
membership. It was also suggested in hypothesis (t) that more
democratic co-operatives would be more likely to make use of
participation agreements. Four in five co-operatives with collective representation employ such agreements compared with about
a third of other co-operatives. A similar, though weaker,
relationship exists with membership level.

It would seem, therefore, that the rewards to labour are greater
in co-operatives, particularly if more democratic, than in industry
generally. To a limited degree, therefore, the endeavour to make
labour a priority over capital does seem to meet with some success
in French co-operatives.

(iv) EFFICIENCY, CHANGE, SURVIVAL AND GROWTH

The bulk of this chapter has focused on themes which have
perhaps constituted relatively subsidiary elements of formal

theories of self-management. In the introductory sections, relatively little has been said about the traditional economic concerns of efficiency, etc. In part, this bias reflects the priorities of the author; but it is also a reflection of important elements in the French tradition of co-operative production, namely, attempts to accommodate to, rather than integrate with, the existing market and social systems. Nevertheless, as members of co-operatives themselves are only too fully aware, they have to accept to an important degree the fact of market demands. Indeed, many critics of co-operatives see this fact as their weakness (e.g. Mandel, 1975; Sirc, 1977).

It has been suggested – and the evidence has broadly supported the view – that co-operatives seek to isolate themselves from certain features of the market in order to pursue more fully goals which are in part at odds with the demands which the market tends to impose. It might therefore be suggested that co-operatives would perform less efficiently than conventional companies. Certainly, at the time this research was undertaken, the rewards to capital were strictly limited. Moreover, the relatively high level of liquidity suggests that funds are not used to what, from a capitalist point of view, would be the most efficient ends. But such an argument has the danger of imposing upon co-operatives aims which are foreign to them.[4]

On the other hand, as has been widely argued, the 'high trust' situation typical of co-operatives suggests that, *ceteris paribus,* internal efficiency (conventionally defined) could well be higher in co-operatives than in the generality of industry. Lower indirect costs in terms of professional management and supervision, greater worker motivation, as well as a higher skill level are all factors which might facilitate such efficiency. There are, therefore, arguments both for and against a superior level of efficiency in co-operatives.

Conventional notions of efficiency, of course, relate not so much to returns on funds as to returns on capital equipment. This fact favours the possibility that efficiency may be superior in co-operatives as compared with industry as a whole. The data on value-added shown in Table 5.3 supports this view, although value-added per unit of labour cost is virtually identical in co-operatives and industry generally (construction and print). Moreover, there is a slight tendency for the high membership co-operatives to demonstrate a performance superior to those with

TABLE 5.3 *Relative performance of co-operatives to industry (Co-operative performance as percentage of industry)*

	Printing (%)	Construction (%)
Value added as % of production	140	118
Value added ÷ net value of capital equipment	146	128

proportionately fewer members. The fact of superior performance along with the 'security sponge' of high liquidity, a commitment to survival (for employment maintenance), and relative labour intensity suggests that co-operatives would indeed demonstrate a superior ability to survive and on average be larger than enterprises generally.

Unfortunately no data are available on the size (in employment terms) of all co-operatives. But several co-operatives do employ over a thousand people, although no co-operative giants comparable in scale with massive multi-nationals exist. However, while the latter may account for a major proportion of total employment, they are a very small minority of all enterprises. In fact, the sample of sixty suggests that co-operatives tend to be larger than the typical French enterprise. Forty per cent of the co-operatives employed more than fifty people, and two per cent over a thousand. In 1971, ninety-seven per cent of French enterprises which employed any workers had a labour force of less than fifty, while only one per cent employed more than a thousand. This pattern exists even within particular industries; for example, ninety-seven per cent of construction enterprises employed less than fifty workers in 1971, while only fifty-three per cent of construction co-operatives were that small (in 1976).

Table 5.4 provides data relevant to a consideration of the survival of co-operatives as compared with other enterprises. Despite the variations in the different sources of co-operative data, it does seem that the co-operatives are, in overall terms, able to survive for longer periods than the typical capitalist enterprise. (For a further discussion of birth and survival rates of co-operatives, see Vienney, 1966.)

Given the preparedness of co-operatives to continue with low returns on capital (if only because of the limited incentive to

TABLE 5.4 *Age of capitalist and co-operative enterprises*

Age	Capitalist firms* (%)	Sample of 60 (1976) (%)	All SCOP Oakeshott (1978) (%)	All SCOP Vienney (1966) (%)
1–5 years	20.8 ⎫	14 ⎫	24[a] ⎫	⎫ 53
6–15 years	34.0 ⎬ 56.6	14 ⎬ 31	⎬ 43[b]	⎬
16–30 years	22.6 ⎭	17 ⎭	⎭	14[d]
>30 years	22.6	53	33[c]	33[e]
Total	100.0	100	100	100

* Fizaine (1968).
[a] = 1–3 years.
[b] = 3–33 years.
[c] = >33 years.
[d] = 16–24 years.
[e] = >24 years.

withdraw funds), this is perhaps not surprising. However, according to SCOP statistics, co-operatives have also demonstrated a superior record of growth of production since the Second World War. Taking 1949 as equal to 100, the SCOP index of production had reached 595 by 1976 while the overall national figure was only 293. While this variation is so strong as to make one hesitant about the reliability of the comparison, other data also suggest the superior growth record of co-operatives. Again, as has been noted in relation to employment figures, there are problems of comparing a changing population for an industry as a whole with a constant co-operative population. It has already been seen that the employment record of co-operatives appears superior; but the same is true of the growth of capital equipment, where between 1970 and 1972 in both printing and construction, co-operatives exceeded the industry growth figure by about fifty per cent. Similarly, it would appear that both construction and printing co-operatives have in recent years considerably exceeded their respective industries in their growth of turnover.

However, it appears that the nature of the growth of production in co-operatives is different from that found in industry generally. Vienney (1966) has shown that between 1949 and 1961, co-operatives grew faster in periods of low inflation. Perhaps of equal interest – and consistent with their stress upon job security – is the manner in which they have grown far more rapidly than has industry generally since unemployment has reached high levels in France. Hence between 1949 and 1970, unemployment doubled in France, industrial production rose by 182 per cent, while co-operative production rose by 356 per cent – approximately double the national figure. Between 1970 and 1976 unemployment rose by more than 250 per cent, national production rose by only 4 per cent, while co-operative production grew by about 30 per cent – nearly eight times the national figure. This pattern is probably explained by two factors: first, the relative success of the security strategy typically adopted by co-operatives; and second, the tendency for new co-operatives to be established as other companies fail. Despite this second factor, much of the preceding discussion indicates the superior survival ability of co-operatives. However, level of democracy does not appear to be significantly related to growth.

IV DISCUSSION

In general terms, the arguments put forward concerning the aims and performance of the French co-operatives receive support from the data presented, although it should be noted that in some places the data are less reliable than one would wish. As a non-economist, I am not competent to discuss in detail the utility of formal economic models, but a number of points are perhaps worthy of brief mention. First, many of the models assume a self-managed economy and clearly the activities of co-operatives in such a situation may be expected to vary somewhat from those in the kind of situation in which the French co-operatives find themselves. Second, and relatedly, it is perhaps true to say that in the French situation the co-operatives are dominantly concerned with their own survival so that questions of relevance to a self-managed economy are of less relevance for them. Indeed, as has been continually reiterated, the co-operatives are seeking in part to reject the demands of the market. Third, if the argument of this Chapter is correct, the co-operative seeks to ensure an especially long-term perspective. Accordingly economic models focusing upon short-term adjustments are missing what appears to be the crucial features of co-operative behaviour (see below). Fourth, the particular constitutional features of co-operatives appear to be important – the requirements for certain levels of plough-back, the limited incentive in capital terms for individuals to leave or for the co-operative to be closed, the limitation upon the powers of outside shareholders – are all of considerable significance in fostering the particular orientations discussed above. Accordingly, the applicability of formal models may often be limited. Finally – and this is suggested by the preceding comments – the over-emphasis upon conventional economic theory can lead to a picture of co-operatives which, from a more general perspective, is somewhat misleading. For example, so far as I am aware, liquidity is not embodied in the formal theories; while security may be defined as an endeavour to maximise income in the long term, this may serve to bias theoretical endeavour against certain elements of co-operative performance, such as continuation even when making what would generally be seen as a loss, which are of crucial significance.

More generally, economists have looked at tendencies for co-operatives to decline either economically or democratically (see Jones, 1976). This theme has of course been much more widely discussed. But the dynamic interrelationship between changes in organisation and in economic performance has not been built into the formal models. And yet the French experience suggests that this interrelationship is important. This is discussed at greater length by Batstone (1979) but it is perhaps useful to outline briefly the main elements of a co-operative life cycle model which appears to explain much of the data on French co-operatives of differing ages (ideally, of course, the model requires data on the same co-operatives over time).

First, it is necessary to note that there is no *steady* decline in the level of membership as one moves from the newest to the oldest co-operatives. Two-thirds of the newest (post-1968) co-operatives have over half their work forces in membership, a figure which falls to 19 per cent for the 1945–67 generation of co-operatives, but then rises to about 50 per cent for the older generations. At the same time, the existence of collective representation rises steadily with age of co-operatives; it exists in 43 per cent of post-1968 co-operatives, but in 78 per cent of pre-1914 co-operatives. Given these facts, the life cycle model can be outlined briefly.

The essence of the life cycle model lies in the interrelated growth of employment, funds and professional management and reactions to these developments (Cf. for conventional companies, e.g. Mueller, 1972). When first established, the co-operative is small and short of funds. Most, if not all, of its initial work force will be members and will be highly committed to the enterprise and its success. Considerable effort will be made to use the best methods possible, but funds will be a continuing problem. At the same time, the very nature of the co-operative's origins in the communal effort of a few will mean that a primitive democracy exists. This may occur as much unconsiously as through a conscious decision.

Assuming the co-operative survives its first few crucial years, funds will have developed through the plough-back of financial surplus, and the co-operative will be more firmly established. The 'frontier spirit' will have declined. The 'founding fathers' now feel more secure, the organisation of the co-operative will have become more routinised, and particular members will have become competent specialists in various managerial specialisms. These tendencies will probably have been strengthened by a growth in size and the recruitment of new workers, many of whom may not become members. There is, therefore, a decline of primitive democracy; management will become a more separate activity and the majority of original members may well have become full-time managers rather than workers. This, then, is the low point for democracy. Relatedly, capital will assume a greater priority over labour in this era so that, for example, rewards to labour become less, liquidity is lower (although funds per worker also tend to fall), and supervision increases. However, value-added/unit of funds reaches a peak.

Assuming the co-operative continues to survive, the model suggests a resurgence of democracy. However, it is significantly different from the primitive democracy of the early days. Its thrust comes from the development of institutions of collective representation which, in part, reflect a growth in size and, in part, the changes in management noted above. Legislation concerning, for example, *comités d' enterprise* in larger establishments plays a role here. But, in addition, it may be that increased scale makes informal, individual processing of grievances more difficult. Along with these factors, collective representation appears all the more attractive precisely because there is a relatively clear divide between management and workers within a fairly routinised organisation.

Another set of factors may also be relevant. The founding fathers retire and new people take their place. Over time, therefore, the authority of some members which derives from being founding fathers declines. The gap between the formal structure of a co-operative and actual experience may grow deeper and, without the charisma of the founders, becomes increasingly more difficult to justify. The gap between rhetoric and reality is considerable and new 'leaders' (along with the existence of collective representation) may, therefore, seek to give the co-operative new direction and energy. The rhetoric and the formal co-operative structure of the enterprise indicate the direction for change. At the same time, size and the importance of professional management make a return to primitive democracy difficult. Another factor may also be of relevance: a shortage of funds. This can derive from two things. First, as the number of members declines, so may the size of share capital, particularly in relation to the current size of the enterprise. In addition, because of lower membership and its concentration in management, the allocation of the financial surplus may be directed more to capital and to management than to labour. Hence, this money may not go into the funds of the co-operative. Second, this problem may be exacerbated by the need to replace capital equipment.

Accordingly, therefore, one finds the co-operative running into the third stage – a resurgence of democracy, not only in terms of members but also through the conventional institutions of collective representation which not only play their conventional, contestatory role, but also act as a partial substitute for more traditional co-operative institutions. A resurgence of labour as a priority reappears, although this is to a degree reflected in aspects of conditions and traditional 'industrial relations' areas.

Such a model is clearly oversimplified and a host of other factors are of relevance to the organisation and performance of co-operatives. Nevertheless, the model does serve to introduce a number of themes which have usually been discussed only in the most general terms and received little recognition in more formal theories or models.

In conclusion, it is important to retain a sense of perspective on the above discussion, and this can best be done by returning to the question of whether French co-operatives are, or could be, democracies of small capitalists' or 'solidary collectivities of workers'. In this context, it should be noted that this study has concerned itself with variations in democracy and orientation within a fairly restricted range of experience. As has been suggested above, and as the case studies undertaken indicated, the extent to which the notion of self-management has been pursued beyond the 'mandator' role is somewhat limited. Similarly, it is obvious that all co-operatives have to demonstrate a considerable sensitivity to the conventional demands of the market and to that degree accept that the traditional aim of profit is important if not primary. In both these senses, co-operatives clearly cannot hope to match up to the demands of writers such as Mandel. Indeed, it seems reasonable to suggest that – at least in their day-to-day activity – co-operatives have to adopt a parochial approach, for example by limiting their growth of employment, in order to achieve the requisite degree of isolation from the market to be able to pursue more labour-oriented goals. Nevertheless, it is clear that many co-operatives have not simply developed into the democracies of small capitalists envisaged by some writers. In brief, the co-operatives in France have failed to match up to the more extreme expectations or fears of both the left and the right

On the other hand, they do prove that workers can run their own firms with as much success as conventional capitalists and that in order to do so they do not have to forego totally their more ideological dream. In this sense, they may have an exemplary value of the kind noted by Coates. While it is clear that in recent years a number of co-operatives have been established in opposition to plant closures, it is worth noting that Adam and Reynaud (1978, p. 319) found, in a study of seventeen fights against closure, that only one chose a co-operative solution because 'a company, particularly one in difficulties, cannot be self-managed in a capitalist context . . . union strategy is to negotiate until a future director appears who accepts their conditions; you shoot the pianist until he plays the desired tune but you do not yourself substitute for him . . . '. Even so, for those who work within co-operatives there is the not unimportant advantage that they do have a greater influence and are less merely appendages to machines than they are in the bulk of French industry. One other point is of relevance here. A more radical discussion of co-operatives compares a rather mundane experience with an unspecified ideal. Such ideals are important but it should be noted that any conception of a socialist society has also to achieve a balance between the democracy of market self-management and the allocative justice which might be achieved by a more co-ordinated planning process (e.g. Wachtel, 1973, pp. 184 ff.). Any society involves constraints and in this sense some caution is required in being overly critical of the co-operative experience. Hence, while they cannot be seen as a major stride towards socialism, co-operatives are able to maintain both a degree of democracy and a reduced emphasis upon capital as a priority over time. The thesis of total degeneration gains little support from French experience; conversly, the French co-operative does not fulfil the dreams of many commentators from the left or the right .

NOTES

1. This chapter is based on a paper entitled 'Some aspects of the economic performance of French producer co-operatives', presented at the Walton Symposium, Glasgow, June 1979.
2. A fuller account of the movement's history may be found in Antoni (1957).
3. This discussion refers to the SCOP constitution in 1976; some modifications have since occurred – see Liaisons Sociales (1978).
4. This argument would be less relevant where co-operatives constituted the dominant enterprise form.

6 Spain: the Mondragon Enterprises[1]

Robert Oakeshott

The group of linked enterprises centred in the small steel working town of Mondragon in Guipuzcoa, the most densely populated and economically advanced of the four Basque provinces of Spain, has lately begun to attract increasing attention. In the space of less than one working life, the Mondragon enterprises have grown from nothing into a formidably successful grouping which employs more than 16 000 people in 70–80 separate undertakings, producing, in 1978, total sales of around £240m. The group includes agricultural and housing enterprises, retail stores, schools, its own social security organisation, a technical college, a research and development unit, and banking and management services (the *Caja Laboral Popular*: CLP). The leading sector from the outset, however, has been its industrial enterprises, which account for more than 80 per cent (currently 64) of all the Mondragon undertakings and include Spain's leading producers of both domestic appliances and machine tools. This chapter outlines briefly the historical background, the institutional structures and comparative performance of these Basque enterprises.[2]

I BACKGROUND

Four main elements in the local background can plausibly be presented as having been positive for the subsequent development of the Mondragon enterprises: (i) a long industrial, particularly metal-working, tradition; (ii) a high level of local political awareness; (iii) an exceptional local church; and (iv) Basque

122

raditions of self-reliance, thrift and solidarity. In addition, two ossibly inhibiting factors were absent: (v) Trade Unions; and (vi) Velfare State arrangements.

Iron and coal have apparently been mined since antiquity at laces within reach of Mondragon. By the middle ages, the town as already a centre for iron and steel making, and its forges were roducing ships' anchors (see Garcia, 1970) and chains, as well as words, for markets throughout Spain. The bereted Basque easant of popular stereotype is misleading, because it neglects he long industrial, metal-working tradition of those remarkable eople. The leaders of the Mondragon enterprises have never een in any doubt about the importance of that tradition.

Metal working remained an important Mondragon activity hrough the 19th century. In the early 20th century came the stablishment of an enterprise which was for many years the most nportant employer in the town: the *Union Carrajera*, which was, o begin with, a manufacturer of locks, but which for the last 60 ears has produced steel and other metal products.

The *Union Carrajera* is also important in the political history of Mondragon. There was a long and bitter strike in 1916. ventually, after three months, the strikers caved in. There is urther evidence of the political awareness of the people of Mondragon in the early 1930s. Outside of the Asturias region, the own was the only one which sent an armed contingent to the help f the mineworkers when they raised a rebellion there in 1934. In Mondragon itself, a prominent conservative was shot dead uring the short-lived rebellion. The readiness of the Mondragon orking class to use its muscle in the way this record suggests elps to explain the strength of the town's opposition to Franco in he Spanish Civil War. Three Mondragon batallions were nustered in that struggle – one socialist, one nationalist and a hird made up of less directly affiliated 'volunteers'.

However, Basque nationalism was probably a more important actor than working class readiness to use its muscle in explaining he strength of Mondragon's opposition to Franco. A leading ole in the projection of that national identity was played then, as was before and has been since, by the Basque Catholic church. mong 14 Basque priests killed by Franco's forces during the ivil War was the Arch-Priest Josquin Avin of Mondragon, a nan deservedly famous locally for his piety (see Thomas, 1961).

Apart from the strength of its commitment to Basque

nationalism, the Catholic church is important in any account o
the background to the Mondragon enterprises because of it
alignment with the Church's progressive social teaching as
sociated most famously with Pope Leo XIII. That is a point whicl
will need coming back to in connection with the inspirer an
originator of the Mondragon enterprises, Fr. Jose Mari
Arizmendi.[3] But the points to stress here are: first the intensity o
nationalist feeling and pride (something which may correlate witl
the unique and uniquely obscure character of the Basqu
language); and second the elements in Basque social and cultura
traditions which favour the values of both sturdy self-reliance an
mutual small group solidarity. Social anthropologists stress th
mutual aid and labour exchange which traditionally goes o
between Basque mountain small-holders. They stress the tradi
tional habits of high personal saving. And they point to thos
small age-group social and drinking clubs (the *Chiquitoes*) whicl
seem to foster high-trust relationships between members, as wel
as being highly convivial.

It seems plausible to suppose that all these factors are o
importance in explaining the later success of the Mondrago
enterprises. So, I believe, was the absence of any independen
trade unions, outlawed by General Franco when he came t
power. Quite apart from the wariness (if not suspicion an
hostility) which most trade unions have shown towards productio
co-operatives for most of their history, an independent trade unio
movement in Mondragon would surely have absorbed th
energies of many of the most hard-working of the people, an
thus have diverted them from enterprise building. The absence o
trade unions allowed those dissatisfied with capitalist structure
to set about building enterprises of a different stamp. The absenc
of a welfare state can only have increased their belief in th
importance and good sense of that task.

That last point can be reinforced. Not only was there no welfar
state in the Mondragon which emerged at the end of the Civ
War. The town was crushed and demoralised, and the unwillin
host to what amounted to an army of occupation, Franco'
troops. That was the scene when Fr. Jose Maria Arizmend
arrived in Mondragon in February 1941, shortly before his 26t
birthday. He, like so many other Basques, had fought on th
losing side in the Civil War. After having been captured b
Franco's forces he is, indeed, said to have come within an ace o

execution. Later he had enrolled as a theological student in the nearby seminary at Vittoria. His bishop sent him to Mondragon with a special mission: to concern himself with the needs of the younger generation. Arizmendi interpreted this mission to mean that he should concentrate his energies in two directions: the promotion of technical education and the propagation of progressive Catholic teaching. After an abortive attempt to persuade the *Union Carrajera* to expand its small existing apprentice school, Arizmendi mobilised community support and built a new one instead. It opened with a first enrolment of 20 students in October 1944.

Fr. Arizmendi's technical school is the ancestor of the subsequent Mondragon enterprises, both directly and indirectly. The direct relationship is very clear. Five of its graduates who had gone on to study part time for engineering degrees at Zaragoza University, and who had then worked for a spell with (and attempted unsuccessfully to launch reforms within) the *Union Carrajera*, were to become the founders of the first and easily the largest of the Mondragon enterprises: ULGOR.[4] The indirect links are also of fundamental importance. Had there been no school, the five would not have qualified as engineers, and so would hardly have been in a position to work at high level in an engineering business. Had there been no teaching of progressive Catholic social thought in Arizmendi's school, they would hardly have attempted to reform the *Union Carrajera* or, having been rebuffed, decided to launch a reformed enterprise on their own.

The technical school and its highly unusual character are thus crucial on any account of the genesis of the Mondragon enterprises. So, I suspect, is the town community's involvement in its creation. In an astonishingly bold exercise, which involved placing urns at street corners and inviting the citizens to indicate what they could offer by way of work or money contributions, Arizmendi had mobilised mass voluntary support for the project: roughly a quarter of all households promised to contribute – a remarkable feat of voluntary social engineering. It was also, I suspect, the beginnings of a high trust relationship between Arizmendi and the Mondragon community, which was to be of inestimable value later on.

Two final points are worth making about the context and origin of these enterprises. Carr (1966) has shown that the European co-operative movement, with its roots in Rochdale and elsewhere, was never a substantial force anywhere in Spain. I suspect that there was almost total ignorance of it in Mondragon in the 1940s and 1950s. Paradoxically, that may have been advantageous in relation to subsequent developments: the European co-operative movement has often diverted people's attention away from the importance of industry and into the direction of shopping (and to some extent of farming). Uninfluenced by this tradition, the men of Mondragon were also free from various difficulties inherent in the co-operative principles and practice: the fixed-value share for example, and the practice of admitting outsiders to membership. A final point, also negative, is in some ways more surprising. Anarchist thinking, so strong in Catalonia and in southern Spain, seems never to have had much direct representation in Mondragon. On the other hand, it was clear from talking to him that Arizmendi's own position was always at the libertarian socialist end of the progressive thinking spectrum.

(a) STRUCTURE

ULGOR, when it first started, worked with an informally democratic constitution. Its basic present structures were adopted only in 1959. The same year saw the establishment of the CLP, the banking and management services enterprise which became the headquarters of the group of co-operatives a whole. ULGOR when adopting its basic constitution, chose registration under Spain's co-operative laws, as did the bank, and all the other Mondragon enterprises. The co-operative form was adopted on pragmatic rather than doctrinal lines. Of the various alternative possibilities, the co-operatives of Spanish law fitted least incongruously with the ideas which the men of Mondragon had evolved for themselves. It is now widely recognised that this Spanish law provides a framework for production (as opposed, perhaps, to consumer) co-operatives which is superior to any other in Europe.

A basic structural uniformity is imposed on the enterprises in the Mondragon group by the provisions of the Spanish law and more particularly by the 'contract of association' which all have entered into with the CLP.

For the base[5] co-operatives, the single most important an

overriding rule lays down, in effect, that there must be an identity or near identity between those who work in the enterprise and those who own and control it. Only a bare margin of tolerance is allowed for sudden and short-term upward shifts in the demand for labour. This sets Mondragon apart from the vast majority of old style production co-operatives elsewhere. It also ensures an optimum level of motivation among the work forces of the Mondragon enterprises, and the closest possible alignment between the individual interests of worker members and those of the enterprises themselves.

A second central idea is that the members' rights to participate in control, and nearly all of their rights to participate in 'profits', derive from their character as enterprise workers, rather than their character as enterprise owners. Whilst, with minor exceptions, all workers must be owners, that is treated as a separate, and in some sense secondary, requirement. For control, and only to a slightly lesser extent for profit sharing, it is work rather than ownership which confers the relevant entitlement. Here too the Mondragon enterprises part company with traditional co-operative practice, and approach in certain respects the Yugoslav enterprise model.[6]

The control structures of the Mondragon enterprises cannot be properly understood unless a clear distinction is drawn between policy making and ultimate control on the one hand, and executive management on the other. Ultimate control and policy making are vested in the sovereign Assembly of all members/workers of the enterprise. The Assembly elects a 'governing board' (*Junta Rectora*), to which it delegates authority over policy making and ultimate control. The Board in turn appoints a chief executive, and sometimes a larger executive management team. The executive management, though subordinate and responsible to the *Junta Rectora* (and through it to the General Assembly), is protected from excessive interference by a fairly clear separation of its functions. It is appointed by and is dismissable by the *Junta Rectora*. The only additional institution on the control side of the 'base co-operatives' structures is a species of elected works council, which tends to exist only in the larger of the 'base' co-operatives. They are important in communication, in welfare matters, and as elements in a complaints procedure. They thus perform some of the functions exercised by trade unions in conventional western businesses.

(b) FINANCE

The financial arrangements of the Mondragon enterprises are more complex, but can probably best be understood under three headings.

(i) Capital contributions

When a group of individuals launches a new Mondragon enterprise, or when an individual joins an existing one, they are required to contribute a significant capital sum. The current figures are rather less than £2000 per head for a group starting a new enterprise; rather less than £1000 when an existing co-operative is joined. Of these 'capital contributions' 20 per cent must be immediately and irreversibly transferred to the co-operative's collectively owned and indivisible reserve account. The balances are entered into personal accounts. These personal accounts are adjusted upwards and downwards after each financial year, in line with results; they are also adjusted for inflation. However, they may not be withdrawn unless the individual leaves the co-operative or retires.

(ii) Wages

The most important rules are that the maximum differential between the highest and lowest rates paid on a co-operative must not exceed 4.5–1, and the lowest rates must be fixed so that they are not lower (normally they are some percentage points higher) than corresponding rates for the same work in neighbouring non-co-operative undertakings. Taken together, these two rules mean that the highest paid people in the co-operative generally receive less than their counterparts outside, while the people on the lower rates receive more. It is stressed that there is nothing magic about the 4.5–1 ratio. It represents an ad hoc balance between the constraints of outside market rates and the need for internal enterprise solidarity and cohesion. Formally wages are as 'advances'.

(iii) Profits and losses

The treatment of these derives ultimately from Spain's co-operative law, which lays down certain minimum requirements to which the CLP, in its 'Contracts of Association', has added. Perhaps the most important requirement is that not less than 20 per cent of any profits must be credited to indivisible reserve funds. A further 10 per cent must normally be allocated for the promotion of social and educational projects in the neighbouring community. Once these allocations have been made, the balance is then credited to individual personal accounts, mainly in proportion to wage rates. There is a special provision for dealing with windfall or excessively high profits: a greater proportion must be allocated to indivisible reserves. As with profits, so with losses. Not more than 20 per cent may be debited against individual holdings. There is thus a realistic symmetry between profit and loss sharing.

A fixed interest rate, currently 6 per cent, is normally paid each year on the personal capital accounts. Provided that cash flow constraints permit, these interest payments, unlike the principal, may be drawn out in cash. There is also an indirect or loose link between the size of an individual's capital holding and the 'profit share' (positive or negative) which he or she receives each year. These shares are distributed in proportion to the sum of 'wages' and interest receivable. Thus a longer serving member in a successful co-operative will receive a slightly larger profit share than his counterpart on the same wage rate. In this way, long service is modestly encouraged and modestly rewarded. These provisions are also seen at Mondragon as a way of acknowledging that inescapable importance of capital (as well as of labour) in the production process.

One major effect of these financial arrangements is to secure a very high level of re-investment, so long, at any rate, as the financial results of the enterprises remain positive. For the position is that, aside from interest payments and the allocations to social and educational projects, the entire cash flow of the enterprise after 'advances' have been paid is re-invested. The policy is deliberate. It is linked to the one unequivocally ideological rule which the men of Mondragon have imposed on themselves: the so-called 'open door' rule, which commits the enterprises which are in association with the CLP to policies of continuous expansion and of job creation.

The other major effect of these arrangements is that they permit individual workers/members to build up substantial capital sums, so long as the results of their enterprise remain financially positive. Individual profit shares may represent on average the equivalent of, say, 15 per cent compared with annual advances. Thus, after 40 years of working in a successful co-operative, a man or woman might well have accumulated the equivalent of six or seven years of annual 'salary': or a sum in excess of £30 000 at 1978 prices. Recently, figures in the £20 000–£40 000 bracket have been quoted for the individual savings which may be accumulated in this way. It should be emphasised that the co-operative's pension schemes, whose funds are invested outside the co-operative grouping, are quite separate from these individual savings accounts. A member's pension entitlement has lately been fixed at 60 per cent of final salary.

The leaders of the group are fully aware that if and when retirement rates match those for recruitment, the present financial arrangements may require adjustment, if a substantial outflow of funds is to be avoided. It is said that various ways of dealing with that situation are being considered.

Whilst the substantial prospective savings accumulations which ordinary worker members in a Mondragon co-operative may anticipate are a significant factor, the workers themselves may put a higher value on their job security. The formal arrangements for ensuring continuous employment start from the rule that everyone must undertake to work flexibly and 'out of trade' if necessary. A further element of security is provided by the facility which the group enjoys for switching labour from one enterprise to another. If all else fails, those laid off are guaranteed 80 per cent of their normal earnings until such time as new work which the co-operatives are under an obligation to find, has been found. The costs of maintaining those who are laid off may be partly defrayed by using money which would otherwise have been allocated to social and educational projects in the community. Until now, these job security arrangements have been successful: one of the proudest boasts of the co-operative is that there has never been a forced redundancy, and with the exception of a brief venture into fishing, none of the enterprises has failed.

(c) 'SECOND DEGREE' CO-OPERATIVES

The CLP, the social insurance organisation (LAGUNARO), the research and development unit, the technical college and others are co-operatives of 'second degree': controlled partly by those who work in them, partly by the elected representatives of the 'base' co-operatives. Their sovereign assembly is composed partly of those who work in them and partly of elected representatives of the base enterprises. The means of appointing a *Junta Rectora* and executive management are the same as for 'base' co-operatives. On the financial side, the provisions covering capital contributions, interest, the fixing of 'advances', the treatment of 'profits' and so on, are formally identical to those of the base co-operatives. However, the actual 'profit' figures used to calculate 'profit' allocations are synthetic, being based on the *average* results of the base enterprises.

The CLP's role as supplier of specialised management and professional back-up, as well as its role as an investment and savings bank, needs special emphasis. These services are supplied by the CLP's 'empresarial division' and are clearly of crucial importance, both in ensuring the good health of existing enterprises and in promoting the creation of new ones. The emphasis on the need for good management, which the existence of the CLP's empresarial division implies, is in line with the separation of the management function from the control function in the 'base' co-operatives. It is clear from studies of traditional production co-operative elsewhere that one of their chief handicaps has been management weakness. The institutions chosen at Mondragon are in part the result of a concern to avoid that weakness.

Although this concern for good management is unambiguous, it is deliberately balanced by a concern to ensure that the democratic control structures are genuine. In practice, the relationship and the balance of power between the executive team and the governing board will vary from co-operative to co-operative, depending on personalities, the enterprise's age and so on. However, it is interesting that the staff of the empresarial division see one of their regular tasks as being to bolster up an enterprise's control board against its executive team. An insistence upon the importance of genuine bottom upwards initiative and power is also seen in the empresarial division's techniques of new enterprise formation. It is an established rule that the first approach must come from the prospective workers/members, and not from the CLP.

One final Mondragon institution deserves mention: the *Escuella Professional Politecnica*, today's off-spring of the little apprentice school started by Arizmendi and the Mondragon community in 1943. It has grown out of all recognition since those early days, and enrolled a student population of some 2000 in 1976. More exceptional than its growth is the range of courses which can be followed in the one institution: from courses at craft apprentice level to the highest level of engineering degree course. It is more unusual still in having successfully launched a productive enterprise (ALECOOP) in which its students may work part-time and be paid. ALECOOP would indeed merit a special study and paper on its own.

II PERFORMANCE

This section reviews some indicators of the size and performance of the Mondragon group of co-operatives. It is particularly helpful to distinguish between the success of the CLP considered narrowly as a banking institution, and the success of the Mondragon group as a whole with the CLP considered as its headquarters. For the CLP as a bank, relevant data is presented in Table 6.1. This rapid growth is also reflected in the increasing numbers of the CLP's branch offices. These reached a total of eighty-four in 1978, by which time there were branches in all four of the Basque-speaking provinces. Some indication of the qualitative success of the bank as a mobiliser of regional savings was

T ABLE 6.1   *Banking activities of Caja Laboral Popular*

Number of savings accounts		Savings total (Pstas m)	CLP's own capital (Pstas m)
1966	21653	659.7	60.5
1967	29 577	1 015.7	73.1
1968	43 979	1 449.9	151.3
1969	64 116	2 359.2	236.9
1970	87 807	3 204.2	311.9
1971	108 502	4 669.3	415.8
1972	126 929	6 355.6	572.2
1973	148 331	8 389.6	778.0
1974	169 000	11 351.2	1 069.3
1975	190 000	14 699.0	1 519.5
1978	283 114	32 232.9	3 377.2

Sources: Numbers of accounts 1966–73, Gorrono (1975).
All others: CLP Annual Reports.

given in a comparative study of several of Spain's regional savings banks, which appeared in the middle 1970s. This showed that the CLP was out-performing its main competitors in most of the measurable aspects of banking activity.

But the clearest indication that the bank is doing its job is based on a rather different point. Since the early 1970s the development and expansion of the Mondragon enterprises has not been constrained by any shortage of financial resources. The CLP's available investment funds have exceeded the needs of the co-operatives, and some have even been invested on the Madrid bourse. Historically, workers' co-operatives have been severely handicapped in terms of their access to capital compared with conventional capitalist enterprise. Now for the first time at Mondragon that position has been reversed. The success of the CLP as a bank has given its associated enterprises a clear advantage in the quality and professionalism of their management. Thus the existence and successful performance of the CLP appears to have solved two of the main problems which have frustrated co-operative development over the last 150 years: poor access to capital and bad management.

A comparison of the performance of the co-operatives with their capitalist counterparts in Spain is not possible because of the paucity (and to some extent, unreliability) of Spanish data. Nevertheless, such data as is available on the co-operatives themselves suggests an optimistic assessment of their performance. Table 6.2 illustrates the growth of value added per

TABLE 6.2   *Value added per head for main Mondragon subsectors (in Pstas 000s)*

	Enter-prises[a]	Employ-ment[a]	1971	1972	1973	1974	1975
Foundries & forges	6	1 809	318	376	454	646	658
Capital goods	14	2 684	243	344	436	549	592
Intermediate goods	5	1 237	226	299	355	420	434
Consumer durables	9	4 324	224	335	407	467	528
Building materials	23	3 483	290	336	448	470	585
Weighted average			247	334	412	496	543

Notes

[a] Numbers of enterprises and employment in mid-1970s.

Source: CLP.

worker from 1971–5 for each of the main subsectors used by CLP. It also indicates the number of enterprises and their employment at the end of this period.

Such crude figures on value-added obscure year-to-year fluctuations in the profitability of the enterprises. These fluctuations have been wide as is illustrated in Table 6.3, which shows profits as a percentage of internally-owned capital in the worst year (1971) and the best year (1973) for the early 1970s.

TABLE 6.3 *Profits as a percentage of internally owned capital by subsectors*

	1971	1973
Foundries & forges	13.4	29.5
Capital goods	5.4	28.6
Intermediate goods	15.4	25.4
Consumer durables	1.7	21.6
Building materials	13.0	29.5

Source: Gorrono (1975).

TABLE 6.4 *Significance of exports*

	Export sales (Pstas m)	Total sales (Pstas m)	Exports as percentage of total sales
1969	503	6 386	7.8
1970	753	7 102	10.6
1971	1 060	8 164	13.0
1972	1 343	10 377	12.9
1973	1 565	12 625	12.4
1974	2 435	16 068	15.2
1975	2 344	19 319	12.1
1978	5 744	43 346	13.3

Source: CLP.

A further measure of the group's success is the growth in its export sales. This has been partly in response to the reduction in protection of the Spanish economy in the 1960s. Such protection allowed home production to expand rapidly. By 1974 the percentage of sales going abroad had doubled on 1969, although there was a levelling off in 1975.

Taken together with the steady, twenty-five year expansion of the group's sales and employment figures, and with some specific successes in export markets – whole refrigerator plants sold to Mexico, Tunis, the USSR – this data entitles us to talk of a group of small and medium-sized enterprises which has been performing with at least average success. The figures for value-added per head indicate at least a respectable level of efficiency by international standards. It may be true that 'profits' or return on capital are rather lower than the other indicators would normally imply. But this criticism, supposing it to be justified, may be explained by the co-operative's concern for job security and other goals, as well as with the objective of maximising return on capital.

This concern with goals other than 'profit' maximisation may serve to point us towards what has probably been the area of the group's most dramatic and important comparative success: enterprise and job creation. Industrial employment on the part of the group increased by more than 13500 between 1961 and 1975 for an average of not much less than 1000 new jobs annually.

The same picture of dramatic and sustained job creation is implicit in the record of the growing number of industrial enterprises year by year, as illustrated in Table 6.5. This expansion in the numbers of Mondragon industrial enterprises includes only a handful of cases (five 'conversions', four splittings off from ULGOR) where genuine new job creation has not been involved. It should further be emphasised that it is the quality of the new jobs created, as much as their quantity, which deserves attention. With those points clarified, the achievement is scarcely less than stunning. Certainly, I know of no comparable achieve-

TABLE 6.5 *Enterprise and employment growth*

Year	Enterprises	Employment	Year	Enterprises	Employment
1961	12	395	1969	46	7 945
1962	18	520	1970	46	8 570
1963	29	1 780	1971	48	9 416
1964	32	2 620	1972	49	10 055
1965	36	3 395	1973	52	11 621
1966	40	4 209	1974	59	12 481
1967	43	5 082	1975	60	13 169
1968	44	5 981	1976	62	14 000
			1978	69	16 161

Source: CLP.

ment of successful enterprise and employment development generated and controlled by a small town, anywhere else in the post-war world. Given the importance of Mondragon's commitment to its 'non-economic' policy of the 'open door', it is perhap no accident that it is in the area of job creation that the group's achievement is most striking.

In terms of conventional measures of job satisfaction, we find that absentee rates are low. There has apparently been only one major dispute.[8] Not surprisingly, perhaps, it was in ULGOR with a work force of over 3500, easily the largest of the Mondragon enterprises. After unsuccessfully appealing to the General Assembly, the ringleaders were expelled from the co operative. However, it is perhaps not so much the absence of strikes as the absence of continuous hassle between shop floor and management, and the absence of systematic 'free riding' which is the most valuable result in Mondragon's experience of industria relations. The amount of management time which is thus released for more satisfying and productive work is said to be prodigious

The size of ULGOR is an acknowledged anomaly within the group. The accepted view at Mondragon is that their enterprise structures work best up to a size of about 500 people. On the other hand, with their characteristic pragmatism, neither the ULGOR management nor its governing board would recommend a major break-up of an enterprise which is continuing to show good results, and which contributes substantially to group exports. There is no evidence, so far as I know, to suggest that co-operatives of a good batallion's size (say 700), or really large co-operative (the size of ULGOR and above) are any less successful than their really large conventional counterparts.

The Mondragon policy is, nevertheless, first to avoid, if at all possible, any more really large enterprises of the ULGOR size, and second to encourage the independent 'base' enterprises to form appropriate subgroups between themselves. The aim is, of course, to achieve the best possible balance between the advantages of small and of large size. On such grouping or federation (ULARCO, in which ULGOR is linked with four other enterprises) was formed in the early 1970s. There is the prospect of more.

Having reviewed this evidence, we should acknowledge that factors other than the energy and intelligence of the group's leaders have made its achievements possible. Basque nationalism, the pride and loyalty of local people and their determination to build up a modern economy, have been immensely positive forces. The state of the Spanish economy and the high level of protection enjoyed in its markets during the 25 years since ULGOR's foundation, have been other helpful factors. So have the various tax advantages which the Spanish state accords to co-operative enterprise. Yet when all these factors have been taken into account, it remains reasonable to argue that the effort and intelligence of individuals have been the key forces at work; of individuals like Jose Maria Arizmendi, like Jose Maria Ormaechea and Alfonso Gorronogoita. The two last were among those who graduated at Zaragoza university and were two of ULGOR's five founders. Since 1959 they have been chief executive and chairman respectively of the CLP. One can only speculate about the number of Ormaecheas and Gorronogoitas there may be, elsewhere in Spain and elsewhere in other countries, whose talents are not being fully developed or used by enterprises.

III DISCUSSION

There is and has to be, I think, a daunting amount of detail in any account of the structures and institutions which have evolved at Mondragon. What is more, this detail cannot at all easily be subsumed under a single catch phrase or formula. We cannot talk about Mondragon as if its enterprises were examples of either 'private enterprise' or 'public enterprise'. In a formal sense, if we imply some reference to the so-called 'principles of co-operation', we cannot even refer to them as examples of 'co-operative enterprise'. The fact is that the institutional structures which have been evolved at Mondragon are too sophisticated to be captured by any single 'overview' catch phrase – whether labour-management or worker-ownership or whatever. The point is that in terms of pragmatic sophistication they make the conventional enterprise structural models, whether of classic capitalist shareholder command, or of classic Morrisonian state enterprise, look like artefacts of the Stone Age.

Nevertheless we can, I think, discern in and extract from the mass of detail the single fundamental idea of people who have been trying to strike an optimum set of balances between divergent interests and values. There are the interests of the shop floor and the management, and an attempt is made to strike the optimum balance between a genuine bottom upwards control and a genuinely efficient professional executive. There are the interests of the people inside the enterprise and the facts of the competitive market-place outside; an attempt is made via the policy of maximum income differentials to strike a balance between the two. There are the economies and the dis-economies of small scale and large scale. There are the interests of the neighbouring outside community to be considered, as well as the interests of the enterprise in its own success and survival. There i the need for job security on the part of those working in the enterprises and the countervailing need to adapt to the constantl changing demands of the market. There are the interests of those working in the group of enterprises at any one point to be se against the interests of those who might work in them in the future: the 'open door policy'. There are the interests of the 'outside' savers, who put their money on deposit with the CLP, a well as those of the enterprises' work force to be considered. There are the interests of the longer serving members of the work force to be set against those of the more recent recruits. Among the existing workers, their interests as toilers and their interests a 'owners' (i.e. the suppliers and creators of capital) have to be se against each other. Of course, there is nothing sacrosanct about the particular equilibrium which has been chosen as the point o balance between the different interest in any of these cases However, a real effort has been made to strike an intelligen balance.

One reasonable criticism which the men of Mondragon will accept is that their enterprises have concentrated for the most par up to now on achieving economic rather than, say, social o personal development goals. Their acceptance of this criticism i emphatically not an admission that the democratic enterpris structures they have evolved are a sham, which they are clearl not. But it is an acknowledgement that the actual work organis ation in those enterprises has tended to be conventional, ever Tayloristic in character. Since the middle 1970s the Empresaria Division of the CLP has launched a number of initiatives with the aim modifying the actual organisation of work in a mor participatory direction. After visits to Sweden, ULGOR invited volunteers in one of its domestic appliance factories to experimen with a system of group work to replace a section of a conventiona assembly line. After a good deal of persuasion, a muster of volunteers eventually came forward, but it would be a mistake to suggest that the experiment has been a tremendous success. The results have been at best mixed, and notably less good than those of a rather similar experiment to introduce more participatory work systems in the very different environment of the CLP's own branch offices. Critics, particularly perhaps Marxist critics, have lately tended to attach great importance to the relative failure of Mondragon enterprises to break away from conventional work organisation, and have even argued that, because of this, the whole Mondragon experience is some kind of fraud. This kind of criticism would be more convincing if the critics could point to any real successes in this direction elsewhere. To those who have visited Mondragon, the implicit charge of bad faith will seem simply preposterous.

At a more basic level of generality, the enterprise structures evolved at Mondragon can be seen, I think, as an attempt to reconcile the individualistic values of the right with the solidarity values of the left. They draw from the good sense enshrined in the idea of owner occupation. They also draw from the good sense enshrined in the tradition of the collectively-owned village green. Some will perversely seek to identify virtue as being exclusively located at one or the other end of this spectrum. Sometimes, contraversially, I find myself arguing that the Mondragon structures reflect 70 per cent individual self-interest and 30 per cent collective solidarity. I am not at all sure that these figures are an accurate reflection of the balance which has been struck. Perhaps the figures 50 : 50 would come close to the truth. What seems important, on the other hand, is the Mondragon insight that the best solution lies somewhere along the line of this spectrum, and not at either of the ends.

The final implications of the Mondragon phenomenon have to do with individuals and small groups, rather than with governments, local authorities, or big institutions – whether large companies, or large trade unions. What we need are groups of bold and imaginative individuals who are prepared to see whether something on Mondragon lines can be successfully created elsewhere: not, I hasten to add, in a spirit of reckless risk taking. The spirit should be based rather on cautious professional determination, plus a belief that with intelligence and effort it may well be possible to achieve something of the kind desired.

NOTES

1. This chapter is an edited version of 'The Mondragon enterprises – an exceptional balancing of interests and values', which was presented at the Walton Symposium, Glasgow, June 1979.
2. For a fuller discussion see Anglo–German Foundation (1977) and Chapter 10 of Oakeshott (1978).
3. His full name was Arizmendiarretta.
4. The name is derived from the names of its five founders: Usatorre, Larranaga, Gorronogoita, Ormaechea and Ortubay.
5. Co-operatives of working members as opposed to co-operatives of co-operative enterprises (see further below).
6. See Chapter 2.
7. The John Lewis Partnership, in the UK, in 1978 paid a bonus to the 'partners' of 18 per cent even though in that firm no more than 40 per cent of net profits is allocated to the bonus.
8. Aside from 'solidarity' strikes in support of Basque nationalist goals.

7 Ireland:
Industrial Co-operatives
Connell M. Fanning

1 BACKGROUND

In Ireland, enterprises are regarded as co-operatives if they are registered under the Industrial and Provident Societies Acts 1893–1978. To register, an organisation must satisfy the Registrar of Friendly Societies as to membership size, objectives of the society and acceptability of its rules. The acts, influenced as they are by the *laissez-faire* attitude of the legislature at that time, leave wide scope as to what may or may not be included in the constitution of 'rules' of the society. There are no compulsory clauses which must be inserted in the rules.

In practice, however, it appears as if two common features are present in the rules of most if not all of these bodies. These reflect the general principles of the co-operative movement. First, each shareholder is accorded one vote irrespective of the number of shares he owns in the co-operative. In this particulr sense, the organisation is democratically structured. Secondly return to capital is limited. The reason for this is that making of a profit for distribution to shareholders is not regarded as a prime objective of these organisations. Members benefit in proportion to the patronage or business they have with the enterprise. These two common elements in the structure point to why the co-operative is extensively used in the agricultural sector where members benefit by higher selling prices for products or lower buying price for materials.

The co-operative movement in Ireland as we know it today has its basis in agriculture and dairying activity.[1] Historically, it may be said to have commenced in 1889 when the first co-operative creamery was established in Drumcollogher, Co. Limerick. The growth of the movement may, in large part, be attributed to the enthusiasm and ability of Horace Curyon Plunkett, who was born in 1854 of aristocratic ascendency stock. Plunkett's main vision was to appreciate the importance and value of the principles of co-operation in the agricultural sector in general and the dairy industry in particular. By 1894, due largely to his enthusiasm there were more than 30 Irish co-operative creameries; he founded the Irish Agricultural Organisation Society (IAOS) as the spear head of the co-operative movement. This society promoted the formation of Co-operative Agricultural Societies similar to the French *Syndicates Agricoles* and the Italian *Consonzio Agrario*. In 1897 a new federation of agricultural and creamery societies the Irish Agricultural Wholesale Society, was set up to supply co-operatives with agricultural goods of guaranteed quality.

Another concurrent and vital step was the establishment of 'village banks' known as Agricultural Credit Societies, which were perhaps the first sources to give loans at reasonable rates to Irish agriculturalists. To quote Plunkett: 'they performed the apparent miracle of giving solvency to a community composed almost entirely of insolvent individuals'.[2]

By 1899 the first state institution – the Department of Agriculture and Technical Instruction – was set up to assume overall responsibility for the development of the agricultural industry This body set up its own participatory, elective structure whereby the ordinary farmer could, in theory, be elected to a Council, but the body was not, in the long term, successful, and waged a bitter war with the IAOS, which, however, thrived until the economic slump of the 1920s.

The 'economic war' of the 1930s ensured that the co-operative movement did not flourish again until at least the mid-forties, and since that date the sector has grown in a manner unparalleled in the agricultural and industrial sector. Interestingly, the IAOS is currently seeking to extend the co-operative idea, and to some degree preserve the ideals of Horace Plunkett in a contemporary agri-business setting. Before turning to an analysis of industrial worker co-operatives, the contemporary situations in the three other areas of the co-operative sector that are significant are briefly reviewed.

a) AGRICULTURAL CO-OPERATIVES

Co-operatives are enormously successful in Ireland, according to
the definition of a co-operative given above. This is due entirely to
the agricultural marketing and processing co-operatives which
have been the major force in Irish agricultural development. Of
the 20 largest companies, ranked by sales, approximately 50 per
cent are currently agricultural co-operatives. In terms of capital
employed, they are also substantial, and several have more than
2000 employees. Membership is over 200 000 (although some
persons are members of more than one co-operative) and 9 out of
10 farmers are members. Their range is from giant marketing
agencies such as An Bord Bainne (The Milk Board) and the whole
range of agricultural activities down to the small fishing,
horticultural, and home produce and handcraft co-operatives.

These agricultural co-operatives are established by farmer-
members needing goods or services to provide various purchasing
and supplying services to members. They are controlled by
member-patrons on the basis of one vote per member. Profits are
distributed amongst members on the basis of the standard co-
operative principles of limited interest on shares or refunds
proportionate to patronage. *Co-operation* and democratic control is then implemented in a very constrained manner in such
enterprises. An employee in an agricultural co-operative is not in
any different a position from an employee in a joint-stock
company. Agricultural co-operatives, from the point of view of
worker participation, are not *co-operatives*.

b) COMMUNITY DEVELOPMENT CO-OPERATIVES

There are about 44 small multi-purpose co-operatives concerned
with social and infrastructural development in the underdeve-
oped peripheral areas of Ireland and the UK. They are mainly
situated in the Celtic fringe of Ireland, Scotland and Wales; 41 are
in Ireland.[3] In Ireland they are mainly located in the gaelic
speaking (Gaeltacht) regions. A total area of about 1m acres with
a population of 70 000 in 1971 is involved. Emigration has hit
these areas relatively worse than the country as a whole.
Population has declined 50 per cent since 1911; the countrywide
decline was 10 per cent. The characteristics of the Gaeltacht areas
are those of underdeveloped regions:

land is very poor, with about 70 per cent of farms less than 40
acres; the number of viable or potentially viable farms is in the
region of 15–20 per cent:[4]
64 per cent of farmers are over 50 years of age;
50 per cent of farmers have no clear heir;
the dependency ratio is 85 per 100 persons.

By any numerical measure of activity they are currently
insignificant. However, their emergence in the middle 1960s, long
after the establishment of the co-operative movement in Ireland,
and their development since then is significant:[5]

> It should be remembered that measures like turnover or value-
> added do not give a good indication of the welfare value of
> services . . . being provided by the various Gaeltacht co-
> operatives. These services are highly varied due to the specific
> needs of individual Gàeltachts but generally they have tended
> to concentrate on local development and social type services
> rather than on the purchase and processing of farm output, as is
> the case in the rest of the country.

The wide variety of activities conducted by those co-operatives, it
has been suggested, are in the nature of local government services
in the peripheral areas of Ireland, which has a highly centralised
administration.[6] Furthermore, in order to have community
support, the founders have to satisfy multiple objectives.[7] The
founder of one such co-operative, Glencolumbkille, referring to
its objectives as community self-help stated that its founding and
operation '. . . illustrated the axiom that the more remote a
community, the more important that it embark on a programme
of self-dependence and self-help . . . peripheral areas with fewer
people get less state attention and support than the more central
and populous areas'.[8] Because of this and the lack of resources
including leadership, the emergence of such co-operatives is 'seen
as a result of the inability of other rural organisations to
develop'.[9] Furthermore, the organisational and entrepreneurial
activity that is taking root is collective because in general the co-
operatives 'have not concentrated on traditional entrepreneurial
activities but in the provision of collective goods and services'.[10]
In the context of the co-operative sector, the community develop

ment co-operatives are of particular interest and the history of three of these is outlined.

One of the longest surviving and best known of the community development co-operatives is Glencolumbkille in the south-west of County Donegal. This is an area ravaged, even more than most in Ireland, by emigration which removed the most enterprising individuals and left a poor base of capital and manpower resources. Glencolumbkille, made up of a number of co-operative enterprises, was started in the early 1960s by Fr. James McDyer who believed that progress would be achieved only by the local people themselves using the co-operative form of organisation. It is an example of the key leadership role played by a small number of clergymen in underdeveloped regions. The example was little followed or supported by fellow clergymen. Furthermore, after the initial efforts, it fell to a small group to pursue their objectives of community development.[11]

The achievements of Glencolumbkille have been quite substantial in this extremely hostile region and illustrate the diverse role such co-operatives play in:

(i) *business development* – agriculture, small industry (including fish processing, textiles), home crafts (including a shop in Dublin), and tourist facilities (a folk village, hotels);
(ii) *social services* – rural electrification, road improvement, piped water;
(iii) *social–cultural* – community hall and park;
(iv) *social welfare* – services for elderly and lonely persons.

The sources of finance for development projects are bank loans, primarily, state grants, share capital and profit (£70 000 income in 1977). The most successful venture of Glencolumbkille is the tourist development. This has made use of their major rural resource, land, which, although extremely poor for agricultural purposes, is, in the words of McDyer:[12]

. . . endowed with a plenitude of beautiful mountains, beaches, lakes and rivers, and ancient prehistoric monuments. It seemed fitting that we ourselves should exploit these natural advantages . . . Thus it has happened that all the major development in our greatest natural resources has been promoted and is owned by a local co-operative.

In the last decade or so, a revival has occurred in community development co-operatives with the founding of new co-operatives, e.g. Comharchumann na h-Oilean (Co-operative of the Islands), Comharchumann Forbartha Chorca Dhuibne (West Kerry Development Co-operative), and Comharchumann Chois Fharraige (Co-operative by the Sea) among a number of others. The latter two in particular have been quite successful. The Chorca Dhuibne Co-operative was founded in 1967 in difficult circumstances:[13]

> Co-operatives had a history of failure in the area, there was a great deal of resistance and cynicism. This was to be a community co-operative . . . in other words concerned not only with economic objectives but also with social and cultural aims.

Because it was in a Gaeltacht area, a five-year management grant was received from the state. In the first two years, two community halls for social and cultural activities were constructed. However, no business activity had been established. In 1969, the co-operative took over running the Gaelic language summer schools. This provided a cash flow and income to participating households, which increased from 200 to 2200 from 1969 to 1978. It was discovered that the sub-soil was highly productive and, if it could be deep ploughed and mixed with the topsoil, land would be highly productive. Over 6000 acres have been reclaimed and holdings have increased by 16 acres, on average, for one-third of the farmers. Incomes have increased by 82 per cent and this has lead to improvements in farming techniques, housing etc. This development was a major turning point, with the result that there is now a two-acre glass house, 56 acres of vegetables, a demonstration farm, and a publishing company (including a community newspaper). Co-operative employment in 1978 was 32 full-time persons with a turnover of £400 000. Income in the area has increased by £2 million per year.

The second co-operative of interest, Chois Fharraige, was founded on a more social basis in 1972 by Gaeltarra Eireann. It now includes printing and publishing (including a community newspaper in Gaelic), a retail stationery shop, boat construction, turf cutting, water and building schemes and Gaelic language summer schools. Employment in 1976 was 42 full-time persons (with 200 part-time during summer) and income was £260 000, of which £40 000 was a state grant. 400 shareholders have subscribed £12 500 in capital.

Although, as stated, the extent of this sector is still small, the establishment of such organisations in such unfavourable regimes is significant and has the potential for a major impact on economic development in Ireland:[14,15]

> In avoiding the numerous pitfalls of the highly-developed society, one of the most hopeful and healthy movements which has gained momentum in Ireland has been the co-operative movement, for through this medium the people of a community largely dictate the extent of their development and preserve the quantity of their environment without having progress dictated to them from without.

(c) INDUSTRIAL COMMON OWNERSHIP

One of the best popularised experiments purporting to introduce the ideals of the industrial common ownership movement in Ireland is that carried on by the Bewley enterprise.

This business commenced before the year 1842 as a small family-run tea and sugar business which has expanded to own five large cafés; and is now a valuable business. It was incorporated as a private limited company in April 1926. In 1972 it had an authorised share capital of £40 000. In December 1972, possibly as a result of the debate about worker participation, a scheme of reorganisation was introduced by the owners.[16] The company, Bewley's Oriental Cafés Limited ('the café') reorganised its share capital. It ended up with nine trustee shares, 100 ordinary shares, and 39 891 12 per cent non-cumulative preference shares. Each share has a nominal value of £1. Only the ordinary shares carry with them the right to attend, speak, and vote at meetings, and receive dividends. The trustee shares empower the holders to vote but carry no rights to capital distribution. The preference shares carry no right to attend or vote at members' meetings.

The Articles of Association are highly unusual, in many respects. They provide that 'the trustees' shall hold 'trustee shares'. A maximum of three trustees are appointed by the directors of the café, a maximum of three jointly appointed by a company called The Bewley Community Limited (the Community), and the directors of the café; and a third by the Committee of Management of the Community (mentioned later). The chairman of the Community is chairman of the board of the café and has a casting vote at directors' and general meetings. The power and influence of the ordinary shareholders is clear. The directors of the company, who are appointed by the ordinary members in the usual way, cannot exercise some of their normal duties save with the consent of the Trustees, e.g. no alteration of the articles can be effected if the Trustees veto it. There are provisions for declaring a maximum bonus to employees of 20 per cent at the AGM.

In such a structure, it is somewhat surprising that there are no worker directors, nor is there formal provision for employee participation in management nor is there any provision for the employees (as employees) to be entitled to membership of the company.

The non-voting preference shares are held by Community. Community is a private company limited by guarantee, which is prevented by law from paying any dividend to its members. Its objects are broadly charitable. Community is run by a Committee of Management. Membership of the Community is limited to 50. The directors of the café are members of the Community. The trustee shareholders are members and have loaded voting rights in certain circumstances, e.g. a proposal to change the Articles of Association of the café. Employees of the Café with over three years service are eligible for membership of the Community. There are no worker-directors of the Café. The participatory structures are informal and the workers employed by the cafe have no direct rights in the running of the company.

(d) INDUSTRIAL WORKERS' CO-OPERATIVES

The fourth and final aspect of the co-operative sector that is currently of interest is that of the Industrial Worker Co-operatives. Like the Community Development Co-operatives, this sector is currently insignificant in terms of its size but, because of the importance of industry, is potentially significant. The remaining sections concentrate on the present state of these co-operatives.

II THREE CASES: ESTABLISHMENT AND STRUCTURE

This section deals with the three extant production enterprises which can be regarded in any way as *worker co-operatives* and is an outline of their origin and legal–organisational structures.[17] The following section is an analysis of their performance using available data.[18]

(a) THREE CASES

The best known industrial workers' co-operative is that of Crannac Co-operative Society Ltd in Navan. This was founded in August 1972 after a period of ownership changes and a fourteen-week sit-in following a proposal of liquidation of the Navan Furniture Company, a private company. It is thought that the proposal to liquidate did not come about as a consequence of insolvency. The 32 existing workers, faced with the prospect of unemployment for the second time in two years, pooled their £5600 redundancy payments and raised a further £25 000 from the local community with the help of local members of parliament and clergy. Foir Teoranta (the state enterprise rescue agency) lent £50 000 on a ten year loan at a fixed interest rate of $10\frac{3}{4}$ per cent per annum.[19] The firm, in its early stages, relied on contract furniture sales to institutions but following a difficult market, during the 1974 recession, it switched to quality domestic furniture through its own retail outlets.

Irish Spring Units Co-operative Society Ltd, Dundalk, manufactures bed-springs and was founded in 1973, again after a sit-in following the closure of its predecessor limited company. The sit-in in this case lasted nine months at the end of which only four of the original twenty-five workers remained. Temporary funding was raised through local community efforts; but only when £10 000 was raised by capital shares did Foir Teoranta give a loan of £18 500. Since Irish Spring rents its premises it had no collateral. Only the four workers who survived the changeover from company to co-operative purchased shares, and this is still the position.

The third co-operative of interest here is Castle Shoes Co-operative Society Ltd, Dundalk. It is the oldest of the three cases and was founded in 1971 when a receiver was put in over Laurel Shoes Ltd (a private limited company founded in 1966).[20] As in the other cases, initial funds to purchase the assets were raised by worker-contributions and from the local community, including a substantial loan from the Catholic Parish. As well as availing of the usual overdraft facilities, this co-operative also has a £13 000 fixed interest loan from Foir Teoranta.

It is interesting to note that in the cases of Castle Shoes and Irish Spring, a local priest played a central role in their establishment. Indeed, the foundation of the three co-operatives:

  (i) followed the failure of private enterprises;
 (ii) depended on a few highly-motivated individuals;
(iii) involved financing by individuals (including workers) un-related to a return on capital,[21] as well as state loans.

(b) ORGANISATIONAL FRAMEWORK

The Industrial and Provident Societies Act 1893–1978 provide for the registration of co-operatives by the Registrar of Friendly Societies. The acts do not set up a specific managerial–organis-ational structure but instead merely specify that a society must be registered with rules; and the rules are to contain provision for terms of admission of the members, method of holding meetings, scale and right of voting and method of making, altering or rescinding rules.[22] It is therefore to the rules to which one must look to discover the formal managerial–organisational structure of co-operatives.

The formal structure is akin to that of a private limited company in many ways. At the bottom are the members. The members (who must not be less than seven in number) are the original subscribers to the rules (called special members) together with all others who have been admitted to membership by the Committee of Management. Membership of the co-operative, according to the basic model rules issued by the Co-operative Development Society Ltd, depends on ownership of a trans-ferable but not withdrawable share. The main rights of member-ship are: a right to attend at the Annual General Meeting and the right consequently to adopt standing orders and minutes, discuss and vote on the Annual Statement and Affairs, adopt accounts, appoint auditor, elect to Committee of Management, authorise loans, declare a dividend to members and employees. Secondly and by virtue of the Acts, a member may inspect his own accounts in the society's books or with nine other members requisition an inspection of the affairs of the society, and requisition a special general meeting if the Committee fail to convene one.

A 'Committee of Management' is the next tier in the hierarchical structure. This committee's functions are to control all business carried on by or on account of the society, to hire and fire within limits, and to fix dividend ceilings. Members of the Committee consist of the special members until the first AGM, and then the AGM elects the Committee. There are provisions for annual retirement and for elections. In Irish Spring, the Committee have special specific powers to enter into agreement with trade unions. Although the Committee must be composed of co-operative members, Crannac is exceptional in that it requires that the majority of the Committee members must be co-operative employees.

The effective management of the enterprise lies in the hands of the manager and secretary who is appointed by the Committee of Management but who may be removed only on a vote by a two-thirds majority of the Committee members present and voting.

Thus, the effective structure here is basically a simple three tier chain. The manager and secretary are the executives who are responsible to the Committee of Management, who in the end answer to the shareholders. The structure has unsatisfactory resemblances to that of a private limited company; and it is clear that the concepts of participation and consultation are not endemic to the structure. In the three cases under consideration, the available data does not indicate workers who are shareholders but only that the number of shareholders does not coincide with the number of employees. In terms of their formal structure, the co-operatives are neither worker-owned nor worker-controlled.

III PERFORMANCE

The readily available data permits only limited analysis of these three cases. In this section three aspects are considered: financial soundness of individual co-operatives, comparative performance, and employment trends.

(a) FINANCIAL SOUNDNESS

The trend in a number of series and ratios, given in Table 7.1, 7.2 and 7.3 are used to examine the financial position of these co-operatives over the short period for which data is available. The most important trend is that of the net operating margin (sales revenue less materials, production and management expenses and bank interest) which is the financial result of production activity. From the point of view of a pure labour co-operative, which does not own assets, this is a crucial indicator of viability as a labour co-operative enterprise.

For Crannac, after the initial period of losses, there is a steady improvement in its position. However it must be remembered that Crannac received a £50 000 loan from Foir Teoranta in 1973. This represented 98 per cent of total cash outflow in that year. This loan was for 10 years at an interest rate of $10\frac{3}{4}$ per cent per annum. Only interest was paid on this loan until 1976–7, when £5000 was repaid on the principal amount. Until this loan, which was for the purchase of the factory, is repaid or extended (from a labour co-operative viewpoint, preferably converted to an ongoing long-term loan), the financial position of Crannac, while optimistic, is constrained. Furthermore, a condition of the loan prevents the firm paying a dividend or share on capital without the permission of Foir Teoranta.

The liquidity and leverage ratios are static indications of performance and it is necessary to examine the trends over a number of years. They are constructed on the basis of standard accounting procedures and are prepared from the point of view of shareholders and creditors who are interested in future profitability. They may not be what is required to assess the financial soundness of self-managed worker co-operatives. But, because of their current structure and the environment in which they operate, these are the standards by which performance will be judged.

The first liquidity ratio given is that for current assets to current liabilities. This is probably the most widely used ratio and is a measure of the short-term solvency of the firm. The textbook rule of thumb is that the optimal ratio is about 2:1. Therefore, in the event of liquidation, creditors would still be paid even if there were a shrinkage of 50 per cent of the value of current book assets. From a lender's point of view, a large ratio is desirable. On the

TABLE 7.1 *Crannac – net operating margins and financial ratios*

| Year | Net operating margin[a] (£) | Net operating marginal/total cash outflows (%) | Liquidity ratios | | Leverage ratio |
			Current ratio[b]	Acid test[c]	Debt ratio[d] (%)
1972	−21 158	38	3.67	1.50	41
1973	−21 329	42	2.20	0.69	41
1974	− 687	19	2.29	0.82	35
1975	+ 4 025	102	1.47	0.74	34
1976	+ 5 118	77	1.60	0.65	35
1977	+10 328	100.3	1.74	0.71	29

Notes

[a] The net operating margin is sales revenue less material costs, management and other production expenses (including wages) and bank interest. If negative, net operating margin is classified as a cash outflow, if positive as a cash inflow.
[b] Current ratio = Current assets/Current liabilities.
[c] Acid test = Current assets minus stocks/Current liabilities.
[c] Debt ratio = Total loans (including bank overdraft)/Total assets.

Source: Annual Returns to Registry of Friendly Societies.

other hand, a high ratio might suggest managerial slack i
running the enterprise. Therefore, an even balance is generall
sought. For Crannac the ratio, while varying, has declined from
high 3.7 to a more balanced 1.6–1.7.

The second liquidity ratio shown is that for current assets les
stocks to current liabilities. This removes inventories, which ar
least liquid and on which most losses occur in liquidation, fror
the previous ratio. The Crannac ratio of about 0.7, taken togethe
with large stocks, suggests a reasonably sound position from
creditor's point of view.

Finally, the ratio of total loans (including bank overdrafts) t
total assets is given as a measure of leverage in financing the firn
Although this ratio, because of the composition of assets, i
probably the least useful for assessing a self-managed firm, it i
still relevant because of the structure and environment of th
enterprise. The debt ratio for Crannac has declined steadily t
about 30 per cent in 1977. From a creditor's viewpoint this is quit
satisfactory: firstly, in the event of liquidation, repayment i
virtually assured since they are first in order of repaymen
secondly, it indicates that the membership of the co-operativ
have a large commitment to the firm. From the data in Table 7.
and the debt ratio trend, it can be seen that assets are being funde
by retained earnings rather than equity.

The position of Irish Spring, in Table 7.2, shows generally
positive surplus from production activity. The only year with
negative net operating margin was in 1976, when it was 18 per cer
of total cash outflows. In that year there was also an investment c
£18 134, representing 57 per cent of cash outflows, in fixed asset
As noted already, however, a loan of £18 500 was received fror
Foir Teoranta, as well as a grant of £4500 from the Industri
Development Authority (IDA).[23] To a somewhat lesser exter
than Crannac, share contribution for Irish Spring has bee
concentrated in the early years.

Both the current and acid test ratios are on the low side, wit
inventories accounting for about 50 per cent of the current asset
In this situation, even if the more liquid assets maintain the
value, a 20 per cent shrinkage in inventory value is all that coul
be sustained if creditors are to be paid. The debt ratio shows tha
less than one-third of assets are financed by loans. In the earli
years, share contributions were the main source, but in the lat
years, retained earnings were utilised.

TABLE 7.2 *Irish Spring – net operating margins and financial ratios*[a]

Year[b]	Net operating margin (£)	Net operating margin/total cash outflows (%)	Liquidity ratios		Leverage ratio
			Current ratio	Acid test	Debt ratio (%)
1974	+4110	n.a.	0.67	0.27	0
1975	+8	3	0.80	0.34	0
1975	+8989	54	1.25	0.96	32
1976	−5662	18	1.34	0.61	34
1977	+23421	100	1.21	0.63	26

Notes

[a] The net operating margin is sales revenue less material costs, management and other production expenses (including wages) and bank interest. If negative, net operating margin is classified as a cash outflow, if positive as a cash inflow.
[b] Two returns filed for 1975.

Source: Annual Returns to Registry of Friendly Societies.

For Castle Shoes, Table 7.3, the picture that emerges is less positive than for Crannac or Irish Spring. Only in 1977 was the net operating margin positive. In that year the factory was closed during which time the stock was sold off. Otherwise, Castle constantly makes a loss. The money to keep it going comes from community share contributions and bank and other loans. In 1976 and 1977, the co-operative repaid small amounts on these loans. Little investment has been made during this period. It should also be noted that Irish Spring made an investment of £4630 in Castle Shoes in 1975.

Turning to the financial ratios, it can be seen that both the liquidity ratios are rather low. Since inventories lose value on liquidation, it is unlikely that Castle could pay their current liabilities. The effect of the shut-down during 1977 can be seen from the decline in the current ratio since 1976. The debt ratio shows a continuous increase, showing that current production activity appears, in the absence of an alternative, to be maintained by loans rather than revenue.

(b) COMPARATIVE PERFORMANCE

The performance of each of the three cases is assessed relative to that of their respective industry averages using production data. The appropriate financial data is not available on an industry basis or by firm/establishment for comparative analysis. The data is summarised in Table 7.4.

The performance of Crannac is shown against that of the average for the furniture etc. industry, which average is taken as a basis for comparison, for the years for which common data is available. Over this short period it can be seen that Crannac improved steadily, from its poor position in the initial year to better than the industry average two years later. This is further emphasised by the comparison of sales per employee. This improvement was due to the combined result of (i) an expansion of sales (83 per cent substantially greater than the industry average, 22 per cent) and (ii) a somewhat larger cutback in the numbers employed (−4 per cent) than the average for the industry (−1 per cent) from 1973 to 1974.

The comparative performance of Irish Spring is below average for the entire furniture industry for 1973 and 1974.[24] This can be seen, in particular, from the net output per employee and earnings

TABLE 7.3 *Castle Shoes – net operating margins and financial ratios*[a]

Year[b]	Net operating margin (£)	Net operating margin/total cash outflows (%)	Liquidity ratios		Leverage ratio
			Current ratio	Acid test	Debt ratio (%)
1972	−11 941	56	0.96	0.57	0
1972	−7 749	90	n.a.	n.a.	39
1974	−11 618	71	1.77	0.85	63
1974	−15 484	95	1.49	0.89	62
1975	−17 005	99	1.91	1.18	103
1976	−27 975	59	1.69	0.83	119
1977	+4 214	29	1.10	0.60	149

Notes

[a] The net operating margin is sales revenue less material costs, management and other production expenses (including wages) and bank interest. If negative, net operating margin is classified as a cash outflow, if positive, as a cash inflow.
[b] Two returns filed for 1972 and 1974.

Source: Annual Returns to Registry of Friendly Societies.

TABLE 7.4 *Comparison of co-operatives with industry averages for common years in current prices (industry averages in parenthesis)*

Year	Materials as % of gross output[a]	Earnings as % of net output[b]	Net output per person engaged	Remainder of net output per £ employee compensation[c]	Sales per employee[d] £
Crannac					
1972	76.4(54.6)	168.2(58.5)	307.8(1902.7)	−0.41(0.71)	–
1973	52.4(52.4)	110.9(65.0)	1 458.4(1934.2)	−0.10(0.54)	3 065(4068)
1974	49.0(54.5)	63.0(65.7)	2 993.9(2280.7)	0.59(0.52)	5 867(5010)
Irish Spring					
1973[e]	66.9(52.5)	75.4(65.0)	729.3(1934.2)	0.33(0.54)	2 202(4068)
1974[f]	74.9(54.5)	94.8(65.7)	754.7(2280.7)	0.05(0.52)	3 000(5010)
Castle Shoes					
1972	121.4(49.2)	253.8(60.0)	−331.6(1269)	−1.39(0.65)	–
1972	48.5(50.7)	78.9(61.6)	1 092(1424)	0.26(0.62)	2 583(4132)[g]
1974	41.4(47.5)	74.1(55.1)	1 512.6(2167.5)	0.34(0.81)	–
1974	59.2(51.4)	128.3(58.3)	842.6(2343.5)	−0.22(0.71)	2 068(4828)

Notes

[a] Gross output is the current value of sales.
[b] Net output is gross output less materials costs.
[c] Remainder of net output is net output less employee compensation.
[d] The average number of workers in the industry during the year is used as the number of person employed in that year.
[e] Firm data from Annual Return of 31 March 1974.
[f] Firm data from Annual Return of 31 January 1975.
[g] Industry data for 1973; firm data from Annual Return of 31 January 1974.

Source: Co-operative data is from Annual Returns to the Registry of Friendly Societies. Average industry data is derived from the Census of Industrial Production, *Irish Statistical Bulletin*, various years.

as a per cent of net output figures. As regards the latter figure it should be borne in mind that, like the other co-operatives, Irish Spring pays Union wage rates. This relatively poor productivity performance is further shown by the data for sales per employee. The percentage increase in sales (58 per cent) and change in numbers employed (16 per cent) were greater than the industry average (22 per cent and −1 per cent, respectively) over 1973 to 1974.

The dismal picture painted of Castle in the preceding tables is further darkened by the performance of Castle *vis-à-vis* the

ndustry average. The reject rate for output dropped from 12 to
).5 per cent in a short period after conversion to a co-operative.
Although the percentage of materials in gross output compares
well to the industry-wide figure, the data for earnings as a
percentage of net output and net output per employee further
indicates that the situation was not healthy. Complementary
evidence of this trend in performance is provided by the data for
sales per employee. During 1973–4, the percentage decline in
both sales (− 31 per cent) and employment (− 13 per cent)
exceeded the change in the industry average (11 per cent and − 5
per cent, respectively). Total employment declined in the
ndustry, which has been facing increasing foreign competition.

c) EMPLOYMENT

The preservation of employment and its expansion are often cited
as reasons for encouraging workers' co-operatives. Data on
employment in each of the three cases are given in Table 7.5. Total
employment in Crannac has not increased from 1972 to 1977,
although it has varied a little up and down. On at least one
occasion the firm's public auditor recommended cutbacks in
employment in order to overcome short-term difficulties. While
employment expanded in Irish Spring, the turnover has been
relatively high, with about 30 workers leaving in a four year
period. Overall employment declined in Castle Shoes.

TABLE 7.5   *Number of employees in Crannac, Irish Spring and Castle Shoes*

Year	Crannac	Irish Spring	Castle Shoes
1972	41	–	36 (34)
1973	46	–	38[b]
1974	44	25	33
1975	40	29 (20)[a]	31
1976	38	25	25
1977	41	32	29

Notes:

[a] Two returns made during 1975.
[b] Data from Annual Return of 31 January 1974.

Source: Annual Returns to Registry of Friendly Societies.

IV CONCLUSION

We saw in the introduction to this paper that the co-operative movement in Ireland emerged from the late 19th century depression of the agricultural sector. The co-operative movement made a major contribution to agricultural development. As we saw, agricultural co-operatives are of enormous economic significance today. However, although drawing from the co-operative spirit, one element is missing. There is a general absence of the involvement of workers in management and profit-sharing in the enterprises to which they are vital. These enterprises are closer to managerial corporations than participatory enterprises. However, the revival taking place in the co-operative movement may result in shifts towards the latter types.

The post-famine agricultural decline inspired the growth of agricultural co-operation. In a similar manner, it may be that the lagging behind in certain regions of Ireland may stimulate the expansion of the nascent community development co-operatives. Again, although employee participation is not central to this type of co-operation, it provides a framework for a community's involvement in its own socio-economic development.

The third group of production-orientated co-operatives, Industrial Workers' Co-operatives, is also weak but again may benefit from the renewed interest in co-operatives and worker participation.

The overall position of the three Industrial Workers' co-operatives analysed here, based on their production activities, is summarised by the net operating margins in Tables 7.1–7.3. A pure labour co-operative does not have fixed assets on its balance sheet with which to secure short-term financing. Liquidity in the sense of a positive net operating margin (which in a labour co-operative does not include wages as a cost of management and production) is essential for the survival of a labour co-operative based on production activity. In the event of difficulties, either labour income bears the brunt, or the enterprise risks the recall of credit. Unlike the pure model, the enterprises considered here own assets and pay union wages. In difficult trading situations, the wage bill does not adjust, unless employment is reduced; but short-term financing may be secured on fixed assets.

From this point of view, the financial viability of Crannac and Irish Spring appears sound.[25] Castle Shoes, on the other hand,

:learly has serious liquidity difficulties. In such a case, the :ontinuing operation of a firm in this position depends on the willingness of institutional and individual lenders to provide oans or subsidies. If Castle Shoes were a pure labour co-operative, it could not overcome continued liquidity difficulties oy borrowing which would inevitably be unsecured.

The limited available information, data and analysis do not oermit strong conclusions to be made about the co-operative sector in Ireland at present. There is clearly a need for further analysis, particularly of the industrial workers' co-operatives.[26] In particular, given the limited sample available, there is a need to search historical records for cases to extend the sample in order to orovide a base for answering fundamental questions:

> when, why and how were they founded?
> why was a particular structural organisation chosen?
> why, above all, when we consider the growth of the agricultural co-operatives, were industrial worker co-operatives seemingly rare and unsuccessful in Ireland?[27]

NOTES

This paper has benefitted from the assistance of David Tomkin and Thomas McCarthy. Financial support was received from the Management Fund, Faculty of Commerce, University College, Cork. The usual disclaimer applies. It is an edited version of a paper prepared for the Walton Symposium, Glasgow, June 1979.

1. One of the very few, and the only substantial study of the co-operative sector in Ireland is Patrick Bolger (1977), *The Irish Co-operative Movement: Its History and Development*. Institute of Public Administration, Dublin. The approach of the study is narrative, and contains a wealth of information, rather than analytical. To date there have been no analytical studies of the co-operative sector.
2. Cited by Bolger (1977, p. 182).
3. O'Brien (1979, p. 2).
4. 'The (EEC) Farm Modernization Scheme classification paints an even duller picture with almost 100 per cent of Gaeltacht farms being classified as transitional, which would indicate that according to European standards a complete farm restructuring is necessary in those areas.' In *Framework for Co-operative Development: 63*, Irish Agricultural Organisation Society, Dublin. January 1979.
5. IAOS (1979, p. 63).
6. O'Brien (1979, pp. 7–8).
7. O'Brien (1979, p. 13).

8. McDyer (1975, p. 2).
9. O'Brien (1979, p. 11).
10. O'Brien (1979, p. 12).
11. McDyer (1975, p. 3).
12. McDyer (1975, p. 3).
13. Lewis (1979 pp. 8–9).
14. The continued lack of attention to educational aspects – other than language schools – in all three cases would seem to be an important constraint on their development.
15. McDyer (1975, p. 2).
16. The analysis is based on the returns and company rules etc. filed with the Registry of Friendly Societies. A somewhat more optimistic interpretation is in Oakeshott (1978).
17. A fourth production co-operative, Farney Footwear, Carrickmacross, ceased to function as a registered co-operative after approximately two years and insufficient data was available to include it in the analysis. The fifth extant worker-orientated co-operative in the Republic is Graphic Arts, which is a small group of process engravers.
18. The data used are from the available annual returns and annual company reports as well as the rules etc. filed with the Registry of Friendly Societies.
19. *Business and Finance*, no. 13, (31 July 1975).
20. Viney (1972).
21. Even if the firms were successful, the return to capital would be limited to 5 per cent or less since all three were based on the co-operative movement's principle of limited return to capital.
22. A more detailed analysis of the framework provided by the Acts for labour co-operatives is in Connell Fanning and David Tomkin, 'Labour co-operatives in Ireland: the legal–organizational framework', *Journal of Irish Business and Administrative Research* (1980).
23. This is not shown on the Cash Account Table but is shown in the Balance Sheet.
24. The furniture industry is used as a comparison base for Irish Spring. However, light engineering might also have been used.
25. The participatory viability of their formal structure is considered by Fanning and Tomkin (1980).
26. Since this paper was completed, a further study has been published by Robert O'Connor and Philip Kelley (1980), *A Study of Industrial Workers' Co-operatives*, Economic and Social Research Institute, Dublin. This is a general survey, rather than an analytical one, of the experience of workers' co-operatives in European countries, including the Irish cases analysed here, and includes a proposal for a state-sponsored Workers' Co-operative Agency.
27. These questions apply equally to co-operatives in other types of activities, e.g. consumer co-operatives which were noticeably successful in the UK but not so in Ireland.

8 Chile[1]

Juan Guillermo Espinosa

Few societies in the western world have lived through such brusque changes in the past two decades, or such drastic reorientations in domestic policy, as has Chile. During this period the Chilean economy has been the laboratory for various development models, providing observers with innumerable lessons for the future. In the midst of these changes, beginning in the 1960s, there were various degrees of effort to build a system of broad participation, including not only political participation but worker involvement in productive and commercial enterprises.

There were three clearly distinguished stages in this process. The first or gestation stage was between 1960 and 1970, during which the ideas and early experiments were developed. A stage of rapid expansion followed between 1970 and 1973: beginning with the establishment of an Area of Social Ownership, and attempts to extend the participation model throughout the economy. The current stage, beginning in 1974, drastically reduced the number of participatory enterprises and imposed political limitations on the free functioning of the participation model, the curtailment of which has conflicted sharply with the training and experience of the population and workers.

This chapter summarises the principal characteristics of these three stages and generally analyses the lessons of the Chilean experience, emphasising the broader trends which could be used to develop and implement a system of worker participation in other places.

I THE GESTATION PERIOD (1960–70)

From the beginning of Chilean industrialisation in the 1930s, workers concentrated their efforts on obtaining economic benefits through their trade unions. Although there was a progressive political development in Chilean society, until the end of the 1950s there were no proposals or experiments in worker participation.

During the 1960s, a combination of international and domestic factors slowly began to inspire and spread the idea of participation. Thus for example, at the international level, the reorientation of the Catholic Church under Pope John XXIII in a predominantly Catholic continent[2] and the rise of the Cuban phenomenon, brought about a new opening in the approach of the intellectual, political and economic elites. Overseas, these factors directly influenced the programme of reform proposed by the Kennedy administration, called the Alliance for Progress. Inside Chile, early experiments in agrarian reform were supported by the Church, which disposed of its land holding in 1962 and 1963. Also in Chile, a new social vision centred on worker participation developed as a result, *inter alia*, of industrial development, growing labour organisation, a general political evolution which initiated some redistributive policies, the growing involvement of the state in net investment as a result of the inability of the private capitalist sector, and in 1965 the expansion of an agrarian reform programme based on the co-operative administration of the land by the workers.

During the presidency of Eduardo Frei (1964–70), the more progressive political elements developed a variety of initiatives for reform, including co-operative enterprises and the participation of workers in the administration of companies. For example, the Technical Co-operation Service of the government (SCT) in 1967 initiated a concrete programme to create and support worker-managed enterprises; but the lack of financial resources and political support led to the virtual abandonment of the programme in mid-1969. In these two years only 22 companies were created or assisted, all of them small and of little significance in the economy. Also during these years, there were demands for worker participation in a number of state-owned enterprises. Among the most salient cases were the state sugar refining company (IANSA), the national petroleum enterprise (ENAP), the state electric company (ENDESA), and the national airline (LAN Chile). Although in some instances, after protracted labour and political pressure, the workers eventually gained small minority participation on the boards of directors of these enterprises, most of the initiatives were unsuccessful. While worker participation did not experience substantial growth prior to 1970, it had been introduced as a major item on the political agenda. The 1970 presidential campaigns of both Radomiro Tomic (Christian Democrat) and Salvador Allende (Popular Unity) emphasised the importance of worker participation and the need to create a social ownership sector in the economy.

This brief analysis of the first stage leads to a number of conclusions. During this period, the number of enterprises and the number of workers linked to a participatory system was insignificant in relation to the overall economy. The political organisation of these workers was oriented more to influencing higher policy levels than to influencing the labour sector itself, where at the beginning they were virtually unknown. Although the few small experiments created during this stage involved a vision (or mystique) of seeking a new type of social and economic organisation of production, in contrast, the majority of outside observers saw them as a laboratory or testing ground leading to decisions about future initiatives. This made it clear, in many cases, that while pilot projects may serve as a practical experience in the creation and management of enterprises by the workers, they do not serve to persuade non-believers. The supporters of the idea are already convinced; for the opponents, each experiment is a particular case, generalisations cannot be drawn from them and it will always be necessary to go on experimenting. This common situation reminds us that no economic system is ever tested or 'proven' until it is put into practice. However, the prerequisite of provability is often used in arguing against a participatory system.

As might have been predicted, there were a variety of factors producing a favourable atmosphere for the diffusion and promotion of the participatory model, which had a greater influence than the expected ripple or demonstration effect of the experiments. One of these factors, worthy of special note, was the crisis or inadequacy of Keynesian policies, which called for the state to provide a permanent solution (with short-term policies) for the inability of the private sector to provide the employment, investment or production that the population required. This fact, and the rapid expansion of the democratic system at the political level, provoked a growing contradiction between the economic and political systems. Moreover, the growth and dissemination of popular participation in trade unions, towns, universities, cities, in the agrarian reform and in the upper levels of the state, reinforced this contradiction. The development of political formation and popular participation without a parallel development in the economic sector, together with other factors, led to the beginning of a new approach to development: a road to socialism, but with the preservation of democratic structures and practices. In this way, the involvement of workers in the management of their enterprises coupled with the participation of the population at all levels, appeared to be at least the logical if not the only way to reconcile the trends in the economic and political system which had become conflictive.

II THE STAGE OF ACCELERATED EXPANSION (1970–3)

The period from 1970 to 1973 in Chile has been studied extensively, and there is an abundant bibliography on the subject. Therefore this section concentrates exclusively on the development of participation and its principal results and problems.

The election of Allende in 1970 marked the beginning of a major government restructuring of economic institutions. The new government expropriated its first factory in December 1970, and its last in August 1973. The *Normas Básicas* or standards of participation for enterprises in the social area were promulgated in June 1971, after being discussed with the workers. This three year period was intended as a transition to socialism. Within the society a bitter struggle raged between old and new ideas, between the preservation of the existing economic system and the creation of a new one. As the struggle crystallised, it produced institutional instability and decay, high levels of mass politicisation, popular mobilisation, and extensive, profound and rapid changes throughout the society.

During this period, there was increasing debate on every aspect of social life. This often led to harsh confrontations between political forces with differing viewpoints. The process of participation was no exception: there were many different proposals and models, as well as indifference and opposition in some cases. Nevertheless, one model did predominate from the beginning: that which had been agreed upon by the Government and the *Central Unica de Trabajadores* (CUT), for a joint administration by the workers and the state of enterprises covered by the Area of Social Ownership which was then being formed. The model took the form of the *Normas Básicas*, or basic standards for worker participation.

At the same time, co-operative enterprises which had been carried over from the preceding period (mostly small businesses employing no more than 35 people) sought to be included in the Area of Social Ownership or at least to develop closer relationships with the workers and leaders of the enterprises in the Social Area. Unfortunately, they received little attention.

According to the *Normas Básicas*, the socialised enterprises were managed by an administrative council which, in theory, was to be composed of five elected worker representatives, five state-appointed representatives, and one state-appointed administrator. In practice, however, only a handful of the largest enterprises actually followed this scheme. In the great majority of these enterprises, worker representatives held more than 50 per cent of the seats on the administrative council. Where there was not such outright control, several state representatives were chosen from among the workers of the factory in question. Indeed, in many instances the workers themselves chose their own administrator. Decisions of the council were reviewed and subject to modification at monthly general assemblies of all workers in the factory.

At the shop-floor level, sectional assemblies met on a monthly basis, and production committees were elected to conduct the organisation of production on a week-to-week basis. Suggestions and information flowed from the shop floor to the administrative council through the co-ordinating committee. The latter was presided over by the president of the largest union in the enterprise. (The typical Chilean firm had at least two unions, one white-collar and one blue-collar. During the Allende period, there was a tendency for these two groups to merge and form a single class-unified union.) Aside from the task of heading the co-ordinating committee, union leaders were not allowed to serve as worker representatives on the production committees or administrative councils. This separation of functions at times created problems, as the more bureaucratic unions generally opposed the formation of parallel institutions to represent the workers. The meetings of the co-ordinating committee were also attended by the heads of the production committees, and by the worker representatives on the administrative council. Schematically, the formal structure of the participatory bodies is depicted in Figure 8.1.

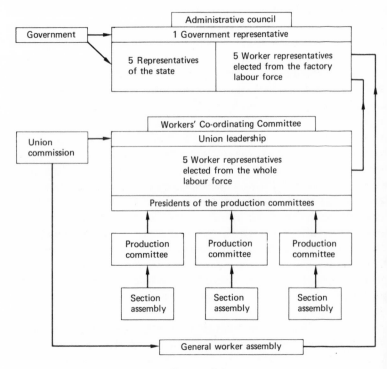

FIGURE 8.1

In the following paragraphs, it is possible only to outline briefly some of the major findings of a study conducted by the author and Andrew S. Zimbalist on the experience of worker participation at the level of the enterprise within the social area. The study, which is based upon an extensive survey conducted in 1973 of 35 randomly selected manufacturing enterprises covering ten industrial divisions of the UN classification scheme, ranging in size from 90 to 1800 employees, is more fully reported and discussed in Espinosa and Zimbalist (1978). The discussion will focus on three dimensions: the structure of participation; the factors influencing the level of participation attained; and the effect of participation on the performance of the enterprise.

A basic methodological assumption of the study was that
worker participation in enterprise management is a measurable
process, at least in comparative terms. The purpose of measuring
the level of worker participation in comparative terms was to find
out what were the main characteristics, the explanatory factors
and the performance of different situations: one, for instance,
with an advanced or high level of worker participation, *vis-à-vis*
another with a very poor or low level of worker involvement in the
decision-making process. In this regard, the following comments
should not be confused with an apology for a process within
which co-existed a diversity of different situations. But in order to
learn from the experiences where participation was higher, as a
normal procedure a greater emphasis was given, at least in our
comments, to those cases where worker involvement was more
developed. However, those comments do not imply that the more
advanced cases were the predominant ones, nor that there did not
exist enterprises where the management did not change, were top-
down in style and where the participation level was fairly poor.

A cumulative index was constructed which allowed an inter-
firm comparison of the extent of worker participation in decision
making, execution of policies, and control and evaluation of these
policies. The index was formed by measuring separately the
functioning of the structure of participation (the existence of
participatory bodies, frequency of meetings, attendance at
meetings, etc.) and the content of participation (range of issues
covered at meetings, workers' influence in forming decisions, etc.)
at three different levels within each enterprise. This information
was obtained from worker representatives, union leaders, state
representatives and administrative and technical personnel within
each enterprise. The analysis of the index and structure of
participation suggest that:

(i) Participation at higher levels within the enterprise (i.e. the
administrative council) was always accompanied by active participation at the base or lower levels (i.e. production committees
and worker assemblies at the level of the shop floor and general
assemblies of the whole enterprise). This finding is consistent with
other studies which find that the participatory process sustains
only itself and evolves into fuller democracy when it develops
from the base.

(ii) A related result is the high correlation we found between
the structure and the content of participation. The existence of

formal participation bodies (structure) does not guarantee tha
workers will exert effective influence (content) in decision making
In fact, experience elsewhere suggests that without the oppor
tunity to have a real impact on the policies of the enterprise
workers lose interest in the formal structure, e.g. they cease t
attend meetings, cease to vote for or watch over thei
representatives, and cease to follow the performance of th
enterprise. Thus the content of participation must not onl
provide for effective worker input in general, but it must provid
for this input in substantive matters. When worker influence i
limited to consultation on inconsequential issues, participatio
will not be dynamic and self-sustaining. However, when th
influence is real and far-ranging, workers will exert pressure t
sustain and deepen the formal structure of participation.

In the next stage of the study, it was hypothesised that th
relative level of participation obtained in each firm was a functio
of the presence, in differing degrees, of characteristics peculiar t
each factory. We considered 29 quantifiable independent vari
ables suggested by previous studies, for which information wa
uniformly available in all sampled enterprises. Our principa
findings regarding the factors influencing the level of particip
ation can be summarized as follows.

(i) One set of variables examined pertained to those charac
teristics traditionally employed to describe the social an
bureaucratic organisation of the firm (size, span of contro
vertical and horizontal differentiation). None of these variables
alone or together, were found to be significant predictors of th
level of participation. Yet other literature on the subject ha
consistently found one variable in particular, horizonta
differentiation, to be positively associated with decentralisatio
of decision making in the firm. However, this literature refer
solely to decentralisation to the level of middle managemen
Since we were measuring participation in decision makin
by workers and not by management, it is not surprising tha
we found this variable insignificantly correlated with partici
pation.

(ii) We considered three distinct measurements of technolog
complexity (percentage of maintenance workers in the firm
labour force), typology of mechanisation (craft, machine tendin
assembly, assembly line and continuous process), and intensit
(capital–labour ratio). Higher capital–labour ratios and great

mechanisation were negatively correlated with participation, while complexity was positively correlated. Although these relationships were statistically significant, they were rather weak, and consequently the relationship between technology and participation was superceded by the stronger relationship between participation and our labour force variables.

(iii) Our proxies for the level of formal schooling were not significantly correlated with participation. Several authors have pointed out that schooling affects not only an individual's cognitive and skill traits, but also his or her affective and ideological traits. These two influences may be offsetting with respect to their impact on participation. It is also likely, however, that our proxies were distorted and inadequate measures of educational level. We also considered a variable representing a broader conception of an individual's education suggested by Freire, namely, the degree of labour mobilisation and consciousness. The motivating notion here is that labour mobilisation and consciousness constitute an active form of education, where the individual learns from mutual interaction with peers based on his or her own life experience. Our measurement of labour mobilisation was based on the frequency and intensity of strikes prior to the enterprise's socialisation and the nature and extent of worker involvement in the enterprise's passage to the socialised sector of the economy. (For instance, was socialisation top-down through government decree, or was it inspired by worker take-over?) Labour mobilisation was found to be strongly and positively correlated with worker participation.

(iv) Our two explicitly political variables, (a) ideology and attitude toward participation of union and sectional leaders, and (b) the composition of political party support in each factory, were very significant and complementary predictors of the level of participation. The more progressive the ideology of worker representatives and the lower the voting support for the parties in opposition or the top-down organised parties in a factory, the greater was the level of participation observed. Worker participation entails a redistribution of power within the enterprise toward the workers, and thus involves a political struggle. The parties and ideological position that stressed the importance of gaining power for the working class over the state apparatus also were able to generate more effective systems of worker power over the enterprise.

(v) The disposition of the enterprise administration towar
participation and the nature and extent of informational flow
within the enterprise were very powerful predictors o
participation. These two variables were classified as intermediat
because their own variance was, in turn, strongly explained b
variables of the central labour force characteristics alread
discussed. The attitude of the factory's administration towar
worker involvement in decision making and the extent an
accessibility of information provided within the firm, appeared t
be a direct function of the level of organisation, interest, an
pressure from the workers.

(vi) Finally, it is important to emphasise that our results fron
multiple regression and factor analysis indicated that the labou
force and political variables were of overriding importance. Th
only technostructure variables significant in explaining the leve
of worker participation were those describing the firm'
technology. However, when the technology variables were con
sidered together with (a) labour mobilisation and consciousness
(b) political ideology and attitude toward participation of worke
leaders, and (c) political party composition, the former lost a
significance. The latter three variables together, on the othe
hand, explained 65 per cent of the variance of our dependen
variable, participation. Finally, when labour mobilisaion an
consciousness, attitude and ideology of union leaders, dispositio
of the administration toward participation and the system o
internal information were considered together, we explained 83.
per cent (corrected R^2) of the variance in participation. Thes
results are impressive and suggest that we were able to isolate th
most relevant factors affecting the development of worke
participation.

In the final part of our study, we analysed the relationshi
between our index of participation and various indicators of th
social and economic performance of the enterprise. We foun
both the social and economic performance of the enterpris
tended to be positively associated with the level of worke
participation.

After the changeover of many firms to the social area, th
elimination of supervisors, the absence of former bosses, th
dissolution, in effect, of the old system of control and disciplinar
pressure, created an atmosphere of social freedom that occasion
ally allowed the workers to take advantage of this new situatior

Iowever, with the establishment of the new participatory system
1 the enterprise, these abuses were slowly brought under control,
nd in most cases there were net improvements beyond previous
:vels of work discipline and organisation. The following are
ome of the major changes observed in performance.

(a) In those firms where a relatively higher level of particip-
tion existed, progress and advances in worker discipline were
gnificant, appreciably surpassing former standards. However,
1 a few firms where the level of participation was low, discipline
eteriorated, weakening internal organisation and team spirit.
~hanges in worker discipline were paralleled by changes in
bsenteeism, strike activity and innovative behaviour, all of
vhich improved with higher levels of participation.

(b) An increase in worker education and training courses was
trongly associated with higher levels of participation. The
pportunity for participation created a demand for more
:aining, and the greater training in turn reinforced the workers'
:nse of efficacy and interest in participation. Increases in training
ourses were also clearly correlated with improvements in
iscipline and decreases in absenteeism.

(c) Correspondingly, higher participation levels were as-
ociated with a change toward more egalitarian and collective
orms of remuneration. Disparities between high and low wages
vere reduced. The number of wage grades was sharply
iminished, and the incentive system was put progressively on a
ore collective basis, as opposed to individual piece rates.

(d) Independent from, and complementary to, the influence of
igher levels of participation, the move toward more egalitarian
nd collective forms of remuneration significantly promoted
ecreases in thefts and defective products, and increases in
nnovative behaviour, investment, and productivity. The magni-
ade of these results was superior to that observed in firms in the
Jnited States and elsewhere where attempts have been made to
nprove worker motivation through controlled stimuli and new
tyles of management.

(e) Whereas the annual increase in capital stock in Chilean
idustry was 3.9 per cent during 1959–64 and 4.6 per cent during
965–70 (Stallings 1975, p. 427), the ·average annual rate of
ivestment in fixed productive assets in our 35 sample firms was
5.47 per cent. Within our sample, firms with higher levels of
articipation also tended to have higher investment ratios. These

results challenge the assertions of many to the effect that worker
run enterprises will opt for current rather than future income and
will therefore invest less than typical capitalist firms. Although
workers might resist innovation and investment in a capitalist
firm because they are perceived as benefiting only the owner and
threatening workers' job stability, in a worker-run firm innov
ation and investment are seen as an important way to secure job
and enterprise stability for the future.

(f) Perhaps the single variable of greatest interest i
productivity. In 29 of the 35 sample firms, productivity either
increased or stayed the same, and in 14 firms, it increased at a rate
superior to 6 per cent per year. Given the generalised economic
problems of the period and the marked tendency for social firm
to expand employment, these results are impressive. In addition
although it was not the most important variable in explaining
increases in productivity, higher levels of participation were
clearly correlated with greater productivity increases.

As indicated previously, collective incentives and narrower
earnings differentials were both significantly and positively
correlated with productivity, both separately and when the level
of participation was controlled for. Also, the positive relationship
between productivity and participation remained when we con
trolled for other variables of the production function and proxies
for changes in product demand. It was also found that higher
capital–labour ratios strengthened the positive relationship be
tween productivity gains and participation. The positive associ
ation between productivity and participation has been found by
many authors under widely varying conditions, and furthermore
no major study has found there to be a negative association
between the two.

(g) Finally, in the area of social results, socialised factories
without diverting resources from productive uses, rapidly ex
panded the social services available to the worker: plant medical
facilities, day-care centres, cafeterias, consumer co-operatives
athletics fields, libraries, and so on. In several factories, cultural
departments were created and sponsored theatre groups and folk
singing groups which performed at other work-places, fairs and
rallies.

Among other interesting aspects, it must be mentioned that the
enterprises of the social area with most advanced levels of worker
participation were the same enterprises that were pushing hardest

or worker participation in sectoral and national planning. That
s, the more participant and mobilised sectors of the working class
were pressuring the most to deepen the democratic forms of the
state.

The foregoing summary, of the principal results and explanatory factors in the process of participation up to 1973,
should not be mistaken for an idealised presentation of a process
without problems. On the contrary, although the experiment of
worker participation in Chilean industry was a new and important historical phenomenon, above all it was a process that was
impelled and lived as an integral and inextricable part of the
political process of structural changes in the economy and in the
society. Given the complexity and intensity of the process
experienced in those years, we should end this section with some
important clarifications.

(i) A process of this nature brings to the surface a number of
hidden conflicts: for example, between bosses and subordinates,
between engineers or technicians and unskilled workers, between
production shops and offices, between the technocratic and the
political mentality, between concern for the defence of the system
and concern for change, etc.

(ii) Naturally, a process of democratisation is not achieved
simply through the good will of those who hold power. In
particular, within the enterprises, a participatory process implies
the diminution of entrepreneurial absolutism, which often creates
great risks and failures within capitalist firms, which must be
shared by all. Managerial attitudes toward participation were
expressed in a wide variety of reactions, from the tendency to
avoid consultation with the workers for fear that their own
opinions would be overridden, to that of exaggerating consultation and overvaluing worker opinions; sometimes authoritarianism was reflected in the flow of information, or in the
evasive action such as creating 'offices for participation' with the
pretext that the new approach was a simple matter of labour
relations which did not affect management of the enterprise
directly.

(iii) In contrast, the most common opinion among the workers
was that participation means a democratising of decision making,
especially with regard to the productive process and discussion of
the work to be done, which was chiefly obstructed by the
resistance of the bosses to the new form of organisation, and their

refusal to collaborate with the workers in a context of dignity and equality.

From a traditional perspective, the most dramatic consequence of the implantation of a system of broad and general participation is the breaking down of traditional authority at all levels, and particularly within the enterprises. In the Chilean case, this was accentuated by the liberating approach towards workers taken by the Allende government, as a result of the capitalist exploitation which the workers had been suffering, which led to its identification as the 'government of the workers'.

In synthesis, the process was not an easy one; the level of participation was not raised in all enterprises in an automatic, homogeneous or generalised way. In some situations the level of participation advanced significantly, while in others it was very poor, as a result of the traditional hierarchical and authoritarian system. What our results show, in sum, is that those enterprises that did show improvements in worker participation also showed positive improvements in other dimensions; and that where participation did not overcome the traditional system, internal confrontation, and indiscipline increased from the pre-1970 level, as a result of the frustration of the workers and the lack of managerial co-operation.

III THE CURRENT STAGE: THE ADJUSTMENT TO AN OPEN ECONOMY AND AN ULTRA-LIBERAL ECONOMIC MODEL

In August 1973 the socialised sector of the Chilean economy comprised approximately 420 enterprises, accounting for upwards of 40 per cent of the total industrial output and over 30 per cent of the industrial labour force.

A month later, the Chilean economy began to experience one of the harshest reversals ever experienced by a country in the western world that was not at war. From then until now, the survival of participation has depended more on the intensity with which the government applied its economic and repressive policies throughout the country, than on the micro-economic situation of each enterprise.

The new economic approach consisted of a return to the most orthodox classical approach, whose application requires the imposition of a high level of political repression, without which it could not be implemented in a civilised society. The economic model now being used is the old and well known theory based on the denationalisation of essential resources, the transfer of enterprises and holdings from the public sector to private groups, and strong incentives for foreign capital. Similarly, their social policy is based primarily on the reduction of educational, housing and health costs, freezing wages and salaries, and suppressing the right to strike. The main instruments of this approach are monetary restraint and public expenditure reduction, which induced the most severe recession in Chilean history as a consequence of its serious negative impact on aggregate demand and on the whole level of economic activity.

There have been three differentiated stages in the implementation of the new policies. The first went from September 1973 to March and April 1975, and it was generally a period of mild application of monetary restraint and government expenditure reduction. It was thought by the economic authorities that after price liberalisation and wage control, inflation would decrease. On the contrary, although prices went up almost ten-fold on average in October 1973, during 1974 the consumer price index still showed an increase of 370 per cent.[3]

The second stage of the process, from April–May 1975 to approximately March–April 1977, might be termed the 'shock treatment' implementation period. In one year, the economic team cut overall government spending by 20 per cent and government capital spending by over half. The result was predictable. In 1975, Chile's Gross Domestic Product (GDP) fell by 16.6 per cent and industrial production declined by 28 per cent. Per capita income declined 24 per cent to roughly the level of 1962. Construction fell 35 per cent and mining output by nearly 10 per cent. According to official government statistics, unemployment in greater Santiago reached 18 per cent at year-end 1975 and Chile's total average wage bill declined by 12 per cent in real terms.[4]

At the beginning of 1976 and as a consequence of the depressed economic activity, the balance of payments showed a surplus, thereby easing restrictions in the foreign sector. However, even with a drop of 14 per cent in the GDP in 1975, the effect on the rate of inflation was insignificant but there was a substantial increase in the already high unemployment rate.

The resulting impact on the balance of payments, instead of producing improvements in the general situation, on the contrary led to new measures derived from orthodox economic theory. There was a drastic reduction in import duties, which, coming on top of the strong drop in real income, ended up practically eliminating the market for national industry.

In the third stage, since April–May 1977, the opening of the Chilean economy to the international capital markets and the deregulation of the internal interest rate, resulted in a growing inflow of international speculative capital, thus inducing a monetary expansion and producing some recovery in the internal economic activity. However, the growing inflow of private foreign credit, resulted in a systematic overvaluation of the national currency in relation to the dollar, thus aggravating the serious new problem of a lack of protection for internal production.

Up to the present, unemployment and idle productive capacity have been concentrated in the manufacturing, construction and public sectors. These sectors, which are often thought to be the main engines of growth in any country, have been left without a market, with practically no short-run credit (there is almost no long-run investment credit) or with interest rates of 7 to 9 per cent *per month,*[5] and disadvantaged by the drastic reduction in import duties and the overvalued national currency. In this framework, which in practice has led to drastic reductions in production for both traditional and participatory enterprises and made imported products artificially cheap, it is easy to explain the large number of defaults and shut-downs of enterprises.[6]

Therefore, it is mainly macro-economic factors that explain the survival or failure of enterprises in the Chilean economy since 1973. The traditional instruments of evaluation at the micro level, though important under ordinary circumstances, have become of minor importance in comparison to the kind of macro problems which affect traditional and self-managed firms equally.

Beginning in late 1973 and early 1974, a variety of groups led by the Catholic and Protestant churches, along with institutions of the co-operative movement and several other groups concerned with worker participation, began to become aware of the level of political persecution, arbitrary firings, and factory closings that the military Junta had begun to impose.

At first they adopted an essentially assistential approach, looking more at individuals than at the whole, thinking that this was a short-range problem. Nevertheless, the increasing volume and massive characteristics of the problem led the groups and especially the churches to seek at least a partial solution at a broader level.

From the end of 1973, the enterprises which had belonged to the Area of Social Ownership in the preceding government, were being returned *en masse* to their former owners. In those cases where the former owners were not interested or did not appear, the businesses were quickly auctioned off.

On the other hand, near the end of 1973, there were about 40 co-operative enterprises with an average of fewer than 40 workers each, which in many cases had previously tried to incorporate themselves into the Social Area but had continued functioning independently. Until late 1973, these enterprises had achieved acceptable or more than satisfactory economic results, despite the limits they faced on their operation. Their annual rate of employment expansion was over 5 per cent, and their annual sales expansion was over 20 per cent (Janneret, Moraga and Ruffing, 1975). The principal deficiency of these enterprises had been their growing employment of second-class workers; that is, the original co-operative members usually began recruiting workers for temporary activities which were then indefinitely prolonged, thus forming a group of workers whose rights were considerably inferior to those of the co-operative members.

In late 1974, the concerned organisations began to work consciously toward more global solutions as a result of several developments: the growing pressure from labour leaders in the former social area enterprises, now about to be sold, for technical and financial support; the churches' involvement in establishing several dozen small co-operative shops as a palliative for unemployment; and a few cases of enterprises which had been put up for public auction and which the workers had succeeded in acquiring through the assistance of an old co-operative financing institution. In this way, a System of Financing Self-management (SFA) was established with financial support from overseas agencies, for the purpose of responding to urgent human, social and economic needs among at least some worker groups, which in general had become the most persecuted sector of the Chilean population. In addition, the need was felt to preserve and save at least some of the broad experience accumulated in this area in the recent history of the country.

Nevertheless, despite the important aid offered by the SFA, between 1975 and 1977 there was a significant number of bankruptcies among the, approximately, 65 enterprises which had survived to the end of 1974 (the old co-operative enterprises and those formerly in the area of social ownership). The principal causes of these failures were, among others: (i) the exceedingly optimistic expectations of being able to acquire overseas financing for all the enterprises that needed it; (ii) the underrating of the general crisis in the country and therefore of needs; but especially (iii) the economic crisis brought on by the economists of the military Junta, which was the determinant factor affecting both the traditional private sector and the enterprises which were beginning to join together in the self-managed or participatory sector.[7]

By way of summarising the situation in the past few years Figures 8.2, 8.3 and 8.4 compare changes in sales indices between the traditional private sector and the self-managed sector of the country. Together, the graphs clearly represent the almost identical evolution of the two sectors, and, in some cases, the relatively higher rate of sales growth demonstrated by the self-managed sector.[8] It is clearly visible that in the three areas of

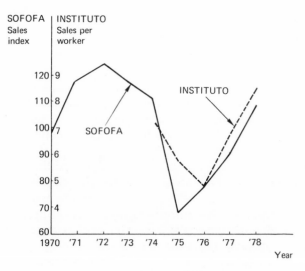

FIGURE 8.2   *Intermediate goods for construction*

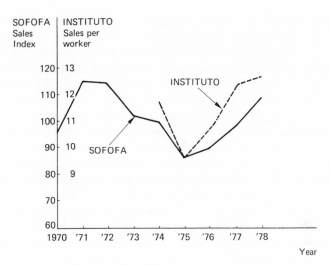

FIGURE 8.3   *Habitual consumer goods*

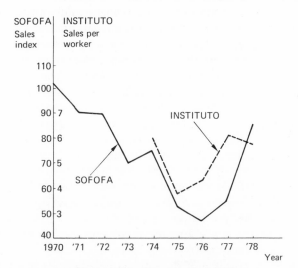

FIGURE 8.4   *Transport materials*

INSTITUTO: The Institute for Self-managed Enterprises
SOFOFA: The Society of Manufacturing Development of Private Firms.

production where the majority of self-managed enterprises are concentrated, starting in 1976 there was a significant recovery of sales; this confirms our original thesis that the crisis faced by the enterprises was due to a large extent to external factors, i.e. the economic recession induced by the government economists.

The current situation indicates that after this process of failures, there were 34 firms associated with the self-managed sector in March 1979, of which 26 were manufacturing enterprises and the other 8 involved in commerce or services. The 34 enterprises together employed approximately 2770 persons and achieved an annual sales level of 31.2 million dollars in 1978.

All but one of these enterprises are classified as small or medium-size enterprises according to employment (10–250 persons) and thus belong to the group of production units most affected by the government-induced economic recession. At the most general economic level, it is possible to hope for a certain stabilisation of the economic situation in the future, and a relaxation of the measures to restrict and concentrate income imposed by the military government. Increasing concern and improved organisation of workers at the national level make it likely that some sort of measures will be adopted to alleviate the exceedingly depressed situation of the lowest-income workers, and also to reduce the incredibly high rates of open unemployment (over 15 per cent of the national labour force in 1979).

In any case, although this slow recovery of the economy may widen the market for the enterprises, the situation is still very unclear because of general economic policies which affect all of Chilean industry in the same way. Thus, for example, the level of imports is at a record high, due to the almost complete absence of tariff protection for all national products, a situation which the most developed and industrialised countries would not permit. This fact is further aggravated by the low value of the dollar, established by the Central Bank as a means of reducing internal price levels. This in turn has been made possible by the strong support in credits obtained by the military government from the international private banks.

The following is a brief summary of lessons derived from the experience of these years.

(a) For the survival of the self-managed sector in Chile, it has been necessary to establish technical and financial support, which confirms earlier theories (Vanek, 1970). The System of Financing Self-management (SFA) has obtained funds free of the abusive norms which prevail in the national and international private financing sector; however, not in the amount required by the prevailing conditions.

(b) Despite the adverse general situation, the data available from participatory enterprises indicate that their productive and financial efficiency has been comparable to similar enterprises in the private traditional sector, and in some cases even higher, which is significant because of their comparatively lower access to financial resources.

(c) In some cases, a contributing factor in the failure of these enterprises was not the inefficiency or ignorance of the workers, but rather their disorganisation or desperation, which appears to have arisen in the moments preceding the enterprise failure, as an expression of their consternation in the face of the irremediable loss of their jobs in a context of widespread overt unemployment.

(d) The average levels of worker participation have clearly diminished as a result of several factors. (i) The climate of political repression which prohibited meetings and made communications and the spread of information difficult. (ii) The extraordinary economic recession has imposed as the top priority a defence of jobs, in many cases forcing the workers to set aside all other concerns. (iii) The general political and economic system has led workers to see their role in society as restricted and unimportant; they are under constant threat from the current system.

(e) The question of ownership of the means of production has been a divisive element not only in the ideological–political sphere, but also in its practical expression: diminishing worker solidarity. The tendency to evade an accurate definition of the problem, or to set it aside as unimportant, has resulted in: greater financial losses for the SFA; a less efficient utilisation of its overseas financial resources; and a 'proprietary' tendency among workers, who perhaps unconsciously abandon solidarity to defend individually their jobs in the face of the acute uncertainty of the economic situation.

The problem of ownership of the means of production is not new. Throughout the gestation stage and from 1970 to 1973, there was acute controversy over the choice between co-operative and state ownership. Some workers and technicians have slowly begun to realise that neither form is adequate, and have begun to experiment with other forms of social ownership such as industrial leasing and the establishment of collective loan guarantee funds.

IV CONCLUSIONS

In this brief summary we have tried to interpret a few of the main characteristics of the Chilean process; many others could be mentioned. In general, we can say that from the results of this experience, and from the findings of many other similar studies, the efficiency and desirability of worker participation in enterprise management and beyond the confines of the plant have been amply reconfirmed.

As a whole, the lessons from the Chilean experience clearly suggest that when worker participation really emerges from below, when workers perceive that they have a say in important matters and can direct the implementation of decisions, then an immeasurable potential seems to blossom from the spirit and capability of the workers. The workers' contribution to the production and general progress of the enterprise grows immensely, not only in hours per day but in the intensity and quality of their work. Human effort becomes the most significant factor, responding to a strong sense of liberation, newfound dignity and a deep perception of equity and self-determination.

Nevertheless, although the idea of self-management refers to a specific method of organising production and service units whose principal characteristic is that labour legitimises the administration of the enterprise, today in Chile at least, the concepts of self-management and worker participation have come to imply an interweave of principles, values and concrete methods, which go far beyond the simple transformation of a business to seek a new kind of society, organised around human labour free of the traditional political, economic and social forms of oppression.

Finally, the Chilean experiment was not imposed from the top down, authoritatively, but through the patient common effort of many people, through many years of searching, dialogue, shared successes and failures, often amid harsh conflicts but more often through consensus.

This process has been restrained and diminished by the hostile atmosphere that prevails today. It cannot fail to re-emerge, perhaps after many years. It can be repressed or ignored, ridiculed or deprecated, but it is a much deeper phenomenon. It is a whole concept of life, of the working people, of human beings and their social organisation.

NOTES

1. This chapter is based on a paper entitled 'The building of a self-managed sector in a capitalist economy: some lessons from the Chilean experience' which was prepared for the Walton Symposium, Glasgow, June 1979.
2. See, for example, the papal encyclical 'Mater et Magistra'.
3. Though the new free-market policies were mild in the implementation of contractionist policies, nevertheless they promptly resulted in an important set-back in the distribution of income. The official figures of the National Planning Office showed that in 1972, wage and salaried workers received 63 per cent of total income, with 37 per cent going to the propertied sector in the form of profits, dividends and rents. By 1974, income shares had literally been reversed: 58 per cent accrued to the propertied sectors and 42 per cent to labour (source: National Accounts, National Planning Office of Chile). Other studies have estimated a much worse reversal in income shares in 1974. For instance, a United Nations study estimated 64 per cent for the propertied sectors and 36 per cent to labour (source: UN Economic and Social Council, *Study of the Impact of Foreign Economic Aid and Assistance on Respect for Human Rights in Chile.*)
4. Sources: World Bank, *Economic Memorandum on Chile* 24 December 1975); OAS, *Situación y Perspectivas de la Economía de Chile*, 25 March 1976).
5. In 1979, after 5 years of this remedy, the prevailing interest rates were between 5 and 6 per cent *per month*.
6. In 1975 alone, the industrial sector suffered a 28 per cent decrease in production, equivalent to a setback of 10–12 years.
7. For lack of adequate data, it is hard to estimate the exact number of enterprises which declared bankruptcy or failed to survive this period. Some estimates indicate that no fewer than 30 of the 65 enterprises disappeared. This figure does not include several dozen small artisan shops promoted by the churches, especially in 1974, few of which survived.
8. Comparsions were made between the Index of Industrial Sales of the Society of Manufacturing Development (SOFOA) for each year since 1970, and an Index of Annual Sales per Worker (in dollars), for which information is available only from 1975. It must be recognised that the private sector index of SOFOFA includes a high proportion of large, and somewhat fewer medium-size, industries, which because of their monopoly power and easier access to credit were not so adversely affected by the economic crisis as were the medium-size and small enterprises. This index therefore represents a particularly favourable image of the traditional private sector. For the self-managed enterprises, we estimated sales values for 1974 on the basis of a subgroup of 16 enterprises. The data for the self-managed enterprises were provided by the Instituto de la Autogestión (INA).

9 Israel: the Kibbutz[1]
Avner Ben-Ner and
Egon Neuberger

The subject matter of this chapter, the Israeli kibbutz, represents a
more comprehensive communal form of self-manged organisation than those discussed in the preceding chapters. In this
chapter we hope that we can:
  (i) show that comprehensive communalism coupled with self
      management is viable;
 (ii) point to some historical factors which gave birth to this type
      of socio-economic organisation and influenced its develop
      ment;
(iii) analyse its economic functioning and some of it
      implications.

I BACKGROUND HISTORY

The development of the kibbutz movement, and that of modern
Israel, cannot be understood except against the background of
the history of the Jewish people in the Diaspora, which in turn
was strongly shaped by anti-semitism, and the general develop
ment of human society.

Some nineteenth century developments form the historical
basis of the kibbutz movement. Rising anti-semitism and the
hardships it brought on the Jewish people, coupled with rising
national movements in Europe and the social restructuring
resulting from the rise of capitalism, all had a significant impact
on Jewish society, primarily in Europe.

The predominantly static and closed European Jewish society
started to ferment and look more actively for solutions for it

redicaments. One segment of it (marginal in numbers at that me, but central to our story and to the future of the Israeli state ome decades later) found the answer in the ideal of a socialist ociety built on a Jewish national basis and on its historical soil, ie land of Israel. This segment, called socialist Zionism, was to ecome the founder of the kibbutz movement and ultimately, of ie state of Israel.

At the turn of the century, the situation of Jews in Russia (who omprised half of the world's Jews) became aggravated, leading o a mass emigration (about two million) from Russia, mostly to .merica. During 1904–14, only a small minority of Jews (some 5 000–40 000, including many from the Austro-Hungarian mpire, Romania and Yemen) migrated to Palestine. The immi- rants who chose to go to Palestine were generally very young, iiddle and lower bourgeoisie, and dedicated to national and ocial goals: Zionism and Socialism.

This immigration wave (called the second 'Aliya') found in alestine about 650 000 Arabs and only 80 000 Jews, an economi- illy undeveloped country, predominantly agricultural, and an cute lack of jobs. Only 10 per cent of the immigrants could find a b, while the rest were driven to despair and many left the ountry (Darin-Drabkin, 1963, p. 60).

The response of the immigrants who chose to stay was to try to nite in small groups, in order to pool the risk of unemployment nd provide all members with basic necessities. (Groups had an dditional advantage in being able to contract large scale works, rovide members with professional training, and serve as a ibstitute for the families most of them had left behind in their ountries of origin.) Consumer and producer co-operatives were lso formed (e.g. communal kitchens and laundries, bakeries and oemakers). The Jewish workers were organised in two (rival) arties, which fulfilled tasks such as mutual aid, sickness funds, nployment exchange, cultural and social clubs, etc.

Under the influence of the ideology which said that agriculture the vocation for the Jewish people returning to Israel, and their esire to escape the exploitative conditions of wage labourers at iat time, workers tried to find employment in agriculture.[2] No inds were available to support individual settlers, and existing :wish farmers were unwilling to help in the further development f Palestinian agriculture (Laquer, 1972, p. 288). Collectives of orkers found employment on a piece-work basis under the supervision of managers, appointed by the Zionist organisation in farms established by the national (Jewish) fund. After bitter quarrels between workers and managers, and a strike, the workers assumed responsibility for the management of the farm Um Juni (renamed Degania) in 1909. This was the first kibbutz, then called *kvutza*. However, this and other *kvutzot* established during that period, preserved until 1920 individual accounting (on the basis of equal remuneration for time worked), and despite collective production, the collective organisation of consumption was not universally adopted.

More *kvutzot* were established in the coming decade (1910s) but not until after the First World War were the *kvutzot* organised in any national organisation, although they kept some loose contacts between themselves, mostly through party (political) ties.

These first *kvutzot* were engaged primarily in agricultural production, but their lack of experience, and financial and technological handicaps, forced them to rely also on other sources of income. The desire of the members to participate in the construction of the country led to groups of *kvutzot* members acting as contractors in public works.

A new injection of membership came with the next wave of immigration (the Third Alia) of 34 000–37 000 young people between 1919 and 1923. This wave was instigated primarily by two events: (i) the 1917 Russian Revolution, which had a double edged effect on Jewish youth: a revolutionary excitement, with its impetus for Jews to follow a similar path in their own society, and a disappointment from the development of the revolution (and its consequences for Jews); (ii) the conquest of Palestine by the British and the Balfour Declaration.[3]

Many immigrants (apparently the majority: see Laquer, 1972 p. 308) wanted to join or establish *kvutzot*. The Zionist organisations did not provide sufficient funds for this purpose, so that by 1927, some 24 established *kvutzot* were in existence, while 60 work groups were waiting for settlement (Barkai, 1977, p. 64). The Zionist leadership decided to divert resources from *kvutzot* for the establishment of a new type of agricultural settlement, the *moshav*,[4] and some even expressed the hope that *kvutzot* will gradually develop into *moshavim*. Thus the waiting list increased and the proponents of the small and intimate *kvutza* had to make room for the absorption of newcomers into existing settlements.

'he need to establish a national network became more evident.
Iany felt that the experience accumulated by various kibbutzim[5]
hould be shared by all, and in view of the ideological interest
xisting kibbutzim had in the propagation and survival of this
istitution, a sort of mutual-help system had to be established.
Libbutzim also had many common interests *vis-à-vis* the Zionist
rganisation and the British government. The increasing anta-
onism between the Arab population and the Jewish immigrants
esulted in some armed Arab attacks on kibbutzim. Thus, a joint
ibbutz defence organisation was also needed. Finally, many of
he kibbutz members felt that their immediate role was to lead the
vhole Zionist movement, and this obviously required an
rganisation. This was accentuated by the establishment of the
.abour Battalion (1920), which grew out of groups which worked
1 public works, with the aim of eliminating competition between
roups, and the establishment of a large army of workers ready to
alfil national needs at the call of the central organs. The goal of
he Labour Battalion was the establishment of a national
ommune, with common and centralised finances, ensuring a
imilar standard of living to all groups and members, and
entralised allocation of tasks. It was hoped that, ultimately, the
ommune would embrace all workers of the country, proceeding
) socialism and skipping the capitalist stage.

After one attempt in 1920, a national organisation of kib-
utzim was finally established in 1925 as *Hever Hakvutzot*
'ehakibbutzim. However, almost two decades after the kibbutz
iovement was born, substantial differences between various
ibbutzim still existed. They were rooted in the different social
nd cultural backgrounds of the members, and in their political
iews regarding kibbutz organisation, the Jewish national ques-
on and its relationship to socialist goals, and the international
ocialist and Communist movement. Thus, the single national
rganisation was short-lived and, in the course of time, four
ifferent national kibbutz federations were established: in 1927
ie United Kibbutz (*Hakibbutz Hameuhad*–KM), and the
Jational Kibbutz (*Hakibbutz Haartsi*–KA), in 1928 the Union
f Kvutzot (*Hever Hakvutzot*–HK), and in 1935 the Religious
Libbutz (*Hakibbutz Hadati*–KD).

We shall now look at the development of the kibbutz move-
ient through its major components: the federations. Adoption of
iis approach does not mean that dissimilarities between kib-

butzim are of extreme importance;[6] it is interesting to identify th
various forms of Israeli communalism, and view some of them i
the light of the economic analysis of Section III.

(i) The *Hever Hakvutzot (HK) Federation* originally consiste
of the settlements dedicated to a small and intimate membershir
whose central economic activity is agricultural. Historically, HI
was associated with the largest labour party in Israel (Mapai,
The member-kibbutzim of this federation assumed a large degre
of independence, and central organs took upon themselves onl
co-ordination and some income-transferring responsibilities. HI
was, thus, the antithesis of the 'national commune' envisaged b
the Labour Battalion, and in fact, was established as a residu;
(after the KM and KA were already established).

In 1951, HK merged with a splinter of KM to form *Ichu
Hakvutzot Vehakibbutzim* (IKK) – the Union of *Kvutzot* an
Kibbutzim. The merger did not change the basic features of th
federation, except that larger kibbutzim were added to the HI
kibbutzim (which were already themselves in the process c
increasing their size). The average population of kibbutzim in th
federation increased from just a few dozen in the 1920s to 139 i
1936, 226 in 1945, 267 in 1951, 326 in 1952 (after the union) an
407 in 1972 (Barkai 1977, Table 13.1, p. 249); a great divergenc
from the 20 families considered as optimal for the *kvutza* in th
1920s.

In spite of the federation's belief in agriculture as the exclusiv
employment for its members, as time passed, it moved toward
industrialisation. In the 1920s and 1930s, most HK members wer
employed in agriculture and related branches, while in the 197(
about half of all the members working in production branche
were employed in industry.

Compared to the other two large federations (KA and KM
IKK (as well as its predecessor, HK) places a relatively sma
emphasis on collective consumption. This is revealed in variou
ways, e.g. in 1975 in about three quarters of its 85 kibbutzin
children did not live in separate communal quarters but with the
parents in apartments; many of them allowed for private dail
dinners, with breakfast and lunch in a communal dining hal
personal money allowances were a relatively high proportio
(around 20 per cent) of total consumption expenditure. Man
members of IKK follow the logic of individualistic welfai
criteria in the current debate in the kibbutz movement on th

'comprehensive budget', i.e. they favour the abolition of the current system of rationing of private consumption items and its replacement by an equal monetary budget for each member. The opposing view is that collective decisions on the composition of important items in private consumption are an indispensible aspect of the kibbutz, which otherwise would be transformed into a *moshav shitufi*.[7]

IKK, like other kibbutz federations, runs its own schools, either in individual kibbutzim, or (generally high schools) run jointly by several kibbutzim. Its activities cover all spheres of life: culture, society and economics. At the federation level, central organs, funded by member kibbutzim, provide services in each of these spheres.

(ii) The *Hakibbutz Hameuhad (KM) Federation* originated from a group of kibbutzim founded in 1921 and was under significant influence of the Labour Battalion. The principles of this federation can be summarised as follows: the kibbutz should be a large settlement and an ever increasing one, open to immigrants regardless of their political or youth movement affiliation; its production activities should be varied, both agricultural and industrial; the federation had in the past a dominant position in the management of its member kibbutzim and centrally-directed resources (mainly new members), according to what it viewed as the needs of individual kibbutzim, the kibbutz movement, and the country. The ideology of KM was a combination of left-wing socialism and activist (and mostly hawkish) nationalism. Its political affiliation was with left-wing factions in Mapai – the Labour party – but growing differences on both national and international political issues led to a split in KM (and a splinter of it jointed HK in 1951 to form IKK).[8]

Like IKK and other federations, KM has a chain of organisations to promote the economic, cultural and social activities of its 25 000 members (in 1975) living in 55 settlements. KM kibbutzim, historically the largest (average size 365 in 1936, compared to 138 in the movement as a whole), include the largest kibbutzim in Israel (with population of over 1000). KM falls ideologically between the relative extremes of IKK and KA.

(iii) *The Hakibbutz Haartsi (KA) Federation* was founded by members of *Hashomer Hatzair*, a pioneer scout-type movement, originating predominantly in Poland and Galicia. Their political and organisational beliefs were developed in the early days of the federation: the kibbutz has to be a comprehensive autonomous unit, organising collectively all areas of life: economy, society, culture, education and politics. In this sense, KA is more extreme than the other two federations discussed above. The KA kibbutz is viewed as an instrument for fulfilling Zionist goals, furthering class struggle and building a socialist society, as well as playing the role of an archetypal socialist society. Most KA members are affiliated with the socialist Mapai party.

KA kibbutzim do not view the question of maximal or minimal number of members as crucial in itself; the important thing is the planned, organic (all-embracing) growth of the kibbutz. (The median population in its 75 kibbutzim (in 1975) with a population of 32 700, was about the same as in KM.) Although strongly involved in general national events, KA members stress the internal affairs of their own kibbutz and the relationship between individual members. While debates on essential principles of kibbutz life are encouraged, once the federation adopts a firm policy, dissent is then discouraged. It has developed to its utmost the notion of 'collectivity of ideas', which in earlier decades meant that those who did not adhere to the exact principles of the federation could not remain as members of KA kibbutzim.

Collective consumption of members, as well as collective activities in general, are highly valued in KA kibbutzim: the collective education of children, who in all KA kibbutzim live in their own separate quarters and lead relatively independent lives, is considered to be of primary importance; social and cultural activities are encouraged, as in other federations, but with more emphasis on their collective and co-operative aspects.

Although agriculture was viewed as the most important activity, KA kibbutzim underwent an industrialisation process, and, in the 1970s, more than half of the members engaged in production activities work in industry. Although opposition to hired labour, which is against one of the basic tenets of the kibbutz – that members have to live on the fruits of their own labour and should not act as capital owners hiring labour –was voiced in all federations, practice differed considerably. KA kibbutzim employ the smallest proportion of the hired workers and IKK the highest (see discussion in Section III below).

   (iv) *The Hakibbutz Hadati (KD) Federation* is a small religious federation of kibbutzim, incorporating the values of non-religious kibbutzim of collective production and consumption, and equality, with religious practice. Its socialism bases many of the egalitarian and communal principles on religious attitudes. In 1975, 13 kibbutzim, with a total population of 4840, were affiliated with KD.

II AN ECONOMIC MODEL OF THE KIBBUTZ

One of the crucial features which distinguishes the kibbutz from most other types of self-managed organisations is that both production and consumption decisions are interdependent and made by the same decision-making organs. It is essential to incorporate this dual nature of the kibbutz into the economic model; to the best of our knowledge, none of the previous models of the kibbutz have done this (see Barkai, 1977; Helman, 1975; Inbar and Peleg, 1976; Rudolf, 1973).

On the basis of the historical and ideological developments described above, and of the description of the economic system of the kibbutz in Ben-Ner and Neuberger (1979), we present a simple two-period linear model which incorporates production and consumption decisions.

The model involves the maximisation of an objective function subject to a set of constraints. This form of the model focuses our attention on the two critical elements: the definition of the correct objective function and the selection of the most appropriate set of constraints.

The choice of objective function has been one of the critical issues in the literature on self-management. Most of the studies have adopted a very simple version: maximisation of income per member (see Chapter 1). This simple objective function is not appropriate for the kibbutz. We present a somewhat more comprehensive function which includes the kibbutz members' goals in both production and consumption.

Our model assumes a fixed number of members (labour force) in the initial period and an exogenously determined growth in membership of 2 percent (natural growth plus a net inflow or outflow). Our reasons for making such a restrictive assumption are the need to keep the model as simple as possible (linear) and the fact that the supply of members to the kibbutz is quite inelastic (they cannot expel members on economic grounds and do not find it easy to attract new members in the short run). The long-run variations in membership are probably influenced more by changes in the wider society than by actions of the kibbutz.

We assume that the kibbutz objective function (representing the preferences of kibbutz members) contains the following arguments: (i) amount of collective consumption of services and goods, which services are predominantly produced on the kibbutz; (ii) amount of private consumption goods, which are mainly purchased on the market; (iii) level of profit, i.e. total revenue from market sales minus non-labour costs in these activities; the role of profits in the objective function is as an indicator of economic success; (iv) the utilities derived by members from working plus an allowance for non-pecuniary aspects of working in different branches of the kibbutz.

We assume the following constraints: (a) the employment in the three branches (industry, agriculture and collective services) cannot exceed the kibbutz labour force; (b) the capital stock used in the three branches cannot exceed total capital stock; we assume that capital can be freely transferred from branch to branch; (c) land is fixed in quantity and is used solely for agriculture; (d) monetary resources can be shifted between two periods at a fixed (4 percent) rate of interest, and at the end of the second period the discounted monetary value of the wealth of the kibbutz should not be negative; (e) the per capita private consumption level of the kibbutz (which is bought on the market) is not permitted to vary by more than 25 per cent from the level in the average kibbutz; this constraint is based on the egalitarian ethic of the kibbutz movement.[9]

The kibbutz modelled here has three linear production activities (with constant production coefficients, which do not change between the two periods): industry and agriculture which produce goods for sale on the market, and collective consumption services and goods produced for internal kibbutz consumption only.

All decisions (for both periods) are made at the beginning of period 1 and we assume perfect knowledge of all present and future parameters. The full specification of the model is given in the appendix to this chapter.

III RESULTS

Even the simplified model outlined in Section II and fully specified in the appendix is much too complex to be amenable to analytic treatment; thus, we are forced to resort to simulation. We chose to perform the simulation (sensitivity) analysis for the 'average' kibbutz in 1965, the latest date for which sufficient data for such analysis were available. Data were derived from Table 9.1 by dividing each individual figure by the total number of kibbutzim. Production coefficients have been calculated and constraint levels specified for this hypothetical kibbutz.

TABLE 9.1   *Size of the kibbutz sector, 1965*

Number of kibbutzim	=	222
Kibbutz population	=	87 753
Land in kibbutz usage	=	1 408 thousand dunams

	Capital stock ('000 1958 IL)	Labour (member-years)	Gross Product ('000 1958 IL)
Industry	47 790	5 589	35 553
Agriculture	393 872	16 876	154 982
Collective consumption	307 497*	17 509	62 125

* Including community structures and durables, as well as private housing of members (yet collectively owned).

Source: Barkai (1977, various pages).

These basic data, when plugged into the model, yield results for levels of output in each branch and the value of consumption goods bought on the market as indicated in Table 9.2. All of these correspond very closely to the actual situation in 1965, thereby indicating the ability of the model (with the chosen values for marginal utilities – see below) to represent the average kibbutz.

Since there is no unique set of marginal utilities which, coupled with the 'technological' data, lead to the actual set of outputs and consumption, we chose the set of marginal utilities that corresponds most closely to our view of the kibbutz members' objective function. The choice was not particularly difficult, since the alternative specifications diverged widely from any reasonable set of marginal utilities.[10]

TABLE 9.2   *Activity levels generated by model ('000 IL 1958)*

Activity	Model result	Actual figure for average kibbutz[a]
Industry, period 1	158.86015	160.14864
Industry, period 2	203.48756	
Agriculture, period 1	696.95604	698.11711
Agriculture, period 2	696.95604	
Production of services for coll. cons		
period 1	280.79727	279.8423
period 2	268.67722	
Private consumption		
period 1	477.85707	473.5
period 2	633.61510	
Net investment	O[b]	(371.509[c])

Notes

[a] Actual figures are 1965 values; no 1966 values were available to compare with year 2 simulation result.
[b] The model compels the kibbutz to replace all used capital which amounts to IL374 000 (including material cost) compared to 371 500 (excluding material cost).
[c] Gross investment.

The potential divergences between our model and kibbutz reality can result from the following factors: (i) the use of linear production functions; (ii) our assumption that the limits on private consumption are 25 per cent above and below that of the average kibbutz (with no such constraint on collective consumption); (iii) our choice of the objective function and of the specific set of marginal utilities; (iv) a number of other detailed assumptions listed in the appendix. If it is valid to assume that none of the above specifications are too far from reality, we can claim to have the ability to specify quantitively the objective function of the kibbutz.

(a) OBJECTIVE FUNCTION

The set of marginal utilities which we have chosen to best represent the structure of kibbutz preferences is shown in Table 9.3. This set exhibits some interesting features of kibbutz preferences, discussed in Section I above: collective consumption[11] is preferred to private consumption, and labour in agriculture is preferred to labour in industry, which in turn is preferred to labour in the production of collective consumption services. Also, marginal utility of labour (given the number of hours worked in the average kibbutz, as well as its distribution of members across branches of production) is positive. This seems to be a confirmation of the kibbutz ideology which views work as a positive end in itself, as a need to be satisfied, and not only as a means toward the achievement of other goals.

Based on the discussion of the differences between federations in their preferences over collective versus private consumption, and agricultural versus industrial work, we have postulated marginal utilities for a 'typical' KA kibbutz and a 'typical' IKK kibbutz, also shown in Table 9.3.

TABLE 9.3   *Relative marginal utilities in kibbutz objective function*

| | MU of consumption | | | | Collective Consump- | |
	Private goods	Collective goods	Profits	Agriculture	tion	Industry
'Average'	1	2.1	0.1	1.3	0.5	0.8
KA	1	2.5	0.1	1.5	0.5	0.8
IKK	1	1.7	0.1	1.3	0.5	0.8

Consider now these 'typical' kibbutzim endowed with technologies and resources similar to those of the average kibbutz. In this case, the following differences in the levels of economic activities would obtain.

KA: (i) private consumption considerably lower than for the average kibbutz, and (ii) production of collective consumption services substantially higher, at the expense of marketable output, mostly industrial.

IKK: (i) private consumption considerably higher than for the average kibbutz, and (ii) production of collective consumption services lower in favour of increased industrial production. (Thus, the fact that IKK prefers labour in agriculture, as compared to KA and the average kibbutz, does not automatically lead to a higher level of agricultural production.)

This experiment shows the crucial significance of the values assigned to the marginal utilities in the objective function, and illustrates the probable differences in the economic behaviour of different types of kibbutzim. (For a more detailed analysis of these differences see Barkai, 1977, Chap. 13, and Ben-Ner, 1980.)

CHANGES IN PRICES[12]

Given the specification of the objective function and the constraints for the average kibbutz, we may examine the impact of changes in various parameters (e.g. prices of inputs and outputs, subsidies and taxes) on its economic behaviour.

Given a small increase in the price index of industrial products, the average kibbutz will increase its output of industrial goods at the expense (in terms of capital and labour) of production of services for collective consumption and in favour of increasing private (bought on the market) consumption. Larger increases in the prices of industrial products cannot be directed toward more private consumption, since this is limited by the egalitarian (upper limit) constraint. As prices increase still further, more resources will first be taken away from agriculture and shifted to the production of services for collective consumption; then, at even higher prices, the income generated by industry is so high that even some resources from industry can be diverted to the production of collective services. Thus, here we see a backward-bending supply curve of industrial products.

Given small increments in the prices of agricultural output, agricultural production decreases immediately. This negatively-sloped supply curve is the result of the high level of production of agricultural goods, where a small price increase results in large additional profits. Since the utility derived from profits as such is rather low, the kibbutz will react by diverting resources from agriculture (and later from industry) in favour of production of collective services, while keeping private consumption at the upper limit.[13]

A crucial role is played by the upper limit on private consumption in determining the kibbutz hypothetical short-run supply curve. In our model, a rise in prices of marketed outputs generally leads to a reduction in supply. This is a rather short-run feature. In the simulation analysis, we allowed prices to increase but did not permit an increase in the level of the upper consumption constraint, which we assumed to be set exogenously. In practice, however, this constraint will be adapted with some time lag (mostly through instructions regarding consumption levels issued by the central organs of the kibbutz federations). Thus, our anticipation is that, in face of increasing prices and fixed limits on consumption, kibbutzim will tend to decrease production of marketable goods in the short run, and then increase them in response to raised levels of consumption limits. Alternatively, on the basis of past experience, kibbutzim might short-circuit this process and thereby save the costs of continuous variations in output levels. Given an expectation that increases in prices will lead to raised consumption limits, they could respond by increasing output of marketable goods immediately. This result is illustrated in Figure 9.1.

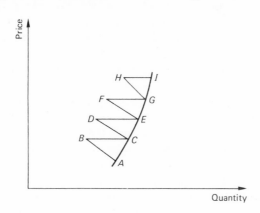

FIGURE 9.1

The movement from *A* to *B*, *C* to *D*, etc. is the hypothetical short-run supply response to increased prices of output; *B* to *C*, *D* to *E*, etc. is the response to the rise in the consumption limit coupled with the increased prices of output. The movement from *A* to *C*, *C* to *E*, etc. represents the alternative, and probably more realistic, response based on expectations.

The egalitarian constraint on private consumption also has a differential impact on the behaviour of different kibbutzim. The above analysis was relevant for a 'rich' kibbutz that is already at the upper consumption limit, or an average kibbutz that becomes 'rich' as a result of price increases. On the other hand, a 'poor' kibbutz would have a positive supply response even in the very short run. Thus, we should expect higher supply elasticities in poor kibbutzim than in rich kibbutzim.

The real difference in consumption between the rich and poor kibbutzim would, of course, be found in the collective consumption area (where the egalitarian constraints either do not operate or are much less binding than in private consumption). This model prediction may be observed in kibbutz reality.

A rise in prices of private consumption goods purchased on the market will lead first to substitution of collective consumption for the now more expensive market purchases. This is accompanied by a decrease in the production of marketed goods. However, the kibbutz very soon reaches the lower limit of private consumption and, at that point, it is forced to increase the production of industrial and agricultural goods, at the expense of the production of collective services, to pay for the more expensive private consumption goods. As the prices of private consumption goods continue to rise, this trend will be accentuated until production of collective consumption services is discontinued. (In reality, of course, there would also exist a lower limit on collective consumption services, so this point would never be reached.)

Obviously, the constraints on private consumption play a crucial role in determining the outcome of price changes. In order to obtain a quantitative, as well as qualitative, idea of the significance of these constraints, we performed the same analysis without imposing the constraints.

Comparing the initial situations with and without the consumption constraints, we find no difference in the production activity levels in the three branches. On the other hand, there is a significant difference in private consumption, which is now concentrated completely in the second period (discussed further in (d) below). Given a relatively small (10 per cent) increase in the price of industrial output, we find a somewhat less than 50 per cent rise in industrial output when private consumption is constrained; without this constraint, industrial output quadruples, at the expense of a complete elimination of production of collective consumption services.

The above results must, however, be viewed with considerable skepticism. First, given the linearity of our model, the marginal utilities of both private and collective consumption are held constant, and the elasticity of substitution between them is zero. In reality, of course, as the pattern of consumption shifts from collective to private consumption, the changing marginal rates of substitution would, most likely, prevent a complete abandonment of collective consumption. Second, the private consumption constraint within our linear model serves a function similar to the changing marginal rates of substitution in a non-linear model. Third, in order to make the linear model more realistic, we should probably impose similar constraints on collective consumption. The form these constraints would take is rather complex. It should combine the proportion between private and collective consumption in the given kibbutz with an egalitarian constraint like the one on private consumption. (This type of constraint could not be used in our model since the proportion part of the constraint cannot be put into linear form.) Fourth, the economic parameters (prices, technologies and resource constraints) favour private over collective consumption (though we should recall that the opposite is true of values of marginal utilities in our model).

Suppose now that the cost of capital replacement in the production of industrial output goes up at the same rate in both periods. The only activity change is, at first, in the level of consumption in the first period, and then in the second period as well, until both reach their lower limits. All production activities continue to be operated at their initial levels. As the price of capital in industrial production increases further, the provision of private consumption goods becomes increasingly expensive, thus leading to substitution. Giving up some private consumption permits a reduction in the production of some marketable goods, primarily the more-expensive-to-produce industrial output. That allows production of services for collective consumption within the kibbutz to rise. The kibbutz reaches an optimum situation when the production of industrial output is discontinued, and the kibbutz is thus no longer affected by price increases of the above sort. The new situation is one of minimum private consumption levels, slightly lower than initial levels of agricultural output, and much higher levels of production of services for collective consumption.

Should the cost of capital replacement in agricultural production go up, we encounter similar trends. Private consumption goes down to the lower limits, while agriculture is gradually eliminated, releasing resources for industrial production and production of collective services.

How would the average kibbutz, as modelled here, react to an increase in the cost of capital replacement in the production of services for collective consumption? When these increases are small, all three production activities will be kept at their initial levels, and the difference in cost will be borne by the first period's consumption. As capital costs increase further, the kibbutz will start diverting resources from the production of services for collective consumption to industry, and the additional profits will serve to reverse the decline in private consumption, raising it above the initial level. Thus, the reaction encountered here is one of substitution of private consumption for collective when the latter's price increases, just as the opposite occurred when the price of private consumption went up. In this case, just as in the other, industry is the 'shock absorber' of price changes; agriculture cannot serve this function because the land constraint is binding.

CHANGES IN OTHER PARAMETERS

The income per member maximising self-managed firm (as outlined in Chapter 1) responds to increases in lump sum taxes by increasing production and membership to share the increased cost among a larger number of members. The kibbutz in our model cannot increase membership, but can re-allocate resources between market and non-market activities, and between purchases of goods on the market and payment of taxes. This is precisely what the kibbutz does. When the level of the income constraint[14] is raised from zero to a positive number, this amounts to demanding from the kibbutz a fixed payment at the end of the two periods. This is equivalent to an increase in fixed costs or an imposition of lump sum taxes. As these burdens on the kibbutz continue to rise, it reacts as follows: first, the kibbutz gives up some private consumption, but as the payment burden increases it reaches the lower limit of private consumption, and must then shift resources from collective consumption services to the production of marketed goods. If the opposite occurs, i.e. subsidies are given in increasing amounts, the kibbutz will increase private consumption to its upper limit, and then receiving more and more money without having to sell industrial or agricultural goods in exchange, it will gradually discontinue these activities and concentrate on the production of services for collective consumption; thus, the result will be a lower participation on the market, accompanied by an increase in the production of non-marketables.

THE INTER-TEMPORAL EFFECT

Production in the two periods is not the same, even though the model assumes no time preference, no technological change, and no price changes *between* the two periods. The differences are: (i) the labour force is assumed to grow by 2 per cent; (ii) the upper limit on per capita private consumption is increased by 10 per cent (the total kibbutz private consumption constraint thus is raised by 12.2 per cent); (iii) a 4 per cent interest rate is assumed. Thus, the kibbutz would tend to concentrate on profit-generating activities in the first period, in order to earn the interest, and thereby have more resources available for private and collective consumption in the second period. This tendency is reinforced by the rise in the upper consumption limit in the second period.

The only example of net investment in our simulation arises when prices of agricultural output more than double. In this case, a rather complex process takes place. Resources are shifted out of the now relatively less profitable industrial branch, which is now discontinued, as well as out of the now very profitable agricultural branch (see our discussion above of the backward-bending supply curve). The very high level of profits generated by agriculture permits a shift of resources to the production of collective consumption services, but agriculture continues to require a substantial amount of capital. Since the collective consumption branch is the most capital-intensive of all branches, its demand for capital, superimposed on the continued demand for capital in agriculture, requires net investment.

As the price of agricultural output increases even more, the level of activity in agriculture can gradually be decreased, and labour and capital can be shifted to collective consumption, thus requiring less and less net investment.

One possible explanation for the almost complete absence of investment activity in our simulation experiment rests on the fact that our linear model does not permit the substitution of capital for labour, i.e. no changes are permitted in capital and labour intensity of the production process. Thus, given our fixed supply of fully-employed labour, the cost of investment is not only the capital cost itself but also the opportunity cost of the labour that must be transferred from one of the production branches to work with the additional capital. Only in exceptional cases is the need for capital stock sufficiently urgent to justify net investment.

IV AN ECONOMIC INTERPRETATION OF SOME CHANGES IN THE KIBBUTZ MOVEMENT

The kibbutz movement was an enterprise of a select few, and has never become a mass movement. This has been both its strength and its weakness. Despite its small size (as illustrated in Table 9.4), its economic, political, social and cultural, and even military roles were at times extremely important.

TABLE 9.4 *Kibbutz population as percentage of total population*

1920s[a]	1948[b]	1953[b]	1978[b]
2.5	7.9	5.0	3.2

Notes

[a] Proportion of Jewish population.
[b] Proportion of Israeli population.

The fact that the role of the kibbutz movement was, in particular prior to the formation of the state of Israel, out of proportion to its size, is due to the dedication of its members to the goals of Zionism and Socialism, and to their effectiveness in most spheres.

After the establishment of the state of Israel in 1948, the decline in relative size was due not to a net outflow of members, but to the change in the composition of immigrants to Israel, and in the conditions which prevailed in the country. Very few participants in the mass immigration of the early 1950s were attracted to the kibbutz way of life, and the situation has not greatly changed in later years. Also, the objective conditions were much less conducive towards communal living. Although economically the kibbutz movement maintains its very high relative share (contributing some 6 per cent of the national industrial output, and over 30 per cent of the agricultural output), its representation, importance and influence in political, social and curtural life are declining.

Some of the major changes in the economic structure of the kibbutz movement were: the growth of industry at the expense of agriculture, the increase of private consumption relative to collective consumption, and the increase in size (population) of the average kibbutz. In addition, a tendency to an ever-growing similarity between kibbutzim belonging to various federations is observed. We may employ the analysis of the previous section in identifying some economic factors which affect all kibbutzim equally. Other, non-economic factors are, however, no less important (see Ben-Ner, 1980).

For a long time, the kibbutzim could pursue agriculture, which was thought to be the most important occupation. Although the total land available to the kibbutzim was fixed, it was possible to absorb new members in the early years by cultivating it more intensively and by bringing more of it into cultivation. Later, the land's productive capacity was further increased through technological change, and as such possibilities were exhausted, a change in the structure of crops took place. Eventually, as more members wanted to join or establish kibbutzim, the availability of land gradually became a binding constraint.

During some periods it was almost impossible to establish new kibbutzim, so that existing kibbutzim had to absorb some of those who wanted to join a kibbutz.[15] Where new kibbutzim were established, the land available for them was limited in size and quality, and water for agricultural usage was extremely scarce. Thus, additional sources of employment in kibbutzim were needed to avoid running into sharply diminishing marginal productivities of labour. This was coupled with the increasing average age of kibbutz members (who found it difficult to perform agricultural jobs) and with growing markets for non-agricultural products. On the other hand, as the incomes of kibbutzim grew, their demand for both types of consumption (private and collective) grew also. Collective consumption, most of which is produced or processed on the kibbutz, placed an increasing direct pressure on the labour force of the kibbutz, while private consumption required an increase in output of marketable goods. Given the slowing down of the growth in the kibbutz labour force after 1948, labour as well as land became increasingly scarce. The obvious economic answer was to substitute capital for the scarce land and labour. However, the rapid rise in capital stock has led to an even greater demand for (and scarcity of) labour since capital is not fully substitutable for labour. Similarly, on the consumption side, industry and agriculture are not fully substitutable for the production of collective services. Thus, the economic logic required a shift of labour from agriculture to industry, and to a lesser extent, to collective services. This is exactly what happened (see Barkai, 1977, Table 5.4, p. 102 and Table 10.1, p. 190). The industrialisation process can be seen in Table 9.5.

TABLE 9.5 *Number of newly-established factories in kibbutzim*

Up to 1950	1951–60	1961–65	1966–70	1971–76	Total in 1976
47	39	43	49	94	272

Source: Golomb (1978, p. 19).

One way to measure the extent of labour scarcity is to determine whether the existing kibbutzim have more or less members than the optimal size kibbutz (given the kibbutz members' objective function defined in Section II above). Assuming that capital is transferable over time from branch to branch, we found that the number of members in the average kibbutz in 1965 was only between 1/3 and 1/4 of the optimal number of members.

The very serious shortage of labour could not be ignored. Since the kibbutzim were not able to attract a sufficient number of new members, the only avenue open to them to increase the supply of labour was to turn to hired labour. Despite the strong ideological opposition to this practice, most kibbutzim did employ many hired workers. The response differed significantly across federations (see Table 9.6). The more socialist KA employs far less hired workers than IKK. Apparently, this entails a choice of more capital-intensive production processes, and thus smaller size of factories in terms of workers in KA.[16]

TABLE 9.6 *Hired workers in kibbutz factories*

Federation	Hired workers 1971 (%)	Average no. of workers 1971	Investment per worker in years of 1961–71 ('000 current IL)
IKK	76	77	19.4
KM	35	40	24.5
KA	21	33	32.8

Source: Zamir (1976, p. 54).

In all federations a small gradual shift from collective consumption to private consumption has taken place. There are many reasons for that transition which are beyond the scope of this paper.[17] However, one impetus for such a transition may be identified in the 'average' kibbutz economic structure. As shown in Section III, a gradual increase in prices of outputs produced by the kibbutz (as well as of consumption goods purchased by the kibbutz on the market) leads the kibbutz away from the production and processing of collective consumption services and goods in favour of private ones. The Israeli economy experienced such a price level increase for many years, and its severity has increased during the past few years. In the long run, this may imply that the kibbutz consumption patterns will gradually shift away from collective consumption in favour of private consumption.[18]

V CONCLUDING COMMENTS

We have discussed in this chapter a few of the important aspects of a kibbutz economic model, the kibbutz economy, and selected aspects of its history. In a nutshell, the major conclusions that can be drawn about these topics are as below.

(i) A strong ideological commitment to socialism and nationalism, financial support by Zionist organisations, and severe economic conditions in Palestine, all combined to bring about the birth of the kibbutz as a self-managed and communal organisation. The development of the kibbutz federations and help from the state and the Jewish Agency have enabled the kibbutz movement to flourish economically despite an increasingly unfavourable economic and social environment in Israel. On the other hand, these conditions have kept the kibbutz as a marginal institution in Israel and have brought about some changes in the extent of communalism in the kibbutz.

(ii) The kibbutz cannot be analysed in isolation from the rest of the economy and society. *A fortiori*, the individual kibbutz cannot be treated independently of other kibbutzim and its federation. We have seen the crucial role played by the egalitarian constraint on the simulated economic behaviour of a typical kibbutz. This point can be summarised as follows: the price elasticity of supply of a relatively 'poor' kibbutz will be higher than that of its 'richer' counterpart for whom the upper constraint is binding. On the other hand, the backward–bending supply curve for the 'richer' kibbutzim will tend to disappear and the response to price increases will become positive as consumption constraints are adapted by the federation in response to the increasing incomes resulting from higher prices.

The response of the kibbutz to changes in subsidies or taxes resembles that of the 'net-income per member maximising' self-managed enterprise, since increasing subsidies will lead to reductions in marketed output. However, the kibbutz, combining consumption with production, will not reduce the total level of effort but will shift resources from the production of marketed goods to internally produced and consumed collective consumption goods.

(iii) The general trend in the kibbutz movement of growing similarities between the federations has been supported by the simulation analysis. Two federations have recently merged (December 1979), and attempts are being made to bring in the third largest federation (KA), which still feels that the differences warrant organisational separation. We argued that the economic structure of the kibbutz, as exhibited in 1965, may lead, in the wake of across-the-board inflation, to an increased share of private consumption in the consumption basket, thus diminishing the degree of communality of the kibbutz.

The kibbutz, after seven decades of existence, has demonstrated that an economic organisation based on self-management, extensive communal sharing of work and consumption, completely egalitarian income distribution, and a lack of internal pricing for resource allocation, is not only viable, but is a very successful economic organisation. Given the crucial role of ideology in the economic functioning of the kibbutz and very special historical circumstances under which the kibbutz developed, it is certainly not a model for all seasons or all countries. While the kibbutz is undergoing some changes, it promises to continue in its essential characteristics and provide a real life case study of a communal self-managed organisation for many years to come.

APPENDIX TO CHAPTER 9

The model described in Section II is fully specified below: A_1, A_2 and A_3 are the activity levels in industry and agriculture and in the production of collective consumption services and goods respectively.

$$A_1 = (a_{11}a_{21}a_{31}b_{11}b_{21}b_{31})$$
$$A_2 = (a_{12}a_{22}a_{32}b_{12}b_{22}b_{32})$$
$$A_3 = (a_{13}a_{23}a_{33}b_{13}b_{23}b_{33})$$

Maximise

$$\begin{aligned}
W = {} & u_1 h_3 b_{33} + u'_1 h'_3 b_{33} + u_2 x + u'_2 x \\
& + u_3(h_1 p_1 b_{11} + h_2 p_2 b_{22} - h_1 r_1 a_{21} - h_2 r_2 a_{22}) \\
& + u'_3(h'_1 p'_1 b_{11} + h'_2 p'_2 b_{22} - h'_1 r'_1 a_{21} - h'_2 r'_2 a_{22}) \\
& + u_4 h_1 a_{11} + u'_4 h'_1 a_{11} + u_5 h_2 a_{12} + u'_5 h'_2 a_{12} \\
& + u_6 h_3 a_{13} + u'_6 h'_3 a_{13}
\end{aligned}$$

Subject to

(1) $h_1 a_{11} + h_2 a_{12} + h_3 a_{13} \leqslant L_o$

(2) $h'_1 a_{11} + h'_2 a_{12} + h'_3 a_{13} \leqslant L_o p$

(3) $h_1 a_{21} + h_2 a_{22} + h_3 a_{23} \leqslant K_o$

(4) $h'_1 a_{21} + h'_2 a_{22} + h'_3 a_{23} - \dfrac{Ie}{s'} \leqslant K_o$

(5) $h_1 a_{31} + h_2 a_{32} + h_3 a_{33} \leqslant \overline{T}$

(6) $h'_1 a_{31} + h'_2 a_{32} + h'_3 a_{33} \leqslant \overline{T}$

(7) $h_1 p_1 b_{11} + h_2 p_2 b_{22} - h_1^s r_1 a_{21} - h_2^s r_2 a_{22} - h_3^s r_3 a_{23} - gx$
$- Ie - h'_1 p'_1 b_{11} + h'_2 p'_2 b_{22} - h_1^{'s'} r'_1 a_{21} - h_2^{'s'} r'_2 a_{22}$
$- h_3^{'s'} r'_3 a_{23} - x'g' \geqslant 0$

(8) $\dfrac{x}{A_0} \geqslant (1-a)M$

(9) $\dfrac{x}{A_0} \leqslant (1+a)M$

(10) $\dfrac{x'}{A_0 p} \geqslant (1-a)M'$

(11) $\dfrac{x'}{A_0 p} \leqslant (1+a)M'$

and $h_1, h'_1, h_2, h'_2, h_3, h'_3, x, x', I \geqslant 0$.

DEFINITIONS OF VARIABLES AND PARAMETERS

a_{ij}: input i into activity j, when A_j is operated at level 1 (i.e. $h_j = 1$), where $i = 1$ represents labour (measured in man-years per period), $i = 1$ – capital (measured in Israeli Lira (IL) and $i = 3$ – land (in dunams).

b_{kj}: output of type k in activity j, when A_j is operated at level 1. Since all activities (branches) produce one type of product, $b_{kj} = 0$ if $k \neq j$, and equals 1 (through standardisation) if $k = j$. $j = 1$ represents the industrial production; $j = 2$ agricultural production; $j = 3$ production of services and goods for collective consumption. The output of A_1 and A_2 is sold on the market, while the output of A_3 is consumed internally on the kibbutz.

x: private consumption goods purchased on the market, measured in IL

I: net investment decided upon by the kibbutz (in IL), $I \geqslant 0$

p_1: price index of industrial output

p_2: price index of agricultural output

g: price index of x

s: purchase price of capital in period 1

s': purchase price index of capital in period 2

r_1: depreciation rate of capital $i = 1, 2, 3$ means capital in industry, agriculture and collective consumption, respectively

e: 1 + market rate of interest for kibbutz borrowing and lending

u_i: represents the marginal utilities of identical individual members

A_0: kibbutz population

L_0: labour force of the kibbutz (= membership) in the initial period (1) (in man-years)

k_0: capital stock in period 1 (in IL)

$\overline{T}$: available land (in dunams)

M: average per capita private consumption in the kibbutz movement in period 1

a: percentage of M which indicates the limits set on private per capita consumption in individual kibbutzim

p: 1 + natural rate of growth of labour force and population plus constant net inflow or outflow

h_i: $i = 1, 2, 3$, activity levels for A_1, A_2, A_3 respectively

h_i, p, g, etc. are first period values, while h'_1, p'_1, g'_1, etc. are second period values.

All decisions for both are made at the beginning of period 1, and we assume perfect knowledge of all present and future parameters.

From the data in Table 9.1. We computed the following technological coefficients and constraints for the average kibbutz:

$a_{11} = 0.1572$, $a_{21} = 1.3442$, $a_{31} = 0$

$a_{12} = 0.1089$, $a_{22} = 2.5414$, $a_{32} = 0.0091$,

$a_{13} = 0.2818$, $a_{23} = 4.9495$, $a_{33} = 0$,

$L_o = 180$, $K_o = 3374.59$, $\overline{T} = 6.3423$, $= 473.5(A_0 = 386)$.

As noted already, we have chosen a to be 25 per cent.

$p = 1.02$: a frequent growth rate for kibbutzim.

$e = 1.04$: although the interest rate fluctuated widely, 4 per cent seemed a reasonable estimate for the 1960s.

$r_1 = r'_1 = 0.1$, $r_2 = r'_2 = 0.15$, $r_3 = 0.07$: the depreciation rates of capital were chosen according to our estimate of commonly accepted levels of replacement costs according to number of years of useful life of each type of capital in industry, agriculture and production of services for collective consumption.

All price indexes were fixed at 1 for both periods. In this model, period 2 refers to one year after period 1.

The above data were sufficient for the calculation (utilising a modified FMPS programming package to solve the linear programming model) of the optimal level of the various activities and utilisation levels of resources.

NOTES

1. This chapter is a condensed version of a paper entitled 'On the economics of communalism and self-management: the Israeli kibbutz' presented at the Walton Symposium, Glasgow, June 1979. The authors have benefited from comments by the participants in the symposium, and from discussions with participants at the Second Bosphorus Workshop on Industrial Democracy in Istanbul, and from conversations with Professor Haim Barkai.
2. It is impossible to exaggerate the impact of Russian socialism on the Zionist Labour movement, not only on the ideological level but above all on its very attitude towards politics. The Jewish socialists inherited from their Russian

mentors unending doctrinal squabbles, as well as the axiomatic belief that it was the first commandment for any Socialist worth his salt to arrange his own life in accordance with his beliefs. The unity of theory and action were not a matter open to debate. From the Populists they took over the conviction that manual labour was a cure for almost all ills; the second aliya was in some ways a repeat performance of the going-to-the-people as practised by the Narodniks.' (Laquer, 1972, pp. 270–1).

3. This recognised and supported the right of Jews to the establishment of a homeland of their own in Palestine. As things developed later, it turned out to be only verbal, not practical support.

4. The *moshav* is an agricultural settlement based on private production and consumption but with co-operative marketing and funding. Similar to the Russian *kolhoz* is the *moshav shitufi*, which combines collective production and equal monetary reward with private consumption.

5. Although the term kibbutz was not applied until a later date we shall adopt it henceforth.

6. It is probable that most Israelis can identify kibbutzim in different federations only on the basis of the national political stances they adopt.

7. See Note 4 above.

8. To get a feeling of the acuteness of the sentiments aroused by the political debates and disputes, it is worth mentioning that, on the eve of the split, kibbutzim were divided and many families were also split. Today, as a reminder of the early 1950s disputes, there are some kibbutzim bearing the same name, with a qualifier noting the new federation affiliation.

9. From the mid-1920s when the kibbutz federations were first formed, until the present time, there has been a common understanding that no kibbutz should become 'rich' or be allowed to be too 'poor'. Although there exists some very limited inequality in per capita disposable income (Gini Index in the 1950s and 1960s was 0.2 or less), the inequality in per capita consumption was even smaller (Gini Index of only about 0.1) according to Barkai (1977).

10. There is an infinite number of sets of marginal utilities, but all are in a restricted range spanned as follows:

$$\lambda' A = MU$$

where λ is a non-negative rotating vector (that can be thought of as a vector of shadow prices of the constraints in the model), A is the matrix formed by the coefficients of the decision variables in the constraints, and MU is the vector of marginal utilities of the arguments in the objective function. In our problem, λ is 1×11, A is 11×9 and MU is 1×9. The actual number of arguments in our objective function is larger than 9, thus causing the identification problem referred to below (see Note 11).

11. It is impossible to identify the marginal utility both of collective consumption and of labour in the production of collective consumption; only their sum is identifiable. Note that because of the linearity of the objective function, some equalities obtained in general models do not obtain here. The marginal utilities in a linear model express 'intensity' of preferences.

12. Since the kibbutz may be considered a price taker, i.e. it faces parametric prices, the structure of our model does not differentiate between changes in

industrial and agricultural prices and changes in physical productivity in these branches, i.e. shifts in the isoquants will give the same results as changes in output prices.

13. What is the source of these predominantly backward sloping supply curves? They arise from both the model specification and from the actual data for our representative kibbutz. It is the difference in the technological coefficients and actual levels of output in industry and agriculture that explains the surprising fact that a relatively small increase in the price of industrial products results in increased output of industrial goods while the same type of price increase in agricultural products results in a decrease in agricultural output. A 10 per cent increase in agricultural prices will raise income (profits) by almost IL 140 000 for the *two periods combined*. The utility gained from this rise in profits is 14 units (the marginal utility of profits is 0.1). An increase of IL 123 will raise private consumption to the upper limit, and the remaining IL 17 will be unused. Thus, the total additional utility of private consumption plus profits is $123 + 14 = 137$. On the other hand, if the kibbutz responds to the 10 per cent price increase in agricultural products by reducing slightly the output of these products, it can still reach the upper consumption limit and release labour and capital to the collective service sector. Since agriculture is very labour and capital intensive (compared to industry), the slight reduction in output will release sufficient resources to increase collective services, such as to raise total utility by more than 137. (This is true even though the utility of working in agriculture is greater than in collective services.)

On the other hand, a 10 per cent increase in the price of industrial products will increase total income by only IL 36, or not nearly enough to reach the upper consumption limit. Therefore, the kibbutz will shift resources from agriculture and collective services to the now more profitable industrial sector. When the price level of industrial products rises sufficiently for the kibbutz to hit the upper consumption limit, then it will act as it did in the case of agriculture and the supply curve will bend backward.

14. Constraint (7) in the appendix.

15. The kibbutzim belonging to KM absorbed the majority of these new members. These kibbutzim were also the first to industrialise and were, therefore, the ones best able to use this new labour effectively.

16. It was argued above that KA prefers more collective consumption than does IKK (with KM in between), and the branch producing collective consumption services is the most capital intensive. Thus, it was no surprise to find that the shadow price of capital is higher in KA and the shadow price of labour lower than in IKK. This amounts to a smaller pressure for hiring labour, and to a higher capital–labour ratio for total kibbutz production. As shown in Barkai (1977, Table 13.6, p. 260), the historical development follows this pattern.

17. Ben-Ner (1980) focuses on that point through an econometric analysis of changes of preferences in the kibbutz movement over a ten-year period.

18. A sharp shift of consumption patterns in favour of private consumption might imply the gradual disappearance of some kibbutzim, to be replaced by moshavim shitufiim (see Note 4 above).

10 West German Co-determination[1]

Jan Svejnar

The German co-determination system constitutes one of the most important forms of employee participation in management. While falling short of a fully self-managed system, co-determination, as it is currently practised in the Federal Republic of Germany, is frequently heralded as the most advanced system of employee control in the western world.

Over the last thirty years, co-determination has been the subject of substantial publicity, controversy and careful reviews by countries interested in its possible transfer to their own environments.[2] Yet surprisingly little is known about the 'economics' of co-determination and, in particular, about the impact of co-determination on relevant economic variables. This ignorance stems primarily from the lack of theoretical work which would lead to testable empirical predictions. The paucity of economic theory, in turn, derives primarily from the difficulty that one encounters in formulating a plausible objective function for representative participatory firm.

In this study we (i) briefly survey the most important institutional features of the German co-determination system, (ii) present a theoretical model which is consistent with these features and leads to testable predictions, and (iii) report on some of the main empirical findings to date. Readers who are interested in a more technical treatment of the latter two subjects should consult two other studies performed by the author (Svejnar 1977, 1979).

I BACKGROUND

Employee participation has a relatively long tradition in Germany. Political demands for co-determination go back to the

214

March Revolution of 1848 and the first participatory institutions appeared at the start of this century[3].

The decisive step toward the introduction of employee participation occurred in December 1916, when the Auxiliary Service Law provided for the establishment of workers' and employees' councils in all industrial enterprises with more than fifty employees. The law of 1916 was passed primarily to maintain industrial peace during the war efforts. Consequently, the councils acted, by and large, as grievance committees with the right to appeal to conciliation boards which were created under the same law.

In the revolutionary atmosphere of 1918, workers' and soldiers' councils sprang up spontaneously in many enterprises and became a major point of contention in the German labour movement. The Works Council Law of February 1920 legalised the works councils but left them with functions in only two limited areas: bargaining and management. The bargaining role consisted of plant-wide negotiations about wages and working conditions within the overall framework of the collective agreement obtained by the trade unions. The managerial function of the works council lay in its right to fill two seats on the company supervisory board with employee delegates. In practice, the role of councils was very circumscribed and after 1923 the pendulum swung decisively in favour of the employers. With the establishment of the Hitler regime, the councils were superseded by appointed work trustees and trade unions, and employer associations were replaced by a government-operated Labour Front.

While the movement for co-determination reached only limited objectives during the Weimar Republic, the worker desire for participation manifested itself immediately after the Nazi defeat as works councils appeared spontaneously in many plants. At the same time, the leaders of the re-emerging, new and unified trade union movement adopted the concept of industrial democracy as a major goal. As a consequence of the relatively extensive legislative regulation of the German industrial relations system, the major subsequent developments with respect to co-determination took place through the legislative process.

The allied occupation authorities legalised the works councils by the Control Council Law No. 22 of April 1946, but granted the councils only limited advisory functions. While individual German states such as Hesse and Wurttemberg-Baden tried to give the works councils greater discriminating powers, these attempts were suspended by the allied government until the German Federal Constitution decided the issues.

The basic structure of the co-determination system was established by the Co-determination Law of May 1951 and the Works Constitution Law of October 1952.[4] To realise the implications of the laws it is necessary to understand the German corporate structure. Unlike the single board Anglo–American system, the German system is based on two boards – the Board of Directors (Aufsichtsrate) and the Board of Management (Vorstand). The Board of Directors usually meets about four or five times a year, appoints and discharges the members of the Management Board, scrutinises the company records, and makes or approves major policy decisions with respect to issues such as mergers and take-overs. The Board of Directors is also responsible for overall manpower planning and (dis)approves the industry-wide labour negotiations between the appropriate trade union and employers' federation. The Management Board formulates the short-term policy and carries out the daily business of the company. It has individual directors in charge of major departments such as commercial, technical and labour affairs.

The law of May 1951 established the so-called 'parity co-determination' in the iron–steel and coal-mining industries. It provided for equal representation of shareholders and workers on the Board of Directors of their companies. All Boards have an odd number of members, as the shareholder and worker representatives jointly co-opt a neutral member to the Board. The neutral member, often an academic or the mayor of the town, is expected to represent the public interest and casts the decisive vote in the case of an impasse between the shareholder and worker representatives. The Co-determination Law of 1951 also provided for employee representation on the Management Boards of iron–steel and coal-mining companies. The labour director on the Management Board cannot be appointed or dismissed without approval of the employee representatives to the Board of Directors. As a result, the labour directors in these two industries are invariably a pro-labour force on the Management Boards. As will be seen later this is an important aspect of the system because the labour directors are in charge of companies' employment and compensation policy.

Except for minor changes, these forms of co-determination

survived virtually unchanged until 1976 when, after twenty-five years of intense negotiations, the Co-determination Act of May 1976 was passed. The new law gave employees parity representation with shareholders on the Board of Directors in all joint stock and limited liability companies with more than 2000 employees. It was implemented by June 1978 and affected between six and seven million workers in 500–600 major companies (about 70 per cent of the German industry)[5]. While the 1976 law also provided for the special position of a labour director on the Management Board, it differed in three important aspects from its 1951 predecessor for iron – steel and coal mining. First the employee and the shareholder representatives to the Board of Directors do not co-opt a neutral member but rather elect a chairman from their ranks by a two-thirds majority vote. If this proves impossible to achieve, the shareholder representatives elect the chairman, and employee representatives elect his deputy. This mechanism is crucial because the chairman casts the decisive vote in the case of a deadlock on the Board. Second, the members of the Board of Directors are supposed to elect the Management Board directors with a two-thirds majority vote. In case of an impasse, however, the chairman has a casting vote. The law therefore permits the appointment of labour directors against the wishes of the employee representatives on the Board of Directors. Finally, the employee representatives to the Board of Directors must represent all employees (not just the union members) and must include at least one senior executive.

As can be expected, the German unions who fought for the extension of the 1951 Co-determination Law into the remaining industries, are critical of the new law. It gives the shareholder representatives the potential for controlling the Board of Directors and the elections of all the directors to the Management Board. Moreover, the unions fear that the senior executive among the employee representatives will tend to vote with the shareholder representatives and hence give the shareholders a *de facto* majority on the Board of Directors. At the same time, the German employers' and shareholders' associations feel that the 1976 legislation went too far in unduly increasing the power of the unions, violating the basic property rights and undermining the democratic system. The law that was designed over the long run as a major compromise has thus been attacked by all parties and seems to have satisfied none. A longer-term experience is clearly needed to ascertain its real effects.

In addition to the developments at the board levels, the early post-war initiatives with respect to the works councils also led to the establishment of important institutions. The 1952 Works Constitution Act (subsequently replaced by a more comprehensive Works Constitution Act of 1972) provided for the establishment of a works council in every plant in private industry and commerce employing more than five persons. While the size and the composition of the council depends on the number of employees, the legislation currently applies to more than 30 000 companies and involves about 200 000 works councillors.[6] The councillors are elected in a secret ballot by all employees in the firm. Neither the electors nor the candidates need belong to a trade union. In practice, however, most councillors are union members. For instance, while about 45 per cent of German workers are unionised, 80 per cent of the councillors elected in the 1978 works council elections were members of an industrial union. About 90 per cent of the labour force participated in these elections.[7] The role of unions in the composition and operation of the works councils is indirect but clearly substantial. The unions pride themselves on this achievement and, together with the overall degree of worker unionisation, they consider the unionisation of the works councillors the most important source of their bargaining strength.

The German works councils bargain at the plant level about issues not covered in the industry, regional, or national level agreements and they also have co-determination (equal say with management) rights in several important areas of management. The most important of these are: piece rates and wage structure, working hours, employment policies, job evaluation, training and accident prevention. The works councils thus clearly have the greatest power in the area of industrial relations where they interact with the labour (personnel) director at the Management Board. In the case of the iron–steel and coal-mining industries, the labour director is a pro-labour force and the labour affairs of the enterprise are hence left almost exclusively in the hands of labour representatives. However, in the other industries the works councils interact with managers whose positions are more adversarial, and the co-determination process is hence more complex. Neither party can resort to industrial actions,[8] however and unresolved cases are referred to compulsory arbitration or, finally, to labour courts.

As the preceding discussion demonstrates, the institutional system of German co-determination is quite elaborate. Several other western European countries[9] have by now established similar, though perhaps not as far-reaching, systems of employee participation. In the following section, we present a general theoretical model of a participatory firm. The model treats explicitly the concept of bargaining power (degree of control) of the various participants and hence applies to all firms of co-determination ranging from no employee control to full self-management.

II THEORY

The major problem encountered in modelling the behaviour of a participatory firm lies in the formulation of a realistic objective function for it. Existing literature often assumes that capitalist firms maximise profits, π, while labour-managed enterprises maximise income per worker, y. Since other goals have also been suggested, a more general approach takes the maximand to reflect the utility function of those controlling the firm. Accordingly, it may be argued that the capitalist firm maximises the utility of its owner-manager, U_M, while the labour-managed firm maximises labour's utility, U_L. These utility functions may (but need not) reflect profit maximisation, respectively. A crucial task in empirical research therefore consists of using institutional information to identify the objective functions, U_M and U_L. The economics of co-determination faces one additional problem, namely, how to use the information about the objectives of the various parties which co-determine the behaviour of the firm to construct an objective function of such a firm.

As the German institutional framework indicates, there are many parties that influence the behaviour of a participatory firm. The most obvious are the blue and white collar workers, the trade unions, the shareholders, the managers and the government. Moreover, depending on the size of the firm, the nature of its product and the historical time period, the relative influence of the various parties differs. A successful theoretical framework must therefore take into account the diversity of participants and the variability in their bargaining power (degree of influence or control over the firms).

For the sake of exposition we shall presently describe a theoretical model in which two parties, labour (L) and management (M), co-determine the behaviour of the firm. The model is admittedly a rough approximation of the real world situation but can be easily extended to an *n*-party framework.[10] We take the utility functions of the two parties, U_L and U_M, to be of the von Neumann–Morgenstern type.[11] If we measure power (control) on the scale from zero to one, we may denote the power of labour γ and the power of management $1 - \gamma$.[12] Hence, in a purely capitalist firm where workers have no control over the decision-making process, $\gamma = 0$ and $1 - \gamma = 1$. Conversely, in a purely labour-managed firm, $\gamma = 1$ and $1 - \gamma = 0$. In general, a participatory firm can be characterised by $0 \leqslant \gamma \leqslant 1$. This characterisation is important and, before proceeding, the reader should realise the restrictive nature of traditional analysis which assumes that either $\gamma = 0$ or $\gamma = 1$. Formal participation aside, in most capitalist firms workers exercise some influence, either directly or through trade unions, and hence $\gamma > 0$. Institutional studies of labour-managed firms indicate that workers usually share control with other parties (e.g. government, credit institutions and managers), which implies that empirically-observed cases of labour management are characterised by $\gamma < 1$. As will become clear later, analytical inaccuracies stemming from the restrictions $\gamma = 0$ or $\gamma = 1$ are greater, the more different are the objective functions of the parties (U_L and U_M) and the farther the true γ is from the imposed constraint.

The behaviour of a participatory firm is determined jointly by the relevant parties within a system which allows them to interact and exchange information. The decision-making process can thus be formally described as one of strategic interaction in a co-operative framework. The parties consider all possible outcomes and jointly select one which is acceptable to both of them. Since both parties can impede the operation of the firm by resorting to actions such as strikes or lock-outs, the observed outcome is acceptable to the parties in that they do not resort to any of these actions. If we assume that the parties in fact select an outcome which is Pareto-efficient and reflects their relative bargaining power, $\gamma/1 - \gamma$, then it can be shown that the behaviour of the firm can be characterised by the objective function:

$$V = U_L^\gamma \cdot U_M^{(1-\gamma)} \tag{1}$$

The two parties act as if they maximise the weighted product of their utility function, the exponential weights being their relative powers. When $\gamma = 0$ and labour has no influence, the objective function becomes $V = U_{M^\circ}$. The firm then maximises the utility function of managers. When $\gamma = 1$, the firm is labour-managed and maximises the utility function of labour, $V = U_L$. In general, the objective function in equation (1) accounts for all possible cases as $0 \leqslant \gamma \leqslant 1$.

A geometric representation of the co-determination process appears in Figure 10.1. For each party the origin constitutes the threat point – the utility level below which the two parties would not participate in the co-determination process. The threat point utility level of a party is often taken to be the utility of the best alternative available to the given party. Since the von Neumann–Morgenstern utility functions are determined only up to a linear transformation, we conveniently set the threat point utility levels equal to zero. Neither party can be pushed below the origin and the outcome that characterises the behaviour of a participatory firm therefore has to lie in the positive quadrant. Given the technological and market constraints faced by the firm,

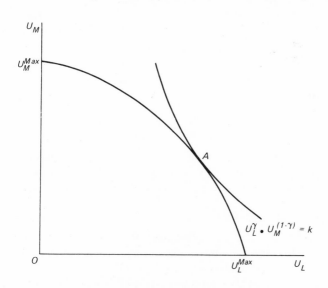

FIGURE 10.1

the set of possible outcomes is limited. In Figure 10.1 we have depicted it as the convex and compact set O, $U_L^{\max}$, $U_M^{\max}$. If, as we assume, the parties select a Pareto-efficient outcome, then the set of relevant outcomes is reduced to the utility frontier $U_L^{\max}$, $U_M^{\max}$. What remains to be shown is how the parties select a point on the frontier.

When labour has total control, we should like the theory to predict the outcome to be $U_L^{\max}$—the firm maximises labour's utility function. Similarly, when labour has no control at all, the outcome ought to be $U_M^{\max}$. When both parties share power, the solution should lie on the frontier between $U_L^{\max}$ and $U_M^{\max}$ and it should reflect the two parties' utilities in proportion to their bargaining powers. The objective function $V = U_L^{\gamma} \cdot U_M^{(1-\gamma)}$ satisfies these conditions. Its contour line, $U_L^{\gamma} \cdot U_M^{(1-\gamma)} = k$, is drawn in Figure 10.1. As can be seen, it has a unique point of tangency, A, with the utility function. This point of tangency corresponds to an outcome of the co-determination process. Its location varies with γ. As γ approaches unity, the location of A approaches $U_L^{\max}$ and the behaviour of the participatory firm increasingly reflects the preferences of workers. A decrease in γ shifts point A to a new location on the frontier, closer to U_M^{Max}. The reader can verify that for $\gamma = 1$ ($\gamma = 0$) the outcome is U_L^{Max} (U_M^{Max}).

Having established the form of the firm's objective function in terms of the utility functions of the parties, it is possible to make equation (1) operational by specifying U_L and U_M. Suppose the workers' objective is to maximise their wage bill over and above the wage bill obtainable in the best alternative (threat point) employment. The utility function of labour can then be specified as:

$$U_L = (w - w^a)L \tag{2}$$

where w is the negotiated wage, w^a is the best alternative wage that a worker can obtain with certainty, and L is the number of workers employed at w. If the management maximises profit then

$$U_M = pQ - wL - rK - mM - \pi_o, \tag{3}$$

where p is the product price, Q is the volume of output, r is the cost of capital, K is the amount of capital used, m is the price of input M, and π_o is fixed cost.

Equation (1) can then be rewritten with the aid of equations (2) and (3) as:

$$V = ((w - w^a)L)^\gamma \cdot (pQ - wL - rK - mM - \pi_0)^{(1 - \gamma)}. \qquad (4)$$

If the parties act as if they maximize equation (4) within the constraints of a standard production technology $Q = Q(L, K, M)$, then the following expressions hold:

$$U^*_L = \gamma \pi, \qquad (5)$$

$$U^*_M = (1 - \gamma)\pi, \qquad (6)$$

$$w = w^a + \gamma \frac{\hat{\pi}}{L^*}, \qquad (7)$$

where optimal values are marked by stars and $\hat{\pi} = pQ - w^a L^*$ $rk^* - mM - \pi_o$ is the net profit of the firm, calculated on the basis of the best alternative wage, w^a. Equations (5) and (6) confirm that the parties will divide net profit in proportion to their bargaining powers, $\gamma/(1 - \gamma)$. The negotiated wage, given by equation (7), will be equal to the best alternative wage plus a share, γ, of the net profit per worker. Rearranging equation (7) yields the increment to the wage bill that workers obtain: $(w - w^a)L^* = \gamma \hat{\pi}$. This result is also evident from equations (2) and (5). Notice that when $\gamma = 1$, the labour-managed firm follows workers' perferences and net profits are distributed totally to the labour force. When $\gamma = 0$, the workers are paid w^a and net profits are appropriated fully by the management. Between these extreme cases lies a full spectrum of participatory firms. Since equation (7) lends itself to econometric estimation it is of interest to explore the effects of the various German co-determination laws on the degree of labour's bargaining power (control), γ.

III EMPIRICAL FINDINGS

Equations (5) and (7) imply that the introduction of co-determination increased labour's power (control), thus implying that we should observe corresponding increase in γ from what it was prior to co-determination.

Using two different approaches and data sets we have tested the effects of the 1951 Co-determination Law and the 1952 Works Constitution Law within the framework of equation (7).[13] Since available data are limited and the immediate post-war years are rather abnormal, the results should be interpreted with caution.

At the same time, these results are as good as we can hope for and provide us with interesting information. The 1952 law appears to have had no noticeable effect on the power and wages of workers in the manufacturing industries. Our findings thus suggest that the minority co-determination institutions set up by the 1952 law were not sufficient to increase the degree of control and wages of the workers affected by this law. The effects of the 1951 Co-determination Law were tested with two data sets in two related frameworks. The resulting estimates suggest that parity co-determination increased wages by 5–7 per cent in iron–steel but did not significantly affect them in coal mining. The results thus indicate that the establishment of a given institutional structure does not necessarily lead to a uniform behavioural outcome. The 1951 law generated identical institutions of co-determination in both iron–steel and coal mining. Yet the effect on wages, holding constant other relevant variables such as output, employment, unemployment, inflation and unionisation, is significantly different between the two industries. This is an important finding because in debates and policy research on German Co-determination and its applicability to other environments, it is often presumed that a given set of institutions gives rise automatically to specific outcomes. Our estimates clearly contradict this notion. A reasonable generalisation seems to be that minority co-determination probably does not have a noticeable effect on labour's power, while parity co-determination may, depending on various circumstances.

A closer examination of the institutional research on the subject tends to support our empirical results. The Biedenkopf Committee,[14] for instance, reported in 1970 that worker representatives on the boards seem to have considerable influence but that this depends on the issues considered, the degree of representation and the type of establishment.

In view of these findings it is clear that more analytical research is needed in order to further our knowledge and understanding in this area. Co-determination is recognised to be an important institutional system with a great appeal in the western world. At the same time, the incomplete understanding of the co-determination process, and its effects so far, limits the potential for its careful evaluation.

NOTES

1. This chapter is a revised version of 'The effect of co-determination on wages', presented at the Walton Symposium, Glasgow, June 1979.
2. For an investigation by a British Royal Commission see Bullock (1977).
3. For a discussion of the historical developments see Blumenthal (1956), Sturmthal (1964), Fürstenberg (1969, 1977) and Almanasreh (1977).
4. Vollmer (1979) presents the most up-to-date description and discussion of the co-determination system.
5. See Vollmer (1979, p. 21).
6. Ibid., p. 10.
7. Ibid., p. 11.
8. The right to strike is reserved to trade unions.
9. Among these are Austria, Denmark, Luxembourg, the Netherlands, Norway and Sweden.
10. See Svejnar (1977).
11. A von Neumann–Morgenstern utility function is determined only up to a linear transformation. This means that if U is such a function so is $U' = aU + b$, provided $a > 0$.
12. Since the scale is irrelevant, this $(0,1)$ normalisation does not affect the model.
13. These results are reported more fully in Svejnar (1977, 1979).
14. The committee was appointed by Willy Brandt to investigate the functioning of the co-determination system. The committee was representative of divergent interests and carried out one of the most thorough institutional studies of the system.

Part III

Overview

Introduction

The two chapters in Part III present, in their different ways, a more normative approach to the labour-managed firm. They are written by two of the highest authorities in the field, whose competence to discuss the subject at this general level is based on their proven competence at the more specific technical level.

Jaroslav Vanek has sought, in a number of papers (see Chapters 1 and 3), to explain the failure of many traditional producers' co-operatives in terms of the worker-owners extracting rents which are due to capital. It is, therefore, not surprising that in Chapter 11, where he presents a framework by which self-management might be introduced in an industrialised western economy, a crucial role is played by a 'fair value' of assets on which a rate of return should be paid to society. This framework is then evaluated against some fourteen criteria. Thereafter, the proposed system's ability to handle questions of investment, inflation, depreciation and decentralisation is examined in detail.

Branko Horvat is an economist with a wide experience of Yugoslavia's self-managed society. In Chapter 12, he presents the view that an economy of self-managed enterprises will satisfy the needs of man better than any other form of society. The argument is based on an adaptation of Abraham Maslow's hierarchy of needs. He argues, further, that the introduction of self-management in capitalist societies will bring about the transition to socialism. The second half of this chapter presents a discussion of the viability of producers' co-operatives as a means of introducing self-management. This part of the chapter is, to some extent, a reflection on the evidence presented in Part II, but it should not be seen as an appraisal of the work presented there. Horvat argues that if appropriate consideration is given to a number of problems which have beset traditional producers' co-operatives (and which are discussed at greater length in a number of chapters in Part II), they can be a viable alternative to capitalist and state capitalist enterprises.

11 A System for Worker Participation and Self-Management in Western Industrialised Economies[1]

Jaroslav Vanek

In many advanced western economies, private and public industries have been in a considerable crisis in recent years. Without any doubt, one of the principal causes for this, if not *the* dominant one, is the archaic top-down governance of these industries, matched by the countervailing power of the labour unions. This writer is convinced, after many years of study, that full self-management and democracy in the place of work is the only viable and lasting solution of the problem; however, substantiation of that conviction is not my objective here. Rather, it is the following: whether I am right or not, those who may have to face and answer the question whether or not to introduce self-management, cannot do so without having a precise conception of what a transition to self-management would involve, that is, without having a concrete project, with some degree of operational detail. The purpose of this paper is to provide one such concrete project which I consider 'optimal' in that it fulfils optimally certain objective economic, institutional and technical requirements emerging from the reality of western economies.

Two qualifications should be stressed at the outset. Firstly, this proposal can in no way be considered final or definitive. On principles of participation according to involvement, others ought to be participating in its design.

Secondly, I emphasise here the economic problems of implementation of self-management from the point of view of the enterprise and structural relations among enterprises. Problems of internal governance of firms and their institutional interdependence and co-ordination including national planning or supporting structures are not discussed here. They must of course also be defined, but these definitions must depend far more on the national political process than on any economists' expertise.

I THE PROPOSED SYSTEM

We shall now present the essentials of the system with respect to a single enterprise belonging to the self-managing sector, for the moment postulating that the enterprise is a single integrated unit.

Suppose at the time of reform towards workers' participation, time zero, our typical enterprise has produced in the last operating period a total revenue TR^0 generating an aggregate labour income Y^0 and incurring other costs (including materials, interest charges and depreciation) of OC^0. A surplus for period zero may be computed as

$$S^0 = TR^0 - Y^0 - OC^0.$$

These calculations are made for the initial period, taken as one year, i.e. the basic accounting period. But because we may want to capture longer-range economic forces, the calculation could be made for an average of several years, say three or five years immediately preceeding the time of reform of the industry.

Further, we postulate some real rate of return on capital, R, which may be a calculated (shadow) price of capital or a policy variable, representing the relative scarcity of that factor in the economy. Using the return R, it is now possible to calculate what we shall call the *initial fair value of capital assets* (i.e. capital or land), F^0, which would yield an infinite stream of incomes S^0, given the yield per annum R, i.e.

$$F^0 = \frac{S^0}{R}.$$

Noting that the other costs OC^0 also include depreciation allowances, the fair value F can be thought of as *net value* of a capitalised infinite stream of returns imputable to the operation of the enterprise, based on the conditions of internal organisation and effort of the working community and to the rest of the economy based on conditions in the product and factor markets. This net value F generally will not equal the accounting or market value of the assets but ought to be understood as an expression of the value of enterprise to the working community, given the thousand and one various factors and forces influencing its operation. It is on that value that the community must pay to society the return R reflecting the intrinsic value of capital within the totality of the economy. Ideally, such returns ought to be destined for further social accumulation. But whether this will happen or other uses will be chosen, such as compensation of original owners, is a political decision which need not concern us here.

In a stationary world there would be no problem left for the participatory enterprise: the community would be paying the return R on the fair value of the enterprise, and the rest of total income, after payment of all costs, including depreciation, would become the earned income of the community. In the real world, however, everything is changing. Our proposed system must take such changes into consideration. It must do so in a simple, straightforward manner, taking into account the net effect of many forces (e.g. changing employment, plant and equipment, the institutionally given prices; and wages may be renegotiated by the labour unions). All of these changes, with a constant fair value, F, and rate of return on capital, R, will tend to produce variation in the actual net income, Y^t over time.

At the end of the first accounting period, there will be two measures of the income of the community:

Y^1: total income actually realised and shown in the accounting data;

$\bar{Y}^1$: a target income, given the union or otherwise determined wage structure. This may be equal to $\bar{Y}^0$ or may exceed it by some negotiated percentage increase.

The difference between Y^1 and $\bar{Y}^1$ is the realised surplus (positive or negative), assuming that the target wages $\bar{Y}^1$ actually were paid to the working community.[2]

The two estimates $\bar{Y}^1$ and Y^1, will normally not be the same. In successful enterprises, the difference between the actual income Y^1 and the estimation using the target wage structure, $\bar{Y}^1$, will be positive, and vice versa for a relatively unsuccessful enterprise.

Our fundamental postulate is that because the income of the enterprise is the result of many forces, the gain or loss in the income per worker ought to be reflected in the fair value of the enterprise to the community, F, and consequently in the rental which the community must pay to society for operating the enterprise. Thus the working community ought to share in some way with the rest of the society its good or bad fortunes. Consequently, some relationship must be established between the difference of the two values, $\overline{Y}^1$ and Y^1 on the one hand and the value F^1 on which the working community will be paying the return R to society following period one. Several relationships are possible, based on different parameters for the distribution between the community and the rest of society. These parameters ought to be made democratically and the relationship should possibly reflect long-run forces and thus be based on averages calculated over several years.

After the increased or reduced rent is paid in the second period on the increased or reduced fair value F, there will remain a differential between wage bills based on the union determined wages, $\overline{Y}^2$, and the total net income of the community, Y^2. The accounting surplus (positive or negative) becomes exclusively the patrimony (or liability) of the working community which must deliberate on and determine its distribution (or financing)[3]. However, that surplus will determine again F^2 on which the social rent must be paid in the third period, and so forth for all successive periods.

The rental return on all the fair values of all the public enterprises ought to be channeled in its entirety to a national self-management development fund, for the development of a progressive and dynamic self-managing industrial and/or agricultural sector of the economy. The logic of such allocation is that this fund is a national patrimony, and as such ought to be governed by and serve the benefit of all the people. It is not our intention to elaborate further on broader issues of national development policy, but it may be useful to know that given the manner in which the fair value of enterprises and the national investment fund are determined, those working in the self-managing sector can share with the others the fruits of their work, and especially the fruits of increased productivity and overall performance. For example, given the income distribution system proposed here, it might be possible to freeze the union-established wage structures for, say, a period of ten years. This would by no means lead to a stagnant income for the workers of the reorganised enterprises because they would be still left with the calculated surpluses. With predominantly positive surpluses, the fair values of capital assets would keep increasing and thus (a) there would be increasing accumulation for new investments, and (b) for reasons to which we shall turn in the next section, there would be an increased inducement for the existing self-managing enterprises to employ additional workers, or not to release surplus labour which otherwise might have been released.

The system proposed here is consistent with the possibility that F^0 would be negative, and consequently that at least initially the enterprise would have to be subsidised (as it was, by implication, in the pre-reform period). But alternative solutions are conceivable; for example, it might be decided that F^0 cannot fall below a zero value and that the initial target wage bills $\overline{Y}^1$, and subsequent ones, $\overline{Y}^t$, must be correspondingly lower. The rest of the system would remain, but starting from $F^0 = 0$ and a corresponding drop in wage rates at the time of the reform.

Alternatively, the government might accept funding a proportion (say 50 per cent) of the deficiency of labour incomes, below a union target $\overline{Y}^t$, with a postulated $F^0 = 0$. In this way, as in the preceding methods, the incentives to improve productivity rapidly would be maintained while the cost to the government would fall by one-half as compared to the main solution of this section (i.e. with F^0 negative).

II EVALUATION

The system for the implementation of self-management introduced in the preceding section is now evaluated according to a number of requirements and objectives. We believe that these represent criteria against which any proposed reform must be judged. We shall begin with some objectives and requirements which have a general validity, and then turn to those which have a specific significance for the concrete case of western industrial societies.

(i) *Allocative and structural efficiency* within the sector to be reorganised is a very important economic requirement of any policy or system. It means that capital, labour and land ought to be utilised in such a way that, with prices given, reallocation of productive factors between industries would not lead to major increases in gross national product.

This requirement is fulfilled by our system, both in the context of static analysis and, what is more important from the point of view of real applicability and implementation, asymptotically. By this asymptotic property we mean that, although subjected to very many changing and different forces, all of the time the system will be aiming at structural efficiency. The static efficiency of self-management is a well known result from theory (see Vanek (1970) and Chapter 1). Under the system proposed here it is met because, given the same collective wage contract for all of the self-managing sector, the fair value of capital assets is so designed that the return to factors exhausts the income of the enterprise. The democratic nature of the enterprise ensures that workers' incomes will be equated to their incremental productivity. The revaluation of the fair value of capital guarantees that, even under changing circumstances, the enterprise will always be converging on the static conditions of structural efficiency.

If the self-managing enterprise sector is surrounded by other, traditional capitalist or public sectors of the economy, our system will also guarantee structural efficiency of allocation as between the self-managing and other sectors, so long as the target wage of the former, $\bar{Y}$, is the same as the union wage in the rest of the economy. Contractual wages in a sector to be reorganised may diverge from union or non-union wages elsewhere in the economy, but this raises issued beyond the scope of this chapter. However, it ought to be noted that the proposed system, if adopted, would also become an important, even if only partial, instrument of establishing full structural efficiency throughout the economy.

(ii) *Maximum employment* is a general objective for most western countries but it must be properly understood and interpreted. As well as implying the need to generate (or maintain) as large as possible a number of jobs, it also implies that employment must be as productive as possible. Employment which does not lead to corresponding increases in output must be avoided and to the extent that it existed in the past it must be, at least gradually, eliminated.

The proposed system meets this objective in two ways. First, given the increasing productivity and improved performance that can be expected from the introduction of self-management, the system will keep readjusting the fair value of assets upwards, thus constituting higher and higher fixed charges on successful enterprises with increasing labour incomes. However, the theory of the labour-managed firm (see Vanek, 1970 and Chapter 1) tells us that with an increasing fixed charge it is rational for the working community to increase its size, and thus employment.

Secondly, with the rental payment increasing over time, the sums thus levied will constitute an ever-increasing capital fund, which, when fully invested in new projects, will guarantee higher employment. Furthermore, since a rental R will be levied, these new projects again will (a) tend to call for high employment by themselves (see the above argument) and (b) generate further capital assets for further investment. In fact, there is a certain exponential character to all this which ought to lead to rapid absorption of unemployment in any economy.

(iii) *Justice and fairness of income distribution within the self-managing sector* must also be fulfilled. By this we mean that people with approximately equal qualifications and seniority ought to receive approximately equal incomes, and that the distribution of income as between categories within the self-managing sector be fair and subject to reasonable and not excessive differentials. However, the latter will always remain more of a political and labour union decision than one inherent in the system proposed here.

The fulfilment of this requirement by the proposed system is more or less implicit in what has been said above. With the readjustment of fair values and rentals over time, and a common wage level or wage structure defined by union bargaining, incomes of all workers and labour categories will tend to converge asymptotically over time. Small deviations over different enterprises resulting from many various forces (including variable labour productivity) will exist, giving a certain degree of individuality and self-expression, as well as generating healthy incentive forces for the individual working collectives of different enterprises.

(iv) *Fair income distribution as between a self-managing sector and the rest of the economy* is also a necessary but, perhaps, more difficult task. Behind it is also the requirement of graduality and continuity in time. In situations where, in the past, incomes in the two distinct segments of the economy have been allowed to grow apart to a considerable extent, remedial action is necessary. However, it must proceed at a speed consistent with a socio-political optimum. As we have noted already, this condition will be fulfilled by the proposed system as long as the target wages in the reorganised sector are comparable to those in the non-participatory sectors (if any). While realising that this may be difficult to attain in the short run, we have already noted that steering the target union wages of the public sector in the long haul towards some national average would produce, as a result, a just and fair income distribution.

(v) *The presence of static incentives* is a requirement with a general validity but it is especially necessary for a satisfactory functioning of participatory self-managing enterprises. By static incentive, we mean an optimal relationship between a worker's or a working community's performance and the fruits derived from such performance. By the term 'static' we mean a relationship which is immediate in time and concerns exclusively or predominantly the working community.

Under our proposed system, the total net income after payment of all costs, including the rental on fair value, constitutes the patrimony of the working collective. Whenever the working community increases its income through the various instruments at its disposal, such increments in any current period will accrue to the community, and thus there will be a strong incentive for the community, and each of its members, to adapt performance to an optimal earning position.

(vi) *The presence of dynamic incentives* is necessary to allow the working community to reap a fair share of its efforts over the long haul, while at the same time recognising that some of these fruits must be also shared with the rest of the society within which the community works and without which the community could not function as an economic and productive entity. It is inherent in the system proposed that, through readjustment of fair values and the corresponding rentals, the working community will reap benefits from increased efforts in the long run, while sharing with the rest of the community and society the fruits of such efforts. This will be the case especially under the normal expectation that the target union wage would be growing at some rate equal to national increments in productivity. Only such long-range gains in productivity as would exceed the national average would be shared with the rest of the economy.

(vii) *A high volume of accumulation for national investment* must be guaranteed, with, if possible, no diversion of surpluses into uses other than accumulation. This is especially necessary in view of the lagging investment rates which have been observed in just about all western economies in recent years. Given the fair value calculation and the rental levied on it of the proposed system, the rate of accumulation would be very high. This notion was implicit above with respect to maximisation of employment. Indeed, it is the rapid growth of investment that would warrant the very rapid absorption of unemployment. To give an idea of the accumulation potential of the system, the following ought to be noted: suppose that the rental rate R is 10 per cent and that it is levied on the totality of national capital stock (assuming, for example, that the entire economy becomes self-managed). A usual statistic in most countries is that total capital stock is at least twice national product. With ten per cent levied on two hundred, we get an accumulation and net investment potential of twenty per cent of national product which would rank with the highest in the world, even excluding accumulation from other sources.

(viii) *The optimal design and utilisation of technology* is also an important objective, but it may require other measures. It must be hoped that, in the long run, western economies can liberate themselves from their dependence on alienating capitalistic technologies which are far too capital-intensive and dehumanised for a healthy national development. The long-run fulfilment of this requirement is probably the greatest single strength of self-management in general, and our proposed system in particular. A good deal of the present drama of the conflict between workers and managers, and of workers' alienation, resides in the wrong and false factor proportions and technologies emanating from profit-oriented developments which either neglect the worker altogether, or attempt to displace him as a burdensome liability. Self-management in conjunction with our system of distribution produces the ideal conditions for a remedy and reparation of this problem in the long run. On the one hand, the rental R and the calculation of changing fair value guarantees that those technologies will be most favoured in the long run which will best conform to such implicit use values and prices of capital assets. At the same time, the system of self-management, especially when its more mature dialogical forms are attained, is the best if not the only pre-condition of finding such appropriate technologies.

These would also be organic in the sense of giving the working person greatest satisfaction (or, at least, minimising his or her hardships).

(ix) *Simplicity of solutions and their practicality* are necessary because the system we are designing is one to serve the development of democratic self-management. Complex formulas and rules can become prohibitive and confusing to the average worker, with very serious, if not fatal, effects on the healthy development of democracy and democratic dialogue in the place of work.

The proposed system is very simple and workable, and involves only four simple accounting definitions and *one* basic relationship. A more complex system, identifying internal productivity, calls for only two simple index numbers and *one* additional relationship. A relatively limited number of statistical data bearing on the operation of the enterprise must be established every year or every accounting period. The number of the data and their definitions are straightforward and thus can be followed and controlled by everyone in the enterprise. The system thus fulfils a certain necessary condition of transparency which guarantees the typical worker that he cannot be misused or exploited.

(x) *Minimum dependence and maximum self-determination for all people, in all walks of life, according to their involvement* are desirable objectives for all systems. Good and effective self-management depends on good and effective information systems. Simplicity and transparency are significant pre-conditions of the latter. Moreover, the proposed system is perfectly adaptable to increased decentralisation and autonomy of working units. What we have defined for the enterprise of the self-managing sector can be perfectly well applied to any plant or department or workshop as long as independent statistical and accounting data can be obtained.

Next come several objectives and requirements specifically inherent in the concrete situations of western industrialised countries.

(xi) *A given system of prices* characterises most western economies, where prices can be thought of as market determined or as institutionally given. Obviously, our system can operate under any pricing mechanism. What is even more important once, and if, the system is applied, is that the public authorities, or they together with the labour unions, can agree on some principles (or formulas) of price determination consistent with the proposed system of income distribution.

(xii) *The existence of the unionisation of labour* in most western countries must be taken into account in any proposal for reform. The reader must have realised by now that the entire system takes into account the existence of labour unions, collective bargaining, union wages, etc. In fact, as we have argued before, and we will argue again in the last section, the labour unions ought to be prominently involved from the outset in the determination of the system and the selection of various key parameters.

(xiii) *Further decentralisation* may be necessary for full self-management in the future. Less hierarchical and more decentralised structures are bound to emerge after several years of operation of workers' participation. Our system, being fully applicable to any degree of decentralisation and autonomy of work groups, thus becomes an ideal instrument of such decentralisation. As we show in the subsequent section, decentralisation would raise the problem of transfer pricing for transactions among departments and workshops; but the problem is also readily solvable.

(xiv) *Consistency with a meaningful and operational method of project evaluation* for enterprise expansion and new enterprise formation is also necessary. This is developed further in respect of the proposed system in Section III below.

III SOME IMPORTANT QUESTIONS

In Section I we defined the basic system of income distribution. An essential role in that system is played by the *fair value of the enterprise*, which is altered depending on the performance of the firm. The value of the enterprise also will change if a new investment or expansion is undertaken. Similarly, there is the problem for new enterprises as to the definition of the fair value. More generally, there is the problem of project evaluation and the investment decision for new investments. In this section we shall first deal with this all important group of problems.

We shall also consider two other related issues from the point of investment and asset evaluation. The first is the problem of depreciation; the second is that of valuation of assets and the performance of the enterprise in situations of significant inflation such as those encountered at present in many western countries. Finally, we shall return to the question of incentives with which we have dealt already: but we shall do so to propose an improvement which might be introduced in due course, aimed at a further enhancement of the justice and fairness of the system.

(a) THE INVESTMENT DECISION

We can make our point most clearly and most practically by speaking in terms of an example. Suppose that the community of an existing enterprise wants to expand its operations by adding a new plant or a new department to its existing facility. The question arises of how to decide whether or not such an expansion is desirable. A second and related question is how the income distribution system deals with such an addition or expansion.

The rental, R, relfects the scarcity of capital for the economy, or at least the sector to be reorganised. As such it ought to be used in calculating the Net Present Value as the discount factor. In that calculation, the contractual wage or income, $\bar{y}$, must also be used. If the net present discounted value with these inputs (R and $\bar{y}$) turns out to be positive, then the project or expansion ought to be undertaken.

Let us now see how the investment ought to be funded and what other institutional and/or accounting arrangements will be necessary. Suppose that a fund has already been established (hereafter referred to as the National Labour Managerial Fund (NLMF) into which the capital rentals ($R.F$) from all self-managed enterprises are channeled. From that fund, the sums necessary to undertake the investment project are now advanced to the enterprise. Let us say that the total cost is 10 million Francs. The value of assets of the enterprise is now increased by 10 million Francs and added to the fair value of the enterprise as it was reckoned at the time of the investment project. The firm now bases the return R on the total value, that is the total fair value ($F + 10$ mil.) thus constructed. From then on in the first, second, third and later years following the investment, the fair value of the totality of investments is derived in the way already discussed in Section I.

Note that provided that the investment evaluation was correct, a positive surplus must have been realised on the 10 million

Francs investment, and thus, on account of that investment, improved economic conditions are to be expected for everyone.[4]

Similar considerations apply to a newly constituted community of workers just about to enter productive operations. The only difference here is that there is no actual operating wage or income. Instead, the project evaluation must be based on the collective contract wage $\bar{y}$ established for that branch of the industry. The initial project cost, say the 10 million Francs of the example, becomes also the initial fair value of assets (i.e. F^0). It is on that value that the working community will have to pay the return R to the national investment fund. Of course, in practice such payments may be required only after a certain grace period agreed between the fund and the investing community.

(b) ADJUSTMENT FOR INFLATION

As we have noted in Section II, one of our main objectives is simplicity combined with practicality of solutions. Inflation, indeed, causes significant problems which may be dealt with in several ways. We shall propose two solutions. Only the first and the simplest one will be presented fully in this subsection. The second and more precise solution resembles the first and is implicit in subsection (d) below, which deals with a more just and fair income distribution system.

The simple solution consists in revaluing for each period, on a continuing basis, the fair value of assets as computed for that period using some generally agreed price index applicable to those assets. More precisely, the calculations proposed in Section I are performed in each period t starting from fair value estimates F^{t-1}, which have been themselves adjusted by the appropriate price index. This yields a new fair value $\bar{F}$.

The same is done in the second method but the prices or inputs and outputs also enter directly the calculation of the factor by which the fair value F is to be adjusted from period to period.

(c) THE PROBLEM OF DEPRECIATION

There are several possible regimes with respect to depreciation. It would seem that given the conditions of the typical western economy and given the requirements of economic efficiency, simplicity and practicality, the following is most suitable. Given the relative scarcity of investment funds and the need to share as broadly as possible the fruits of economic activity throughout the population, it appears desirable to channel depreciation allowances of individual enterprises into the general national (or social) pool of investment resources (the NLMF). This is not to say that the depreciation funds of a specfic enterprise should never be used by that enterprise: but rather that, except for replacement purposes, society ought also to be permitted to pass judgement on whether or not the funds ought to be used in the enterprise of origin.

What I am proposing is that every enterprise establish a fund for depreciation as an account with the NLMF and that all depreciation allowances be deposited into that account. In case of inflationary changes, such deposits should be revalued by the same price index as the fair value of assets. On such deposits, the enterprise is not bound to pay the return R on that portion of the fair value which has been written off as depreciation. Suppose that the fair value of the enterprise at the beginning of an operating period is 1 million Francs, and that depreciation allowances for the current operating period are 100 000 Francs. The fair value at the end of that period (except for adjustments of the type proposed in (b) above) still remains 1 million Francs, but 100 000 of these are assets on deposit with the sinking fund of the national agency and on which the enterprise now begins to earn the return R. Consequently, in the subsequent period the enterprise will be paying the net return R on only 900 000 Francs.[5]

Of course, when the enterprise needs its funds for replacement of plant or equipment, it can directly, and without anybody's power of control, draw on its fund. If however, the enterprise would like to use such funds for new investment, that is, expansion projects, it should go through some procedure of joint project evaluation with the officials of the national fund. Applications by a firm to use its own depreciation funds, and possibly to use the rental paid on the fair value of its assets, might be subjected to less bureaucratic procedures provided some minimum criterion, such as a labour absorption requirement, were met.

(d) FURTHER CONSIDERATIONS OF A FAIR INCENTIVE SYSTEM

While designed to conform to the requirement of simplicity and practicality, the system proposed in Section I may at some time prove to be too simple. A significant improvement which would not be too difficult to implement is now outlined. The method of revaluing the fair value of the enterprise from period to period is based on the postulate that many factors which cannot be separated from each other influence the performance of the enterprise. A division between changes within the enterprise and changes coming to the enterprise from the outside, primarily as recorded by market forces, is now proposed. It is desirable to design the income distribution and incentive scheme so as to make the working community benefit as much as possible from improvements in performance and productivity imputable to its own effort. By contrast, changes in profitability imputable to external forces, and in particular market forces, ought to be primarily translated into benefits to the national community at large, that is, into changed rental payments on a changed fair value.

This can be accomplished by introducing a new magnitude, $\overline{F}_0$. This magnitude measures, for a given period t, the fair value of the enterprise which would be obtained on the assumption of wage payments given by $\overline{y}$ (as for F) and on the assumption that prices at which the enterprise is selling output and buying its factors of production did not change during the current period as compared to the preceding period.

The fair value of the assets in period $t+1$ is now given by

$$F^{t+1} = F^t + a(\overline{F}^{t+1} - F^t)$$

where the coefficient a has two components: A, which is the distributional parameter discussed in Section I; and B which ensures that the collective does not appropriate gains due to extraneous factors. The value of B depends on the difference between $\overline{F}^t$ and $\overline{F}_0^t$.

If, for example, prices did not change at all and the performance of the enterprise improved considerably thanks to an improved internal productivity, the two terms $\overline{F}$ will be equal: thus the term B will be 0, and consequently the fair value F will be adjusted upwards by only a relatively small coefficient A. By contrast, if all or most of the improved performance (profitability) is imputable to external markets and there is a considerable excess of $\overline{F}$ over $\overline{F}_0$, the term B will be significant and positive and consequently the upward adjustment in the fair value will be considerable. And, consequently, as would seem fair and efficient, the fair value of the enterprise will increase a good deal and so will the payment at the rate R going from the enterprise to society.

Even if the two terms $\overline{F}$ cannot be exactly estimated, the term B can be defined directly in terms of index numbers of product prices on the one hand and factor prices on the other. In either case, the method thus improved will tend to render the enterprise humanly and economically more effective. In particular, the workers will feel that their remuneration more closely reflects their performance and is less dependent on extraneous factors. The method also has the considerable advantage of discouraging the use of monopoly power to increase product price. This is so because such increases would be translated primarily into benefits accruing outside the working community, and not to the community and managerial personnel itself.

(e) DECENTRALISATION

As with the question of pure effort incentives discussed in the preceding subsection, the subject of decentralisation may arise only gradually in any participatory economy. However, the subject is of considerable importance because inherent in an optimal form of self-managed production is a far higher degree of decentralisation of enterprises than we find in capitalist or state-run enterprises. The working communities of participatory enterprises would have to become conscious of this necessity first and then democratically decide on the appropriate degree of work and enterprise decentralisation.

It is necessary, therefore, to show how the proposed system of income distribution can be adapted for decentralisation of enterprises. The first and rather obvious thing (noted already) is that the system proposed here is not specific to an entire enterprise but really is defined for any subgroup, subdivision, department or plant of an enterprise as long as such a unit possesses or can be endowed with an independent accounting system.

If such independent units or departments are engaged in economic transactions of buying and selling only outside the enterprise, then of course we need add nothing to our analysis. This is a trivial case. Normally a department of an enterprise will be dependent economically on other departments and other sections of the enterprise: it will be receiving goods and/or services from other departments and supplying its own goods or services to other departments. If such a workshop or a department then is to become independent under a decentralising reorganisation, such goods and services, whether received or supplied further, must be reckoned as internal purchases or sales. What is most important from our point of view is that *such transactions in goods or services must be priced* using some transfer prices. It is a technical matter as to how to define these transfer prices and it has been dealt with theoretically elsewhere.[6] Here let it be noted only that the problem is solvable in terms very much in harmony with the spirit and principles of workers' participation and the system proposed here. The essence of such determination is to define transfer prices in such a manner as to approximate (more or less precisely) a situation where incomes in different departments are comparable. But at the same time, as in the system proposed in Section I, there must be a certain stability, or slowness of adjustment of the underlying parameters so as to make sure that improvements in productivity stemming from increased effort of a community in a given department are translated into benefits for that working community.

This can be secured by a system of transfer prices throughout the enterprise which equalises incomes (of equally skilled people) among the decentralised departments at the time of the decentralisation. Thereafter, the transfer prices must be allowed to vary with a certain degree of slowness so as to have increments in effort of a given department translated into, first of all, its own benefits; and such benefits only over time, through appropriate variation of the transfer prices, are passed on, to a degree, to the other departments.

IV CONCLUSIONS

In this study I have presented what I, as an economist, involved and concerned with a successful development of a democratic participatory economy, consider the optimal solution to the central problems of economic organisation of the enterprise. The multiple objectives and requirements underlying the analysis are carefully stated in Section II.

Because the objective of this study is to assist the formation of participatory enterprises and a participatory economy, it is *indispensable* that *all* those involved, not only the author, but also and above all those involved directly in work in any future participatory enterprises, take part in the final formulation and resolution of the problems dealt with here. The workers of the enterprises, as individual working communities and through their labour unions, and the managerial and technical staffs all must participate in this elaboration.

Besides those directly involved in work, there are others less directly involved, such as the members of the national community who supplied and created the material resources and the consumers and users of the industry's products. There is also the scientific community, like the author, and many others who may, in the future, remain involved with the participatory reforms in western countries, as scientists, experts or educators.

If a process of reform were to be seriously embarked upon, all these groups must take part in a positive and creative dialogue leading to a final proposal. It is for this reason, to make such a dialogue possible, that I have stated the underlying premises in Section II and shown how they are met so as to allow anyone to participate in either questioning the premises or initially evaluating the analysis.

The form that such further participatory dialogue should take is primarily a process of participatory educational dialogue in conferences, workshop and other media. In such a dialogue, all will learn, as they create knowledge, and as they evaluate critically the materials at hand. To be useful, this chapter ought to be understood as a draft with the understanding that nothing is final and all is subject to discussion, its only purpose being to assist the process of participation and democratisation in production and, in final analysis, to contribute to a more just organisation in our western economies.

NOTES

1. This chapter is based on a paper presented as a working draft to the Walton Symposium, Glasgow, June 1979.
2. In practice, if declining incomes are expected, advances on income, W^1, smaller than $\bar{Y}^1$, might be paid out during the first year.
3. Normally, with increasing productivity and improved utilisation of resources,

positive surpluses can be expected. The working community will often want to establish reserve funds, perhaps funded from surpluses in some years, which would permit the weathering of lean years and possibly operating losses (at union established wages).

4. In fact, if at the time of the investment the current income realised by the working community is far in excess of the statutory income based on the collective contract, y, the working community might prefer to use the actual current (higher) income in the present value calculation. In this way, some projects might be foregone by that (very successful) community and reserved for other working communities where current incomes are less high, or for new communities about to establish themselves. Of course, this may be an additional advantage of the system proposed, even if, probably, not a very significant one.

5. The payments of R on the depreciation fund are not an essential part of the depreciation system proposed. It should be decided by the authorities or by the participatory process itself whether they are warranted. Either way, the effect ought not to be too great on the smooth performance of the self-managing enterprise.

6. In particular, see Chapters 5 and 6 of this author's study 'Through participation and dialogue to a world of justice', unpublished manuscript.

12 Labour-managed Firms and Social Transformation[1]

Branko Horvat

The earlier chapters of this book have been concerned with documenting the performance of labour-managed, participatory or self-managed sectors in a number of economies. This chapter is addressed to two question, one of which is not explicitly dealt with earlier in this book, and the second of which is only partially raised. These are:

(a) Is there a need for self-management?
(b) Can producer's co-operatives play an important role in socio-economic transformation?

The answer to the second question requires something of a synthesis of the earlier chapters of this book, whilst the former requires a consideration of individual and social needs.

1 THE NEED FOR SELF-MANAGEMENT

If any social system is to be viable, it must satisfy human needs better than any of the alternative systems. In such a case, people will be motivated to achieve that system. The present writer believes that socialism is such a system and that the main vehicle for effecting the transition to socialism will be that which best satisfies human needs. The pioneering work on human needs is that of Abraham Maslow. This provides a starting point for the argument presented below that since socialism satisfies the need for self-actualisation, more than capitalism or etatism, it is a

249

demonstrably superior social system. It is then argued that self-management is a fundamental institution of socialism.

(a) THE HIERARCHY OF HUMAN NEEDS

Maslow's research on individual human needs identified a hierarchy (see Maslow, 1970) of such needs. The hierarchy is such that the higher needs do not emerge before the lower needs have been gratified to a certain extent. Maslow identified five basic needs:

1. physiological;
2. safety;
3. belongingness and love;
4. self-respect and self-esteem;
5. self-actualisation.

They are presented here in order of prepotency. It has been pointed out, however (see Davies, 1963), that the second of these, *safety*, is incongruous with the rest since it is not a real need but simply a precondition: a means, not an end. We are, thus, left with four basic needs to be gratified under conditions of relative safety. The first of these relates to mere physical survival, the next two are due to the fact that people live in societies, whilst the fourth reflects personality development, which is a specifically human quality.

Maslow has characterised these needs in the following way:

> The higher the need, the more specifically human it is . . . The higher the need the less imperative it is for sheer survival, the longer the gratification can be postponed and the easier it is for the need to disappear permanently . . . Higher need gratifications have survival value and growth value . . . . (Maslow, 1970, p 98).

How do we know that the needs on the list are really basic human needs and that they are not simply neurotic or socially conditioned? Maslow offers four possible proofs:

1. The frustration of these needs is pathogenic, i.e. makes people bodily and mentally sick.
2. Their gratification, on the contrary, is healthy. This is not the case with the gratification of neurotic needs.

3. It is also spontaneously chosen under free conditions.
4. These needs can be directly studied in relatively healthy people.

If Maslow is right, thwarting the gratification of four basic needs will produce sick individuals who will make up a sick society. What the symptoms of sickness at the societal level are and how such a sick society functions, has especially been studied by Erich Fromm (1941,1955). On the other hand, a society which satisfies basic human needs substantially better than other societies must, in some fundamental sense, be a more progressive society.

So far, Maslow's original theory of motivation has not been well supported by empirical evidence (except in the case of the self-actualisation need). Empirical investigations failed to identify five independent needs and to confirm a simple ordering of needs.[2] Consequently, attempts have been made to eliminate the overlapping of Maslow's categories by reducing their number to two or three and, while retaining the hierarchy, to introduce more complex ordering. The most successful revision along these lines has been achieved by Clayton Alderfer.

Alderfer (1972) compressed Maslow's five needs into three which he called Existence, Relatedness and Growth. People must first keep alive, they must relate to each other and, in order to be human, they must be creative by changing their environment and themselves. Thus existence needs subsume material and physiological desires. When resources are limited, as they are in the scarcity world in which we live, one person's gain is another person's loss. Relatedness needs involve relationships with significant other people and include acceptance, confirmation and understanding. Here the activities do not represent a zero-sum game; the satisfaction depends on a process of sharing or mutuality. The satisfaction of growth needs 'depends on a person finding the opportunities to be what he is most fully and to become what he can' (Alderfer, 1972, p. 147). Alderfer tested his theory in different organisational settings and his three-need hierarchy more or less survived the test.[3]

It is obvious that, while questioning the simplicity of Maslow's theory, Alderfer upholds its essential idea: human needs are objectively identifiable and are hierarchically ordered. The ordering is not rigidly determined. By manipulation of environmental factors, individuals may be oriented towards lower needs. By contrast, since all needs are always present, at least in a latent form, individuals may be induced to reach the growth stage faster and then experience the self-reinforcing satisfaction–desire process. If Maslow and Alderfer are right, thwarting of the basic needs not only makes society sick but also generates the motivation for change. The change implies satisfying the basic needs more fully.

(b) A HIERARCHY OF SOCIAL NEEDS

How do we find out which type of society most satisfies the basic needs? The hierarchy of needs makes possible a simple solution of the problem. A society which better satisfies a higher need, *eo ipso* better satisifes all other needs down the list. Consequently, it suffices to show that socialism satisfies the self-actualising needs more than either capitalism or etatism in order to prove that it better satisfies all human needs and is, in this sense, a superior socio-economic system.

Before we proceed, a difficulty must be removed. The classification of the basic needs from the point of view of individual development is not the same as that from the point of view of social system design. We must discover how to transform the four-stage scheme at the micro-level – physiological, affective, self-esteem and self-actualisation needs – into one applicable at the macro level. An analysis of historical experience provides the answer.

(i) Since physiological needs have a survival quality, neither an individual nor a society can exist if they are not satisfied. At the societal level, this category is enlarged to include all *physical needs* such as food, clothing, and shelter.

(ii) Once basic physical needs are relatively satisfied, a category of need arises which we may call *cultural needs*. People are first concerned with their bodies; next they become concerned with their minds, education, entertainment, art and science belong under this heading. Health ought to be included here as well. At the lowest stage, health is often traded for increases in material comforts. It is only after a certain minimum level of living is achieved that health as such becomes of primary concern.

(iii) The first two stages make for the level of living. The next two stages make for the quality of life. In a relatively affluent society people become increasingly concerned with the so-called political liberties. *Political needs* (freedom of speech, conscience, assembly, etc.) correspond to Maslow's needs of self-esteem.

(iv) Finally, in an affluent and politically-liberated society, the main concern is focused on the growth of personality, on the full development of inherent potentialities and capacities of every individual. It is not sufficient to simply survive, enjoy life and be recognised as a separate and (formally) equal member of the group; it is also necessary to live one's own, self-determined and authentic life. This need for *authenticity* and *self-determination* corresponds, of course, to Maslow's self-actualisation need. It includes affective needs since personal life cannot be authentic if solidarity, love, friendship, etc., are thwarted or alienated.

Stages (i) and (iv) are the same at both individual and societal levels. Stages (ii) and (iii) are not. Besides, the historical evidence is not straightforward. The periodisation above corresponds to etatist development. In capitalist development, political liberties were established before cultural needs of the broad masses of population were satisfied. The explanation for this historical indeterminacy is not difficult to find.

The precondition for the development of capitalism was the establishment of a free market. This, in turn, required that political restrictions of feudalism be removed and political freedoms be made available for the bourgeoisie as well as the aristocracy. On the other hand, the proletariat could not improve its position vis-à-vis the bourgeoisie unless political freedoms were extended to all members of the society, regardless of their origin and the ownership of property. In this way, the class struggle generated political democracy while cultural needs remained only rudimentarily satisfied.

Consider now a different historical situation in which, due to a revolution, economic growth is substantially accelerated and the benefits are fairly evenly spread throughout the society. People will now tend to be more concerned with the improvements in the level of living than with politics. This explains the social stability of etatism. It is, of course, unlikely that the absence of political democracy can be preserved for long without an overt political repression. However, the repression is not a *differentia specifica* of etatism. It exists in capitalism as well, but there it takes the form of *economic* repression. When, on occasions, the oppressed refuse to tolerate the continuation of economic exploitation, economic repression is immediately replaced by political repression.

As consumption and cultural levels of populations increase, it becomes less possible to prevent a full development of political democracy in an etatist environment. Similarly, material affluence and political democracy lead to a gradual satisfaction of cultural needs (free education at all levels, health insurance, setting up of museums, art galleries, etc.). In this way, both systems converge to a state in which a relative satisfaction of material, cultural and political needs will generate pressures for radical social changes in the direction of self-determination.

(c) HUMAN NEEDS AND WORK

We now turn to a consideration of work in relation to needs. Needs are satisfied by work. This is true not only in the trivial sense that work produces goods and services for consumption. It is also true in a more important sense, that work is an essential human activity. Thus, there will be some correlation between the types of need satisfaction and the types of work. In the first three need-satisfaction stages, work is only instrumental and, consequently, alienated. One sells one's labour power and works in order to achieve something else. Work as such is a pain, a cost, something to be avoided. In the fourth need-satisfaction stage, the situation radically changes: work becomes an enjoyment, a need, an end in itself. Let us take a somewhat closer look at this process.

Work is a complex activity with several dimensions. The development of capitalism and etatism is accompanied by a decomposition of work along its various dimensions. The totality is broken up into components, the components become independent, and the process results in alienation. The labour of an artisan or a peasant is an undifferentiated whole. The first step in the process is to separate the producer from the means of production. This is also the most difficult step and sometimes it extends over centuries. In Britain, it implied enclosures; in the Soviet Union, collectivisation. It meant transforming human beings into appendages of machines, into a factor of production along with other factors such as capital and land. Labour was reduced to manual labour – pure and simple, workers were reduced to 'hired hands'. The producers, of course, refused to work, resisted, tried to combine in order to control their destinies. The owners knew better.

Combination among workers was visited with brutal punishment; flogging, prison and banishment were the penalties for strikes. Workers were bound for long terms of service, often extending over several years, and were hounded down like military deserters if they left their employment . . . There was frequently forced recruitment of labour for privileged establishments of all kinds, and parents who did not send their children into industry were threatened with heavy fines. (Dobb, 1963, pp. 234–5.)

These methods, characteristic for the Europe of the sixteenth to eighteenth centuries, reappeared in the European colonies in the nineteenth and twentieth centuries.

The separation of the producer from his means of production meant not only a differentiation of labour into free and hired but also its decomposition into manual and non-manual. The latter was retained by the owner for himself. Economic development and the ensuing division of labour pushed the decomposition one step further. The owner began to hire persons with expertise necessary to cope with various production problems in the undertaking whose complexity was growing. In this way, hired manual labour was supplemented by hired mental labour. The owner retained only entrepreneurship, i.e. the overall control and supervision, for himself. Eventually, the supreme supervisory labour was also hired and the owner remained just an owner, pure and simple.

This process of decomposition generating several partial workers resulted in at least three important consequences. First, the sequence of decompositions – manual labour, hired mental and hired supervisory labour – is at the same time the order of socio-economic positions or social strata in contemporary class societies: manual workers occupy the lowest position, business and political bosses the highest. Secondly, however paradoxical it may seem, up to a point, various strata have a common interest in preserving the existing system. For the ruling stratum that is obvious. Manual workers, on the other hand, still find themselves in the region of lower needs whose satisfaction is quite compatible with the existing social system. In the United States, this is reflected in the conservative attitudes of the unions, which are primarily oriented towards improvements in the material well-being. In the Soviet Union, intellectuals receive little support from the workers in pressing for political freedoms. Thirdly, ownership pure and simple – either private or state – is devoid of the productive function and is becoming growth-inhibiting, which renders it dysfunctional. Function-less or dysfunctional institutions are sooner or later replaced by those which are positively productive. On the other hand, labour pure and simple, i.e. alienated labour, cannot be tolerated any longer once the lower basic needs have been relatively satisfied. Thus, the next evolutionary step can consist only in reversing the past trends. The decomposition of labour has reached its ultimate limits. What one can expect in the future is a reintegration on a new basis. This new basis can consist only in self-determination.

How is this reintegration of producers and the means of production, of various components of labour, to come about? Which is the social force which will carry it out? The traditional Marxist answer is that this social force is the proletariat. We have seen, however, that the proletariat does not transcend the trade union consciousness, i.e. that it remains *within* the confines of the system of decomposed and alienated labour. This is particularly true if the system leaves sufficient room for the gratification of lower basic needs. Two solutions to the problem have been offered.

The first solution is by Lenin. Consistent with his idea of the working class being unable to produce socialist consciousness by its own efforts, he urged the creation of a disciplined party of political activists, headed by revolutionary intellectuals, which could lead and educate workers and would rule by dictatorial methods until socialist consciousness is established. This strategy proved technically efficient but socially self-defeating. It generated etatism, not socialism.

The second strategy is to look for another revolutionary force outside the proletariat. This force is found in students, radical intellectuals and exploited minority groups in developed countries and in peasants in undeveloped countries. Leaving the problem of peasants for later discussion, the second strategy is well-represented by the work of Herbert Marcuse.

By virtue of its basic position in the production process, by virtue of its numerical weight and the weight of exploitation, the working class is still the historical agent of revolution; by value of its sharing the stabilising needs of the system, it has become a conservative, even counter-revolutionary force. Objectively, 'in itself', labour is still the potentially revolutionary class; subjectively, 'for itself', it is not. (Marcuse, 1972, p. 25).

See also Birnbaum (1969, p. 94). While workers are becoming conservative, small and weakly-organised groups of militant intelligentsia cut loose from the organised working class, 'by virtue of their consciousness and their needs function as potential catalysts of rebellion within majorities to which, by their class origin, they belong' (Marcuse, 1972, p. 57). Elaborating this idea to its final consequences, Marcuse ends in an impasse:

> . . . the established democracy still provides the only legitimate framework for change and must therefore be defended against all attempts on the Right and the Centre to restrict this framework, but at the same time, preservation of the established democracy preserves the *status quo* and the containment of change. Another aspect of the same ambiguity: radical change depends on a mass basis, but every step in the struggle for radical change isolates the opposition from the masses and provokes intensified repression . . . thus further diminishing the prospects for radical change. . . Thus, the radical is guilty – either for surrendering to the power of the *status quo*, or of violating the Law and Order of the *status quo*. (Marcuse, 1972, pp. 71–3.)

Unlike Lenin's, Marcuse's strategy has not proved successful and, clearly, never will.

(d) TRANSFORMATION THROUGH SELF-MANAGEMENT

Where do we go from here? Is socialist transformation intrinsically impossible, like squaring a circle? If a particular solution fails, it is always a good rule to look first for the reasons of the failure. Since the working class represents one-half of the population, an exploited half at that, no socialist transformation is possible without the working class. Both Lenin and Marcuse would agree with this proposition and it is, in fact, generally accepted. Here, however, the agreement also ends. Where Lenin and the Old Left err (notwithstanding all verbal pronouncements to the contrary) is to treat the proletariat as an object of change; it has to be taught and led. While, in fact, the emancipation of the working class must be conquered (not by inspired leaders or an elite party but) by the workers themselves, and this in the most real sense of the word. Where Marcuse and the New Left err is a simplified dichotomising of reality: either Law and Order or a radical change. Why not use Law and Order *for* the change?

A historical parallel will clarify the issue. Suppose we find ourselves in a feudal society and contemplate how to speed up capitalist transformation. What do we do? The most sensible thing to do is to discover the fundamental capitalist institution – the one that essentially governs the system – and try to transplant it into the feudal environment. The institution we are looking for is clearly a universal market, i.e. a free market for both products and factors. The transplantation, of course, has its problems and the social body may reject the transplant. But suppose we succeed. The institution will gradually corrode the feudal structure from the inside and the structure will begin to crumble. If everything can be bought and sold, then feudal estates and aristocratic titles soon will be offered for sale and the lords soon will prefer to receive monetary rents from free tenants rather than labour services from their serfs.

The fundamental institution of socialism is self-management. The main task of the present study was, in fact, to examine and validate this proposition. If universal self-management (in both market and non-market sectors) is introduced to either capitalist or etatist societies, it will gradually resolve the old production relations, and eventually the disintegrating system will have to be replaced by something more compatible with the institution. By participating in management (and in local government), by fighting for a continuous extension of participation until it reaches full self-management, workers learn in their daily lives how to control their destiny, how to overcome fragmentation and decomposition of labour, how to achieve meaningful social equality, how to destroy antiquated hierarchies. They do that without the tutorship of omniscient leaders. They prepare themselves for self-determination. And they use Law and Order for exactly that purpose. Self-management clearly cannot be established overnight, but neither was the capitalist market. And, similarly, as the development of the market, however gradual or irregular, could not be anti-capitalist, the growth of participation from its primitive forms of joint consultation towards full-fledged self-management cannot be anti-socialist, in spite of the attempts to misuse it for the preservation of the *status quo.*

Self-management may be introduced by violent (revolutionary) or peaceful (reformist) means. It may be attempted in undeveloped or industrialising or developed countries. It can grow up in a capitalist or in an etatist environment. One can thus theoretically distinguish twelve transition profiles. However, not all of them have empirical content. A violent revolution is not likely to erupt in a developed country. Besides, it is an historical fact that no such revolution has occurred. This reduces the number of possibilities by two. Next, the undeveloped countries are so much dominated by their poverty that the distinction between capitalism and etatism is of lesser importance. This makes for a further reduction of two profiles. Finally, it is generally easiest to build socialism in developed countries, and most difficult – if at all possible – to effect socialist transformation in the poor, least developed countries. If these two polar cases could be handled, the intermediate case of industrialising countries need not represent special difficulties. In the next part of this chapter we consider producers' co-operatives as a vehicle for this social transformation in developed countries.

II THE ROLE OF PRODUCER CO-OPERATIVES

Since the days of Robert Owen, social reformers have from time to time advertised producer co-operative as a suitable means for socio-economic transformation. However, the history of British and American co-operatives has been quite unimpressive (see Jones, 1975, 1977, and Chapter 3 of this book). Nowhere else have producer co-operatives attained more than negligible importance. Thus, one might be tempted to conclude that, although desirable because of their self-governing features, producer co-operatives are not likely to play an important economic role, and thus special attention need not be paid to them. This would, however, be an erroneous conclusion for at least three reasons.

   (i) Contemporary co-operatives seem to be more productive than their capitalist twins (see, for example, Chapters 4, 5 and 6 above).

(ii) In an era of disintegrating capitalism, the social environment is more favourable to co-operative experiments than at any time before.[4]

(iii) There is no need to perpetuate old mistakes. Co-operatives may be shaped organisationally in such a way as to ensure their survival and expansion.

Co-operatives are usually small or medium-size firms. They are established in three different ways. (a) Traditionally, a group of workers would pool their resources and, with a possible outside loan would establish a co-operative; as a rule these are very small establishments. (b) More recently, and increasingly, workers have often taken over firms about to become bankrupt or sold and run them on their own in order to preserve their jobs;[5] such firms are often larger and workers are occasionally able to secure community support. (c) Progressive employers hand over their stock to the employees and the firm is transformed into a co-operative; the process of transformation is usually conducted in stages over a number of years. In what follows I shall concentrate on case (a), although most of the analysis is also applicable to the other two cases.

Producer co-operatives provide an intermediary link between privately-owned and socially-owned firms. They are based on collective property, which is not a very precise category. This provides for organisational flexibility. A co-operative may be organised in such a way as to be indistinguishable from a private partnership firm, or its organisational structure may be chosen from the other end of the continuum where we find the pure worker-managed firm. Due to this flexibility, a co-operative can usually be organised even within a rigid bourgeois legal framework.

The co-operative strategy we are looking for must satisfy two conditions: the firms must be economically viable even in an alien environment and they must provide for a smooth transition to a socialist economy. If one studies the successes and failures of producer co-operatives in developed capitalist countries, one will realise certain regularities which could be used in designing the desirable strategy. The following seven factors seem to be of crucial importance.

(i) *Member contributions.* A person joining a co-operative ought to 'buy' his job. The down payment must be substantial in order to matter, but not too great in order not to prevent possible applicants. The membership deposit serves three purposes: it is a source of capital, it has an educational value as evidence of commitment, and in the market economy it provides incentives for aligning personal interests with the long-term success of the firm. If the applicant does not have ready cash, he may be provided with a loan, or the membership contribution may be deducted from his earnings over a certain period of time. Part of the contribution should be transferred to the co-operative's indivisible reserve account. In Mondragon, for example, this is 20 per cent. The balance is entered into a personal account which may be credited annually at a fixed interest rate. The personal balances may not be withdrawn unless the individual leaves the co-operative or retires. When a person is entitled to withdraw his personal balances, he may be paid in debentures or shares and not in cash. Shares are non-voting but may carry honorific privileges (such as attending the assembly with consultative rights), as long as they are not transferred. In this way, capital of the co-operative is kept intact and the retired member retains an active interest in – and preserves emotional ties with – the community in which he spent an important part of his active life.

(ii) *External funding.* Modern capital intensive technology requires rather high investment per worker. This investment cost cannot be matched by member contributions alone. The balance must be funded out of external sources. For this purpose, the usual financial instruments may be used (loans, bonds, non-voting stock).

(iii) *Non-members* are second-class citizens and, in principle, must not be allowed, in order to prevent the degeneration of the co-operative. There are two possible exceptions to this rule. Co-operative wage differentials are always narrow, and in a capitalist environment, with much larger earnings differentials, that might prevent the co-operative from securing high quality managers. Thus several managerial posts may be reserved for non-members and these managers are hired as employees. This, of course, reverses the usual procedure – when managers hire workers – but such is the nature of co-operatives. The experience of the American plywood co-operatives shows that this can be done. The other exception is seasonal production, when non-members are employed in order to iron out seasonal oscillations.

(iv) *The supporting structure.* An isolated co-operative is unlikely to survive very long. National co-operative associations are helpful, but do not solve the problem. Co-operatives can develop only if economically integrated into a sector. It need not be large, but it must represent an integrated system. In a national economy there may be a number of such co-operative systems. For that purpose, co-operatives need what Jaroslav Vanek calls *supporting structure*. This sheltering organisation is a co-operative of the second degree. Since co-operatives are usually starved of capital because they lack access to the traditional capital market, the most important part of the supporting structure is the co-operative bank. The bank is a source of investment capital, provides short-term credits, underwrites loans and provides a market for shares and debentures issued by the co-operatives. The two other important sectoral activities are education and rendering legal services and management advice together with the availability of the managerial personnel. The phenomenal business success of the Mondragon system is to a large extent explicable by good organisation of the supporting structure, with all three ingredients present. As the co-operative sector grows, it becomes possible to guarantee employment by switching labour from one firm to another.

(v) In order to reduce risks, *pension and insurance* schemes ought to be operated separately. At the beginning, small amounts of insurance money may be channelled into co-operative investment through the co-operative bank. As the number of co-operatives multiplies and the entire sector grows, an increasing percentage of insurance funds may be invested in the sector, increasing thereby the availability of investment capital.

(vi) *Expansion as a precondition of survival.* Technological improvements require continuous reinvestment. Market competition requires an increase in size and in financial strength, which necessitates expanding capital investment. It is too risky to rely for that on external sources. Thus a substantial part of net profits must be earmarked for investment. A certain percentage of normal profits (in Mondragon it is again 20 per cent) and a higher percentage of windfall gains should be credited to indivisible reserve funds. A part of profits should be distributed as additional wages (positive and negative), a part should be spent on social and educational projects; the balance, if any, should be credited to individual accounts. The indivisible reserve fund of a co-operative, financed out of the prescribed percentages of member contributions and of profits, represents the nucleus of social property.

(vii) *Communal ties.* The co-operative is also a work community. It is, therefore, natural that members will – and ought to – take an active interest in communal affairs. Part of the earnings should be spent on various communal projects. On the other hand, in times of need, they will legitimately expect help from the local community. One obvious need is underwriting loans.

In all other matters, the organisational principles of a self-managed enterprise apply also to producer co-operatives. It hardly needs to be stressed that the basic principle of self-management, one man, one vote, retains full force.

One cannot expect that by following the above seven commandments every co-operative will be a roaring success. It is people and their actions that determine success or failure. But it is possible to say that a contemporary producer co-operative has a reasonable chance of succeeding.

Since in exceptional cases, co-operatives are not likely to be a major, or even very important, instrument of social–economic transformation participation within private and state sectors and wage earners' funds appear to be much more important. The co-operative movement can, however, greatly contribute to the creation of an appropriate atmosphere, to consciousness raising, to deligitimisation of private ownership with its social hierarchy and authoritarianism. Apart from that, co-operatives can solve many individual existential problems. For these two reasons, producer co-operatives form a part of the general strategy of socialist transformation.

NOTES

1. The first part of this chapter will appear in a more extended form in Horvat (1980).
2. For a detalied examination of this empirical evidence see Alderfer (1969) and Wahba and Bridwell (1974). Results more in tune with Maslow's theory have been obtained by Mitchel and Mondgill (1976).
3. These results are more fully reviewed in Chapter 15 of Horvat (1980).
4. In 1978, the US Congress passed a bill creating a co-operative bank and encouraging worker and community groups to buy capitalist enterprises. In an opinion poll in 1975, two out of three Americans said that they would

prefer to work for a worker owned and controlled company if they were given the choice (Stokes, 1978, p. 42).

5. The two recent European examples, both in 1974, are the *Triumph* motorcycle plant in Meriden, England, with 1750 workers and the watch-case factory *LIP* in France, employing 1300 workers. Japanese competition compelled the *Triumph* management to close up shop. Workers occupied the plant, got a government loan, and preserved at least 700 jobs. The production of motorcycles per worker increased from 14 to 22. *LIP* was sold to Swiss interests, whereupon the factory was closed. The workers struck, and later continued to produce and sell the watches. The government sent the police, but the population gave support by buying the *LIP* watches. The Chilean case is rather bizarre. Here the Junta attempted to sell off state-owned enterprises. In the prevailing chaos, not many businessmen were willing to assume political and economic risks, thus often the workers were the only interested buyers. In some 50 firms, more than 5000 workers assumed management and ownership responsibilities in order to preserve their jobs.

Bibliography

The books and papers listed below are those cited in the text. The list is not intended to be a comprehensive bibliography of the literature, although it contains most of the more important works.

ABRAHAMSSON, B. (1977) *Bureaucracy or Participation* (London).

ADAM, G. and REYNAUD, J. (1978) *Conflits du Travail et Changement Social* (Paris).

ADIZES, I. (1971) *Industrial Democracy: Yugoslav Style. The Effect of Decentralisation on Organisational Behaviour* (London).

ALDERFER, C. P. (1969) 'An empirical test of human needs', *Organizational Behaviour and Human Performance*, pp. 143–75.

ALDERFER, C. P. (1972) *Existence, Relatedness and Growth* (New York).

ALMANASREH, Z. (1977) 'Institutional forms of worker participation in the Federal German Republic', in D. Heathfield (ed.), *The Economics of Co-determination* (London).

ANGLO-GERMAN FOUNDATION (1977) *Worker Ownership: The Mondragon Achievement* (Anglo–German Foundation for the Study of Industrial Society).

ANTONI, A. (1957) 'Workers Co-operatives in France', Annals of Collective Economy, no. 3, July–December 1957.

ATKINSON, A. B. (1973) 'Worker management and the modern industrial enterprise', *Quarterly Journal of Economics*, vol. LXXXVII, no. 3.

BARKAI, H. (1977) *Growth Patterns of the Kibbutz Economy* (New York).

BATSTONE, E. (1978) 'Arms-length bargaining: French plant Industrial relations and the theory of institutionalization', mimeo. (Industrial Relations Research Unit, University of Warwick).

BATSTONE, E. (1979) 'Organization and orientation: A life cycle model of French producer co-operatives', mimeo. (Industrial Relations Research Unit, University of Warwick).

BELLAS, C. J. (1972) *Industrial Democracy and the Worker-owned Firm* (New York).

BEN-NER, A. (1980) 'Changing values and preferences in communal organizations: Some evidence from the experience of Israeli kibbutzim', paper presented at the Symposium on the Economic Performance of Participatory and Labor-Managed Firms (New York).

BEN-NER, A. and NEUBERGER, E. (1979) 'On the economics of self-management: The Israeli kibbutz and the Yugoslav enterprise', *Economic Analysis and Workers' Management*, vol. 13, no. 1–2, pp. 47–71.

BERMAN, K. V. (1967) *Worker-owned Plywood Companies: An Economic Analysis* (Washington).

BERMAN, K. V. (1975) 'The Worker-Owned Plywood Co-operatives' in *Self-management in North America: Thought, Research and Practice*, Cornell University Program on Participation and Labor–Managed Systems, unpublished study no. 11.

BERMAN, K. V. (1978) 'The role of labor unions in worker-managed firms', *Self-Management*, vol. VI, no. 1.

BERMAN, K. V. and BERMAN, M. D. (1978) 'The long-run analysis of the labor-managed firm: comment', *American Economic Review*, vol. 68, pp. 701–5.

BERMAN, M. D. (1977) 'Short-run efficiency in the labor-managed firm', *Journal of Comparative Economics*, vol. 1, no. 3, pp. 309–14.

BERNSTEIN, E. (1909) *Evolutionary Socialism* (New York).

BERNSTEIN, P. (1976) *Workplace Democratization* (Kent State Press).

BERNSTEIN, P. (1977) 'Worker owned firms steadily outperform industry', *World of Work Report* (May) pp. 49–57.

BIEDENKOPF, K. (1970) *Gutachten Mitbestimmung*, Bundestags, Drucksache, VI, 334.

BIRNBAUM, N. (1969) *The Crisis of Industrial Society* (London).

BLUMENTHAL, W. M. (1956) *Co-determination in the German*

Steel Industry (Industrial Relations Section, Princeton University).

BOLGER, P. (1977) *The Irish Co-operative Movement: Its History and Development* (Dublin: Institute of Public Administration).

BULLOCK, L. (1977) *Report of Committee of Inquiry on Industrial Democracy* (London: Department of Trade).

CARR, R. (1966) *In Spain: 1808–1939* (Oxford).

CARSON, R. (1977) 'A theory of co-operatives', *Canadian Journal of Economics*, vol. X, no. 4, (November) pp. 565–89.

CHENERY, H. *et al.* (1974) *Redistribution with Growth* (Oxford).

CHEVALIER, Y. (1974) 'Les co-operatives ouvrieres de production', *Archives Internationales de Sociologie de la Co-operation*, 35, pp. 167–92.

COATES, K. (1976) 'Some questions and some arguments', in K. Coates (ed.), *The New Worker Co-operatives* (Nottingham).

CULLEN, J. (1956) 'The inter-industry wages structure 1899–1950', *American Economic Review*, vol. 46, pp. 353–69.

DAHL, H. E. (1956) 'Worker owned plywood companies in the state of Washington', unpublished manuscript (First National Bank of Everett).

DARIN-DRABKIN, H. (1963) *The Other Society* (New York).

DAVIES, J. C. (1963) *Human Nature in Politics* (New York).

DEWAN, B. and FRIEDEN, K. (1978) *Preliminary Recommendations on Worker/Community Ownership Structure for Re-opened Campbell Works* (Washington: National Center for Economic Alternatives).

DIRLAM, J. (1979) 'Some problems of workers' self-management specific to integrated cyclical, oligopolistic industries: steel', *Economic Analysis and Workers' Management*, vol. XIII, no. 3, pp. 339–54.

DIRLAM, J. and PLUMMER, J. (1973) *An Introduction to the Yugoslav Economy* (Merrill).

DOBB, M. (1963) *Studies in the Development of Capitalism* (New York).

DOMAR, E. (1966) 'The Soviet collective farm as a producer co-operative', *American Economic Review*, vol. 56, pp. 734–57.

EATON, J. (1979) 'The Basque workers' co-operatives', *Industrial Relations Journal*, vol. 10, no. 3, pp. 32–40.

ESPINOSA, J. G. and ZIMBALIST, A. S. (1978) *Economic Democracy: Workers' Participation in Chilean Industry, 1970–73* (New York).

ESTRIN, S. (1978) 'Industrial structure in a market socialist economy', (University of Southampton, Discussion Paper no. 7717).

ESTRIN, S. (1979a) 'An explanation of earnings' variation in the Yugoslav self-managed economy', *Economic Analysis and Workers' Management*, vol. XIII, no. 3, pp. 175–99.

ESTRIN, S. (1979b) 'Income dispersion in a self-managed economy', Discussion Paper no. 7906 (University of Southampton, Dept. of Economics).

ESTRIN, S. (1979c) 'The utility maximising self-managed firm', mimeo (University of Southampton, July).

ESTRIN, S. (1980) 'The theory of the self-managed firm reconsidered', Discussion Paper no. 8018, (University of Southampton, April).

ESTRIN, S. (1981) 'Income Dispersion in a Self Managed Economy' *Economica*, vol. 48, pp. 181–94.

FANNING, C. and TOMKIN, D. (1980) 'Labour co-operatives: the legal-organizational framework in Ireland', *Journal of Irish Business and Administrative Research*, vol. 2(2) (October).

FERGUSSON, C. E. (1969) *The Neoclassical Theory of Production and Distribution* (Cambridge).

FIZAINE, F. (1968) 'Analyse statistique de la croissance des enterprises selon l'age et la taille', *Revue d'Economie Politique*, 78, pp. 606–20.

FOX, A. (1974) *Man Mismanagement* (London).

FRISCH, R. (1965) *Theory of Production* (Reidel).

FROMM, E. (1941) *Escape from Freedom* (New York).

FROMM, E. (1955) *The Sane Society* (New York).

FÜRSTENBERG, F. (1969) 'Workers participation in management in the Federal Republic of Germany', *International Institute for Labour Studies Bulletin*, no. 6 (June).

FÜRSTENBERG, F. (1977) 'West German experience with industrial democracy', *Annals of the American Academy of Politics and Social Science* (May).

FURUBOTN, E. G. (1971) 'Toward a dynamic model of the Yugoslav firm', *Canadian Journal of Economics*, 4(2), pp. 182–97.

FURUBOTN, E. G. (1976) 'The long-run analysis of the labour-managed firm: an alternative interpretation', *American Economic Review*, 66(1) (March) pp. 104–23.

FURUBOTN, E. G. and PEJOVICH, S. (1970) 'Property rights and the behaviour of the firm in a socialist state: the example of Yugoslavia', *Zeitschrift fur Nationalokonomie*, 30(3–4), pp. 431–54.

GALENSON, W. and FOX, A. (1967) 'Earnings and employment in eastern Europe', *Quarterly Journal of Economics*, vol. 81, pp. 220–40.

GARCIA, Q. (1970) *Les Co-operatives Industrielles de Mondragon* (Paris).

GOLOMB, N. (1978) 'The relationship between factory and kibbutz', in *Al Hashimir*, Supplement of the Kibbutz Industry (31 March) (in Hebrew).

GORRONO, I. (1975) *Experiencia Co-operativa en el Pais Vasco* (Bilbao).

GORUPIC, D. and PAJ, I. (1970) *Workers' Self-Management in Yugoslav Undertakings* (Zagreb: Ekonomski Institut).

GREENBERG, E. S. (1978) 'The governance of producer co-operatives: the case of plywood firms', unpublished manuscript (Institute of Behavioural Science, University of Colorado).

HELMAN, A. (1975) 'The distribution and allocation of consumer goods in the kibbutz', PhD Dissertation (London School of Economics and Political Science).

HORVAT, B. (1971) 'Yugoslav economic policy in the post-war period: problems, ideas, institutional developments', *American Economic Review*, vol. 61, no. 3, part 2, Supplement (June) pp. 71–169.

HORVAT, B. (1980) *Political Economy of Socialism* (New York).

IAOS (1979) *Framework for Co-operative Development: 63* (Irish Agricultural Organisation Society, January).

INBAR, I. and PELEG, D. (1976) 'Aspects of an economic model pertaining to the productive sector of the kibbutz, MA thesis (Tel Aviv University) (in Hebrew).

IRELAND, N. J. (1980) 'The behaviour of the labour-managed firm and disutility from supplying factor services', *Economic analysis and Workers' Management*, vol. xv, no. 1, pp. 21–43.

JANES, G. M. (1924) 'Co-operative production among shingle weavers', *Quarterly Journal of Economics*, vol. 38 (May).

JANNERET, T., MORAGA, L. and RUFFING, L. (1975) *Las Experiencias Autogestioriarias Chilenas* (Departamento de Economia, Universidad de Chile).

JAY, P. (1976) *Employment, Inflation and Politics* (London: Institute of Economic Affairs).

JONES, D. C. (1975) 'Workers' management in Britain', *Economic Analysis and Workers' Management*, vol. IX, pp. 331–8.

JONES, D. C. (1976) 'British economic thought on associations of labourers 1848–1974', *Annals of Public and Co-operative Economy*, 1, pp. 1–32.

JONES, D. C. (1977) 'The economics and industrial relations of producer co-operatives in the United States 1791–1939', *Economic Analysis and Workers' Management*, vol. XI, pp. 295–317.

JONES, D. C. and BACKUS, D. K. (1977) 'British producer co-operatives in the footwear industry: an empirical evaluation of the theory of financing', *Economic Journal*, vol. 87, pp. 488–510.

KATOUZIAN, M. A. (1980) *Ideology and Method in Economics* (London).

Laquer, W. (1972) *A History of Zionism* (London).

LAW, P. J. (1977) 'The Illyrian firm and Fellner's union-management model, *Journal of Economic Studies*, vol. 4, no. 1 (May) pp. 29–57.

LEWIS, F. (1979) 'West Kerry development', *Cope News: Journal of Co-operative Enterprises in N. Ireland*, vol. 2 (1).

LUCAS, N. (1974) *The Modern History of Israel* (London).

LIAISONS SOCIALES (1978) 'Statut des SCOP', Supplement au 7828.

MCDYER, J. (1975) 'Resurgence in the west', *Ireland Today: Bulletin of the Department of Foreign Affairs*, 899 (June).

MCGREGOR, A. (1977) 'Rent extraction and the survival of the agricultural production co-operative', *American Journal of Agricultural Economics*, vol. 59 (3) (August), pp. 478–88.

MACHLUP, F. (1969) 'Positive and normative economics: an analysis of the ideas', in R. L. Heilbroner (ed.), *Economic Means and Social Ends* (Englewood Cliffs).

MCLACHLAN, H. V. and SWALES, J. K. (1978) 'The positive/normative distinction in economics', Discussion Paper 78/3, (University of Strathclyde, Department of Economics).

MANDEL, E. (1975) 'Self-management – dangers and possibilities', *International*, 2/3, pp. 3–9.

MARCUSE, H. (1972) *An Essay on Liberation* (Harmondsworth).

MASLOW, A. (1970) *Motivation and Personality* (New York).

MEAD, W. J. (1966) *Competition and Oligopsony in the Douglas Fir Lumber Industry* (Berkeley).

MEADE, J. E. (1972) 'The theory of labour-managed firms and of profit sharing', *Economic Journal*, vol. LXXXII, (March), pp. 402–28.

MILENKOVITCH, D. D. (1971) *The Plan and Market in Yugoslav Economic Thought* (New Haven).

MILLIS, H. A. and MONTGOMERY (1945) *The Economics of Labor* (London: McGraw).

MIOVIC, P. (1975) *Determinants of Income Differentials in Yugoslav Self-Managed Enterprises*, PhD Dissertation (University of Pennsylvania). Published as Cornell University Program on Participation and Labor-Managed Systems. Unpublished Study no. 14.

MITCHEL, V. F. and MONDGILL, P. (1976) 'Measurement of Maslow's need hierarchy', *Organization Behaviour and Human Performance*, pp. 334–49.

MUELLER, D. (1972) 'A life cycle theory of the firm', *Journal of Industrial Economics*, vol. XX(3), pp. 199–219.

NEUBERGER, E. (1970) 'The Yugoslav visible hand: why is it no more?' Stony Brook Working Papers no. 23, (New York).

OAKESHOTT, R. (1978) *The Case for Workers' Co-ops* (London).

OBRADOVIC, J. (1973) 'Distribution of and participation in the process of decision-making', in *Proceedings of Dubrovnik Conference*.

O'BRIEN, T. (1979) 'Non-dairy multi-purpose rural development co-operatives', mimeo. (March).

O'CONNOR, R. and KELLEY, P. (1980) *A Study of Industrial Workers' Co-operatives* (Dublin: Economic and Social Research Institute).

PAULY, M. and REDISCH, M. (1973) 'The not-for-profit hospital as a physicians' co-operative', *American Economic Review*, 63, pp. 87–99.

PEJOVICH, S. (1969) 'The firm, monetary policy and property rights in a planned economy', *Western Economic Journal*, 7, pp. 193–200.

PERRY, S. (1978) *San Francisco Scavengers* (Berkeley).

REYNOLDS, L. G. and TAFT, C. M. (1956) *The Evolution of Wage Structure* (New York).

RUDOLF, A. (1973) 'A theoretical analysis of the kibbutz as a producers' co-operative', PhD Dissertation (Columbia University).

272 *Bibliography*

RUSINOW, D. (1977) *The Yugoslav Experiment 1948–1974* (London).

SACKS, S. R. (1973) *Entry of New Competitors in Yugoslav Market Socialism*, Research Series no. 19 (Institute for International Studies, University of California, Berkeley).

SACKS, S. R. (1979a) 'Divisionalization in large Yugoslav enterprises', mimeo. (University of Connecticut, January).

SACKS, S. R. (1979b) 'Vertical integration and divisionalization in Yugoslav enterprises', *Economic Analysis and Workers' Management*, vol. XIII, no. 3, pp. 327–38.

SERTEL, M. (1978) 'The relative size and share price of a workers' enterprise facing competitive capitalism', Applied Mathematics Division Technical Report, (Marmara Research Institute).

SHIROM, A. (1972) 'The industrial relations systems of industrial co-operatives in the United States, 1880–1935', *Labor History* (Fall) pp. 533–51.

SILVESTRE, J. (1974) 'Industrial wage differentials: a two-country comparison', *International Labour Review*, 110, pp. 495–514.

SIRC, L. (1977) 'Workers' management under public and private ownership', in B. Chiplin, *et al.* (eds), *Can Workers Manage?* (Institute for Economic Affairs, London).

STALLINGS, B. (1975) 'Economic development and class conflict in Chile 1958–73, unpublished PhD Dissertation (University of Stanford).

STEINHERR, A. (1978) 'The labor-managed economy: a survey of the economics literature', *Annals of Public and Co-operative Economy*, vol. 49, pp. 129–48.

STEPHEN, F. H. (1976) 'Yugoslav self-management 1945–74', *Industrial Relations Journal*, vol. 7, no. 4 (Winter) pp. 56–65.

STEPHEN, F. H. (1979) 'Investment in labour-managed firms', unpublished PhD Dissertation (University of Strathclyde).

STOKES, B. (1978) *Worker Participation Productivity and the Quality of Work Life* (Washington: Worldwatch Paper 25).

STURMTHAL, A. F. (1964) *Workers Councils* (Cambridge, Mass.).

SVEJNAR, J. *The Effect of Employee Participation in Management on Bargaining Power and Wages: A Generalised Nash Solution and Econometric Evidence from Germany*, Working Paper No.

106 (Industrial Relations Section, Princeton University, December).

SVEJNAR, J. (1979) 'The Effect of Co-determination on Wages', paper presented at the Walton Symposium, Glasgow, June 1979.

SVEJNAR, J. (1981) 'Relative wage effects of unions dictatorships and co-determination', *Review of Economics and Statistics.*

THOMAS, H. (1961) *The Spanish Civil War* (London).

TIVEY, L. (1978) *The Politics of the Firm* (London).

TYSON, L. D'A. (1979) 'Incentives, income sharing and institutional innovation in the Yugoslav self-managed firm', *Journal of Comparative Economics*, vol. 3 (September) pp. 285–301.

VANEK, J. (1970) *The General Theory of Labour-managed Market Economies* (Ithaca).

VANEK, J. (1971a) 'Some fundamental considerations of financing and the form of ownership under labor-management', Working Paper No. 16 (Ithaca: Cornell University Department of Economics). Reprinted in H. C. Bos (ed.), *Economic Structure and Development, Amsterdam* (North Holland).

VANEK, J. (1971b) 'The basic theory of financing of participatory firms', Working Paper no. 27 (Ithaca: Cornell University Department of Economics). Reprinted as Chapter 28 of Vanek (1975).

VANEK, J. (1975) *Self-Management: Economic Liberation of Man* (Harmondsworth).

VIENNEY, C. (1966) *L'Economie du Secteur Co-operatif Francais* (Paris).

VINEY, M. (1972) 'Up by the bootstraps', *Irish Times* (23 May).

VOLLMER, R. J. (1979) 'Labor relations and industrial democracy in the Federal Republic of Germany', (Washington, DC: Embassy of the Federal Republic of Germany, December).

WACHTEL, H. M. (1973) *Workers' Management and Workers' Wages in Yugoslavia* (Ithaca and London).

WAHBA, M. A. and BRIDWELL, L. G. (1974) 'Maslow reconsidered: a review of research on the need hierarchy theory', *Academy of Management Proceedings,* pp. 514–20.

WARD, B. (1958) 'The firm in Illyria: market syndicalism', *American Economic Review*, vol. XLVIII.

WARD, B. (1968) *The Social Economy* (New York).

WARNER, M. (1975) 'Whither Yugoslav self-management?', *Industrial Relations Journal*, vol. 6(1) (Spring), pp. 65–72.

WEBB, S. and WEBB, B. (1930) *The Consumers Co-operative Movement* (New York).

WILES, P. J. D. (1977) *Economic Institutions Compared* (Oxford).

ZAMIR, D. (1976) 'The hired labor and the structure of the factory in kibbutz industry', in Hakibbutz Haartsi Council, *The Industry in the Kibbutz* (Social Research Institute and the Industry Bureau of Hakibbutz Haartsi) (in Hebrew).

Index

The numbers in bold type indicate the most important references to the particular entry.

275